The Water Above

*'Falling from mysterious heavens
on all creatures equally'*

A Memoir

David Holdridge

Cover credit: **Gray Jacobik** is a painter and poet who works in various mediums and styles. The cover art, "The Water Above the Firmament" is one of her encaustic (hot wax) paintings. She invites viewers to her website: grayjacobik.artist.com.

ISBN: 979-8-218-96903-5

David Holdridge writes with a gritty realism that sometimes feels like a punch in the gut. You don't so much read about his characters as you experience them as they seek love, adventure, danger and meaning in an always perilous post World War II world, one he knows well from his lifelong predilection to bed down with the benighted in God Forsaken places. His are not imagined or armchair descriptions of survival in the war-torn Middle East or being blown up in combat. He's been there, and he brings you along with him with gripping prose.

W.E. "Bill" Barnes views the world from his perspective as former political editor and columnist for the San Francisco Examiner, and Contributing Editor for Time magazine.

"The call to service is something that some ignore, others do when it's convenient or easy, and still others do regardless of the risk or cost because it's the right thing to do. David Holdridge is in that third, and most admirable category. Serving both in combat and in humanitarian roles, he has volunteered to be in some of the most hazardous places on earth, yet he has managed to maintain both his humanity and his humility. I met David when he was serving in the chaos of a crumbling Iraq, struggling each day to help civilians caught in the middle and risking his life on a daily basis to do so. Those who have engaged in service as well as those who might not be able to imagine what that life is like, will gain insights and perhaps inspiration from David's personal example and writings.

Congressman Brian Baird served 12 years in the U.S. House of Representatives and is the founder and chair of the National Museum and Center for Service, an organization dedicated to honoring and inspiring service in ALL its forms. During his time in Congress Dr. Baird visited Iraq, Afghanistan, Gaza, and Sarajevo among other places. Dr. Baird holds a Ph.D. in clinical psychology, specializing in neuropsychology, and he has served as a university president and department chair.

───◁◫▷───

A brilliant, moving, globe-hopping memoire, The Water Above bravely chronicles the journey of a man who is trying to make sense of America's role in the world, raise a family and lend aid to the victims of the violent civil war in Lebanon – all at the same time. Author David Holdridge, follows up on his award-winning Avant Gard of Western Civilization with a deeper, more personal account of his life – that of an idealistic young man intent on advancing the best of America values. What he meets along the way – in Vietnam, Connecticut, Lebanon and in the offices of relief agencies throughout the Middle East – is intense, frustrating, heart-wrenching, and inspiring. And makes for a rich and rollicking read that reminds me of a modern-day Candide by Voltaire with echoes of the film A Year of Living Dangerously.

Ralph Pezzullo is the bestselling author of over two dozen books including Jawbreaker, Zero Footprint and Saigon, an award-winning playwright, and host and producer of the popular podcast Heroes Behind Headlines.

―⊂⫙⫙⊃―

David Holdridge has written an irresistible tale of war, madness, love, devotion, and the moral quagmires of American imperialism and international aid. A story of "recuperative wanderings" after Vietnam and work overseas, his protagonist's personal, familial, and political agonies are powerfully rendered, and triumphs hard-won. Our grand narratives, thought to be over, are brought back to life through his voice, whose thoughts, visions, and dreams of hallucinatory intensity contemporize the genius of the greats (Dickens, Joyce, Twain) while giving the reader a rare insider perspective into today's crises of military intervention and masculinity. *The Water Above* is a masterpiece.

Virginia Konchan is the author of four poetry collections and a collection of short stories. Her work has appeared in *The New Yorker*, *The Atlantic*, and *The New Republic*.

Table of Contents

'FOR MISTER HARRISON'

Preamble

I first met Botanicos in his freshman year at an elective,
a literature class—quite a surprise, given that students
in the engineering channel rarely indulged such
fantastic stuff. He seemed a caricature to me, like a
baseball catcher. Easy to imagine him whipping off his
face mask and pegging the ball to second or blocking
the plate as the runner tried to steal home.

He was square, with strong forearms and a stack
of brown hair. And refreshing, since amidst all the
gratuitous flapping going on about this and that
symbol or double entendre, he, seemingly, could stay
clear of it and speak his own mind.

It was at one of those periodic homecoming
events where he had spotted me clopping across
the campus on a personal errand and diverted his
father and fiancé from the activities to shake my
hand. They were from a farming community in

1

Western Pennsylvania. Not as farmers, but engaged in "off-farm" activities: his dad in tractor supply and his fiancé from a grain and feed family business. What they were usually called was pillars. Meaning, if it was at all like Northbrook, they sat in the front pews of the Lutheran church and had for several generations.

His fiancé Mary was notably plain—plain and proud of it. She was a confident young woman with no embellishments or exotic accentuation. She did the talking, with an unblinking interest in a friend of Botanicos. This gave me no ground to go off on any wild expatiations involving my ride a couple of years earlier through her neck of the woods on that flat-bedded Ford, planks jumping in the back as we had moved through the summer haze, much less the drama that had unfolded in the Scranton Y toilet with those glossy nudes.

In any case, the college agenda soon drew them back to their circle and I returned to my errand, wondering at the time whether any sickness or other assorted pathogens could possibly circulate around their lives: whether any of them, in adolescence, had ever been dragged out of secret tunnels by Mr. Riker and been called "sick "for what they were doing. Surely, they must have, but not so as any outsider could detect. There was only the twitch of his eye that he told me later had been the result of a nerve injury incurred in a clash of wills at home plate; his chortle, one pitch higher than expectations; and his name, which seemed very un-Lutheran but, as I was told later, was attributable to a Greek connection on his father's side around the time of the civil war, and the great turbulence in general within the town.

The Rathskeller: Thick-pillared, dark and Romanesque. Smoking steaks, piles of fries and pitchers of beer.

Botanicos: Turning away from the cashier, and advancing toward me sitting alone. He was quietly outlandish, all the buttons buttoned, and a garnet tie dotted with the university emblem. Which might have invited taunts, had it not been for those magnificent forearms of his and his forthright countenance.

I objected to his caution. That he seemed absent during bouts of personal degradation and that his ties to his fiancé back home showed no strains of being corrupted by doubt or imagination. And then there was the issue of inheritance, his plans to join his father's company.

Nevertheless, left alone to consider it, I couldn't help but be charmed by Botanicos' guileless, uncursed manner. He was a durable, if occasional, friend who naturally trod the path between frugality and extravagance, between the reluctant and the daring.

Botanicos found me slouched in a booth, clad in my habitual ragged army air corps jacket.

Botanicos- How are you, friend? Sorry to keep you.

Rutherford- Good to see you. It's been a while. Good idea to check in, don't you think, being in the home stretch and all?

B- (with an all-encompassing smile and a stare, held too long): So, tell me, counselor, what's new?

R- Actually, old news. Just mooning, friend. Mooning over Peggy. Little good that it will do me. Too much water over that dam for any resurrection now. You remember her, that girl who laughed with such endearment when I told her that I had written the definitive work on Jean-Paul Sartre.

B- Yes, I do. The lady from Avenue J. And so what finally stopped it?

R- Who knows? Little things. Perhaps because her lipstick always stained her teeth or because she was one of those girls who closed their eyes before a kiss. Maybe it was just that she looked foolish when she danced. Still, she was probably the best. Best behaved, in any case. In the end, more exotic sights, a French girl in a plum orchard, a poor creature in Pigalle, lured me away. And, while I was away, I am sure her dad had her ear. In any case, my calls have not been returned.

B- Lipstick on her teeth? Christ, I'd say you're a bit lacking in heart.

R- Heart? Tell me, Botanicos, who's got heart? I suspect it's just an organ. Take a look at the article (pushes the campus newspaper over to him). Just twenty-one years ago, speaking of my Peggy, Jewish kids like her got snatched and cremated. Kids, Botanicos...as in kids who played with pretty dolls and jumped rope. Put in ovens as casually as your mom bakes apple pies.

That's our world Botanicos, a world with absolutely no fucking beating breast large enough to care. Just hold on (laying his hand on his friend's arm) ...think about it. Just when our daddy's sperm was wiggling up the old uterus to make us--you and me--elsewhere, millions of humans were being systematically starved. Just skeletons with skin like cellophane stretched over them and then crammed into extermination sheds and we knew it, Botanicos. We knew it. And we did fucking nothing. And more, ten years ago when all the evidence was there of the genocide, spread all over the covers of magazines, we still had big yellow warning signs on our Atlantic shore that said 'no jews or dogs allowed'. I mean how can we live with that? We knew and we did nothing. Oh yes, we went to war and bombed Germany to smithereens but we did that with absolutely no thought of the Jews. Botanicos, we didn't care. I mean...Heart? I mean sometimes, I just try to imagine starving, my sister starving, the ribs, the hollow eyes, the teeth and hair falling out and then fathoming the horror when the cyanide was dropped. Yes, Botanicos, we were cozy in the womb by then, just growing nicely-- putting on the ole baby fat, if you please, and that was going on.

B- My friend, I know...I know we don't care. Not enough in any case. Not most of us. No doubt, it is our collective black heart. It will happen again and I am pretty sure both of us, in our own ways, would die before letting it pass. But we would be a small hindrance I am afraid.

R- I just can't get it out of my mind. And the way it comes down for me is my ache to kill all those fuckers who put up those signs on the beaches. I mean, Botanicos, I would love to slip into a KKK hall and slaughter them ...just leave a pile of bloody meat.

B- Reaches across and covers Rutherford's hand, now shaking with his hate.

R- (distraught)...Sorry Botanicos, I just started thinking of the girl from avenue J and then without purpose started reading the newspaper left here and then the article and had some beers and I just lost it. Sorry, you didn't sit down for this...sorry, sorry. I mean I think about it too much lately. Obsessed with it (raising his voice). All of it. It's like a fucking global black cancer, a melanoma, lying in wait until metastasis. Ha, Just like this little baby the doc. found last week...only global (lifting his shirt) ..

B- God, is that serious? What did the Doc say?

R- `Watch it for growth'.

(He fills his own glass from the pitcher and offers to top off that of Botanicos, but he places his palm over it.)

R- Still a sipper, heh Botanicos? Anyway, enough of this. Put my mole aside. What else was our heritage? Black women selling some squeeze for our little squirts of white excitement. Trying to keep warm on a winter night...Lovely black women...my

Pearl. Pathos, pathos everywhere I turn...Khadija, in her alleyway...Pearl in her shack...Daisy in Piccadilly, scrapping for tips and my phony tidbits.

B- Hiroshima--our birthday bang.

R- Yesssiree, no flies on us, still growing like topsy in mama's womb. We were nice and plump as can be, the sun gleaming on its fuselage, we incinerated 100 thousand civilians and radiated countless more. Yep. The ruthless white man. Stalled at the apex. White men, us, staring around, licking their chops, bursting with bloodlust, fenced in, coast to coast, with barbed wire, with too many live babies and our energy stuck at the Berlin wall.

B- And what can we -- so fresh from the womb -- do about it, beyond lament, beyond guzzling foreign beer and offering up wild tirades helter skelter in a posh liberal university. We're not exactly bleeding at the barricades here. Or, if you please, marching with candles for peace.

R- (choking on his beer) Touché. Time will tell. I'm feeling a decision coming soon. There's a reckoning...candles or arms. That, or we're just more liberal slosh sliding down to nonchalance. Meanwhile, as you no doubt suspect, I'm bent on using you friend tonight for some sort of respite; since with all these damn deadlines breathing down my neck, such indulgences are running out of time. As of today's mail, if events unfold the wrong way, I am looking at service before self or something along those lines. Yep, you have here sitting before you a bona fide red white and blue '1-A'.

Hold on. Let me take a piss. I'll be back.

(Rutherford pushed off past the tables of assorted clientele; some with heavy beards, others still pimply. It was a varied crowd: stale sons of the old line; intimidating Jews from Brooklyn in transit to the all-night study hall; hostile cloaked radicals; and a sprinkling of flunkies, barely hanging on, over their heads.

In a few minutes I returned, flushed and weaving slightly, amused with how many holes I had hit in the commode, and rejuvenated with the stretch I felt across my shoulders. Botanicos had bought some more fries.)

B- Help yourself.

R- And so, Botanicos, in less than three months, one way or the other, we're out. You still headed home?

B- At the risk of your smirk--yes, to small business. My dad's firm.

R- And the marriage?

B- Of course. That too. But what about yourself?

R- Well now, counsellor. Assuming no uniform in my immediate future which may not be a practical assumption, well, let's take a second, if you will, to examine the ledger. I have no capital for small business. Zero. Spent it all on debauchery and other assorted flights of fancy over the last four years and am too curious for extended cafe life or the professions. And, certainly no steady on my arm, these days.

B- (Smiling) The corporations are interviewing.

R- You wouldn't wish that on me, would you? I already had my fill in that air-conditioned insurance company; that no-risk anathema with all its pink carbon copies floating around and phones ringing with the latest catastrophe. Forty years of that and I'd be ready for the old men's section in the 'Y' and the boob-tube. And just what have you heard from the companies that have come to campus?

That there's big money to be had by selling glamour.

B- Don't make me self-conscious.

R- Ha Ha, cute... (Pushing some loose change toward Botanicos) I know you think I'm exaggerating. But you remember this. I'll bet you all these coins. You watch our mates here in their middle years. And then call me. That's right, pick up the phone and call me when you are thirty. Tell me who's right. By then, they are all urbanized, au courant; patrons of liberalism, foreign films, experimental sex and mild marijuana. Hell, if shit were chic, for Christ's sake, they'd dine on it. Nary a thought of Hiroshima and Auschwitz. And Botanicos, worse...what about the ridicule they will heap on those of us who revolt? Who make fools of themselves, go over the edge, spill drinks, get sick, etcetera, and sleep with folks who do likewise. And can on occasion become emotionally unhinged by all that black heart. Everywhere.

B- Don't forget, they're buying these drinks and your degree, and the books you're so fond of. We live off them and they tolerate us, sometimes. Gadflies. Think of us as unwelcome bugs which when we become annoying enough, they just shrug us off, like a dog shedding rain water.

R- Providers. Yes, my father is a provider. I sure would be a failure as a provider. The Dow, strokes, clubs, awards, quotas and all of it, it seems to me, at the expense of what my lit prof calls 'the noiseless hunt'.

B- Noiseless hunts. I suppose you mean butting your head up against the enigmas of the black heart.

R- That's it. The human condition. Rail against it or put a bullet in their head or your own head. These days it seems those hunters he talked about end up shooting themselves and being discovered days later by some disinterested cleaning lady.

B- How can you be so exceptional? Afterall our mates over there are all humans; they share this human condition with us. There is a stream though it called humanity, why we feel sick about the collective black heart, why some naturally find kindness within the condition, notwithstanding that I too fear it may come to no good end, candles or not. With or without me. But along with that black heart we discussed, most of us have a life force, almost regardless of circumstances and for those who don't, it's not as if the 'natural laws' are going to pivot because of our bit of outrage or early demise.

R- NOT me. Shit, friend, I can't live this way. I know them. If I am going to be humane, it should be for the likes of Daisy or Khadija, not for them. Just like you I've been sitting next to them in classes for eight years now. I've heard them conniving. Take those gentlemen over there, those idle sons of invested wealth. I feel it in my bones that we'll see them pass their early years as East side dandies with impeccable draft deferments. While the lumpen masses put on their uniforms. You know what really separates us Botanicos. You think there is a progression, if you will, that with time will alter the chemistry, affect the natural laws, make hate vestigial. Yet you, far more than I, know that is so far out of our hands that …a fool's errand. (big breath) Anyway, counsellor, as for my next job -- it's moot. I'll probably fall into the impatient hands of the war mongers. They've been a year in Danang already.

B- Hopefully, they're not looking for the likes of you.

R - Let's get out of here.

B- Where to?

R- I'll take you to Pearl's.

B- Oh no, you won't.

R- Why the hell not? Your convictions will survive, perhaps even grow. I mean…there's our elusive 'beating breast'.

B- That's what I'm afraid of.

R- At least shake hands with the woman. Her living room, albeit a little dark, is actually quite comfy.

B- There's nothing there for me, except to twiddle my thumbs while you finish.

R- While I'm under the covers you can have an aperitif with toothless Jane. Practice your humanity. Test your humanity. Sober as you are, I assure you, she won't be much of a temptation.

B- Ok, I suppose so, but on one condition: it's understood that I'm there to keep you company and under no circumstances to indulge.

R- I wouldn't want it any other way.

B- Alright, but I've got to make a call home in about ten minutes.

R- At this hour?

B- It's our habit.

R- Ok. Fine. We'll finish this pitcher.

(Rutherford pours out the remaining beer. Botanicos raises his glass and toasts)

B- Here's hoping you're spared the Army.

R- If not, it's my choice. I had the same opportunity for exemptions that you did. Actually, I'm unsure about the experience -- the so-called engagement with the godforsaken. It's the Goddamn organization behind it that scares me.

B- And the cause?

R- I'm no patriot. Look it, as we said, for millennia man has organized to hunt each other. Natural laws again. The costumes and the chants have been different but he has never stopped keeping national movements paramount. It's his way of breaking out the lunacy on a very weak leash. Look it, the Auschwitz's and Hiroshima's have suffused our history, strong black currents in the evolution of man. As for me, I can't resist seeing them better though hating them more. I am too curious about man. About his inheritance, our inheritance. War, it seems, is one of the fundamental aspects of the human condition, if not the essential one. How can we look past it. We are war, Botanicos. Look how I, even with the proper inclination, handled Khadijeh and Daisy.

B- So, this is your world--'we are war'-- in 3 words or less?

R- I assure you this is no finished composition. Not from me. I've never been able to wrap the world up for myself, much less for others but from the little I have managed to learn, I noticed that the world tends to pull in upon itself, a pendulum, -- create intense confusion -- an implosion of sorts until it ultimately explodes causing havoc at first and then a brief peace. Usually very brief before religion boils up again, this last time however, binding technology to its will. And the saddest aspect, Botanicos, is how willingly the victims `sell the pasture to buy the horse'. You've seen the newsreels from World War II. By the glint in their eyes, you'd swear they had been saved by some evangelist instead of marching on to war.

B- My God has to be within that 'brief peace', those intervening stalemates, such as they are and, God willing, they will endure and grow their time and space.

R- (Shaking his head) I'm afraid its false hope. You see, it's much larger than a ceasefire built on mutually assured destruction; larger than our world, even. From the beginning, it was always the dark and infinite cosmos, not our planet, that enticed man. It encouraged his refusal to recognize limits and encouraged him to dote on marvelous and hideous exaggerations.

B- You seem to be conveniently forgetting the society of men who mistrusted the mystical and used the acceptance of their own ignorance as the foundation for a more measured harmonious life.

R- And what did your Enlightenment accomplish except to rob the primitives of their spirituality and replace it with ad hoc refinements that were quickly shaken off by a new burst of unmasked savagery? The Ardennes. Ring a bell?

B- Well, thanks for the stump speech. Seriously, I think you'd be a hit in Hyde Park. You need to slow down and maybe spend more time on those footnotes you love so much.

R- Momentum, Botanicos. It shouldn't be slowed when I'm running on all eight. As an engineer, you must sympathize.

B- (Laughing) Go on then. Since you will, anyway. Let the catharsis continue.

R- It's just that your God, as you worship Him with your Mary on Sundays is outside our inheritance, other than for those brief episodes. Your God is Still; the God you pray to... too stable to exist. What you have mistakenly called calm and peace -- living within limits -- is only, collectively, the busy restoration of concentrated energy. My childhood friend and I on the stoop in August, cooking up excitements.

It is our ambition halted, finally frustrated, left lurking within the press of a stronghold where eventually it is impelled by more potent powers to change colors and brazenly gallop forth in disarray till it is once more stopped by the cold dark and drawn back inside.

B- Very Good. Right out of your term paper. I suppose... Right? You and your dark prisons, dark heavens -- why not dote on the light for a while? I believe that with time and effort humans can evolve from beast toward angel. That, if studied, there is nothing a priori in natural law to preclude that.

R- Yes, my term paper, my mind is inflated with this stuff, these days. Finals around the corner and all that. Here's more, in response, direct from my paper.

The so-called age of enlightenment -- according to you a time for an incremental step forward. Some step. And I quote from my paper. 'By the 20th Century, Europe was again celebrating the epic of the shadow. Reasons machinations turned in relief to national religions; to Art Deco and anarchical jazz; classicism to brutish, prowling, dark notions. Germany, too long contained and exasperated by thought steamrolled over its neighbors with shouts of self-sacrifice and final solutions.' And while I'm at it, don't forget, Botanicos, that we too avoided our national depression, our inward muddle, with war. (wagging his finger) You'll see. We're taking a rest now, healing our wounds in the warm aftermath from the last global convulsion; diverted from another fight by a preoccupation with worldly distractions and producing a lull. Not a permanent progression.

And, friend, just so you don't forget. This is not all stump speeches and thesis. In purely a physical sense, I am closer to it than you...troop levels keep growing in southeast Asia.

B- And isn't your own inclination to 'leave them stewing in a pile of bloody meat' inseparable from the situation you're attacking -- your bitterness toward hate and uniforms a hollow outburst?

R- It doesn't seem that way to me. Or to all those classics read to me at bedside by my mother. Of all those stories, save one, the message was overpowering. Individual warriors with Jesus in their hearts slay the beast, not a multitude of candles. I won't die for everyman's sullied national religion and their particular bomb. I want the right to follow a personal religion that's in step with my disposition. With the naturally ordained movement but free from the evil administration of others.

B- Still the black prince against the devils who profit from the dark.

R- Right on, friend. Rid the temple of the money changers. The dark defined as that condition which prevents mankind from peering 'in or out' too long; encourages them to jam up around temporary excitements like buying things, burning crosses or war itself where they first sacrifice the unsure and the unproud among them and last trade gold stars on their screen doors for dead sons. Not a bad deal, eh Botanicos?

B- (Draining his glass and bundling up, preparing to leave) God bless our children that they may have a different conversation. I believe there is a human progression because I have to believe it. Who could live with those images of the

Jewish children thrown in the cattle cars on their way to extermination, if they thought they were never-ending.

R- OK, I'm sure you do. I can see you all too easily in a crowd with those big hands of yours, thumb and finger pinching a candle.

I'll meet you outside the north gate.

———⋖⫘⫘⊖———

We looked up at the lop-sided street sign: 'Corporal D'Angelo Square'.

"There you go Botanicos", I exclaimed. "What a tribute. See how they bleed them."

Botanicos looked at me, baffled. "There I go, what", he responded.

"Look at it. They hung the same plastic flowers on it as they use in that restaurant. For a commemorative, a state issued condolence."

Botanicos was ignoring him. "Are you sure you know where you're going? It doesn't look as if there's anything down here."

I muttered something about 'garlanding the sign, with smelly bandages'.

Botanicos persisted in looking puzzled. The neighborhood was changing, radically. Most of the buildings were warehouses now and bore the names of wholesalers for olive oil and pasta shells. Further on, there were some empty lots strewn with refuse. Then a rusted out old Ford, sunk on its axle into the road, a foot of old snow covering the carcass. "See that grey tenement down the end?"

"Yes."

"That's hers."

He looked disappointed. I guessed that my friend had expected something a little more cheerful - at least a light. Something other than a shabby grey tenement stuck between an empty lot and a warehouse. As they approached, he saw that the bottom windows and been replaced by cardboard panes - Garafolo Distributors, Schenectady, N.Y. in large red print, sealed to the frames with dirty strips of yellow masking tape. I took Botanicos past some battered shrubs, once a hedge, and up to the back stoop. I knocked and the two of us stood facing each other. Ruddy, wind burnt, noses wet. Botanicos uneasy, I beaming - the guide ready to supply my friend with a memory. Still, they heard nothing. Then the door opened, a couple of inches. The chain was on.

"Who's that?"

"Me."

Then the door opened. "Why honey, I thought you had forgot Pearl." Black Pearl with a summer sweater buttoned down the front over her faded green cotton dress and two pairs of woolen socks pulled up to her calves. "Come in. Who's your friend? He sporting? Did you bring me a present?"

They stepped into an unventilated warmth; into smoke and smells that would have gagged the fastidious. "You know that charity is bad for your dignity, Pearl," I said.

She laughed. "Oh you college boys, aren't you smart. Never mind, come in."

She took us through the kitchen into the dusk of the living room, where she offered us seats. Across the room there were two other people sitting at separate ends of a couch. One was Jane, looking especially hideous this evening and there was a gaunt older man. Both of them appeared almost dead from drink. Pearl ignored them and sat down close to me and Botanicos. She was pure black. She reclined into the easy chair, her legs astraddle, heels akimbo on the musty carpets. It was late. She laid back against the headrest, holding her glass of gin and milk in her lap. She half closed her eyes and asked, "You in a hurry to go with me?" I said no, that I was still cold. I thought she was beautiful - a warm African, with no extra...with bleak eyes, who presided over a saloon of winos and college boys with no particular ambition for anything better. Still young, I thought. Last time, when she hadn't yet become unsteady from too much drink, she had brought in a clothesline from the kitchen, doubled it up, and silenced those present by jumping rope to a childhood cadence in the middle of her carpet...slapping up years of dust.

My toes were starting to thaw. There was a wood-burning stove in the corner with its exhaust pipe running toward the kitchen, over my head, through slings of piano wire hooked to the ceiling. Through the soles of my boots I could feel the heat trapped in her carpets. There was no wood to her floor. She had found remnants - over many years, now - and regardless of shape, had laid them where it suited her. They had over time melted into this matty carpet, now several inches thick.

The old man had muttered something to Pearl.

"This nigger's", she answered, "gonna run you out into the cold if you don't shut up about your God-damn money."

She had threatened him without stirring an inch. Without being angry. I stared at the man and through the impoverished light saw what looked to me like a scarecrow - his pants open, bile on his lips.

I was fascinated. The old man shifted toward Jane - chancres on his bony shins. Then came the old man's grumble, "I didn't get my satisfaction." He paused as if in suspension, troubling what was left of his mind for another word. Something persuasive. "Bitch," he finally added. Jane showed no sign of receiving the communication. Blighted, toothless Jane. She was looking like some gaudy pastry that had been left out in the sun too long. Her brain was shot. Perhaps only a bit of it remained in the base of her tongue to wag some old curses. "Fucking liar. You sure as hell got something all over me."

Pearl giggled. I looked over at Botanicos to see how he was taking it. He was a long way from Mary and her Shetlands. Pearl looked at me and I nodded. Then she directed herself to Jane. "Get my bucket. Can't you see we got customers?" Jane roused herself - as if a distant alarm had just rung, an indistinct call to duty and began to grope along the wall like a blind woman till she found the door to her bedroom. She soon reappeared, stumbling about with her load trying to get it to the backdoor, till she half fell and landed the pail so hard that some of the douche sloshed out on the rug and against the stove where it sizzled and went up in steam. Pearl looked disgusted. "I ought to kick your ass, you helpless whore."

Meanwhile the wino was trying to get the attention of Botanicos. "A man ought to know if he got laid or not." Botanicos was pretending not to hear and involved himself in loosening his scarf and looking elsewhere. The man slumped back in some sort of rumination for a minute and then reached down and pulled out his lifeless penis, peering expectantly at the head of it - as if he hoped it would settle the dispute in his favor. He looked up. "I ain't paying," he said.

Pearl stood up. "You better stick that ugly thing of yours back in your pants or I'll get my knife and cut it off." She was shouting - measuring out some rage - tired of him.

Botanicos had his pipe out now and had begun to work on a bowlful, tamping the mixture with deliberation. I was nervous about leaving my friend alone in the midst of this circus. If only there was something civilized for him to do - a magazine even. As it was, with Pearl in the other room, the old man might take to smacking Jane around or Jane, who had already eyed Botanicos, might get it into her head to make a foolish lunge for his stuff. I half expected him to leave.

She led me into her room but not before holding me back a minute at the door while she bent over in the pitch dark and shook her sleeping daughter. A brown child of perhaps nine that Pearl now was trying to wrest from the hollow in the bed. She wrapped her in one of the blankets and walked her, still mostly asleep, past me. The girl was rubbing her eyes. I saw her see me and drop her head again.

"Make yourself at home," Pearl said as she passed. I sat down on the edge of the bed and started pulling off my boots, putting the socks and wallet inside, pants beside them. I was cold again and could feel the goosebumps. My hand went between my thighs and, tugged on it a couple of times to get the blood moving. I blocked a thought of what was under the heap of covers behind me. Her blankets were probably like her rugs - she added them, perhaps shook them, swept them; but she didn't replace, didn't scrub. I got under them and sank into a slightly punk, musty warmth. I could hear Pearl's voice next door; gathering force, bringing up a loud complaint against the old man. "You get your sick ass out of here...Here take your fucking money... You come back, I'll cut you." "Nigger bitch" he answered..."Nigger bitch is it, Mike? Where's my knife." Fading commotion finally punctuated with the back door slamming.

A few moments later she opened the door and came in. "Crazy-assed Jane. I ought to throw her out too." She closed the door. She had the bucket in her hand. I felt her hands patting the bottom of the bed. "Which side you on honey? There you are." I wanted a cigarette. I still had the shivers. I sat up and pulled the pack from my shirt pocket, then struck a match and held it, looking for an ashtray. There was a small silver tree on the bureau - the type my grandmother Mable used in Saxon Gardens at Christmas time. I turned my boot on one side, blew out the match and laid it on the heel. She was getting in bed, not touching me. "That's right," she said. "Light me one too." I took another out and lit it from the ember. I heard her reach. Then she put a saucer between us and we smoked in silence for a while until she broke it abruptly with her laugh. "You know anyone in West Virginia?" She asked it as if she were talking about someplace down the street. I knocked off the ash in the saucer. Briefly I could see that she had pulled up the blankets to her chin. "I got relations down there," she continued. "That's where I'm from." I just listened. She went on about brothers, sisters, the mines, Charleston, this dump, that honky King, hillbillies, her father's shotgun. Her rambling was so soothing - apparently endless - nothing to do with that moment. And each time it slowed she rejuvenated it. "Why you ask? Well let me tell you why."

I offered short concurrences as other images tumbled in my mind...the miniature Christmas tree, stacking presents under it with Grandma in her hairnet, excursions to F.A.O. Schwartz with its floors of drumming, whirring, beckoning toys, Bethlehem, a brilliant shot from the night sun to the manger, her sleepy-eyed daughter, cookies for Santa.

She showed no signs that her conversation would stop. I was warmer now. I lifted off the saucer and rolled toward her. "Why, honey, why didn't you tell me you was ready for Pearl?"

Easily, she led me over her leg. Yet so dark was it, I could see nothing. my hands were beneath her slighter back. She was humming a child's song. Yet, still the thoughts - her daughter. I closed my eyes and moved in her fluids. And I had soon outstripped thought - left it behind - unmuddled, unwasted. Till, for me, no more, nothing - just the surge while I rocked in her song in her arms in the dark.

Soon after, she left the bed. I heard her splashing over the bucket. Then I felt her sit next to me. She laid her hand on my forehead for a moment. "Do you think your friend wants to go with Pearl?" she asked. I couldn't imagine it and said no. I felt very warm and drowsy. Very happy. "Come on lazy bones," she said, "I've got to get my daughter back in bed."

When we entered the living room, we found Jane passed out on the couch, snoring through her hairpiece; now lying askew on her shiny, hairless skull. Botanicos had apparently gone into the kitchen and was enjoying some coffee with a book he had found on songs for a fourth grader. The little girl was curled up in the armchair, closest to the stove, sound asleep. Botanicos rose and began to put on his coat. "I hope you don't mind my making myself some coffee." "God no," she laughed. "Anytime you're looking for a good cup of coffee, you just come down here." Pearl led her visitors to the door, stopped and shook her finger at us. "Next time you boys remember to bring Pearl some gin. It's too cold now for a Southern girl like me to go out." Botanicos stepped out onto the steps.

I lingered to give her the money and what I thought to be, a romantic kiss - the delicate variety. She giggled and pushed me toward my friend.

We were out of the soup and into the thin winter air; roused again. Botanicos stopped at the hedge. "Greasy spoon," he enquired, smiling. "Of course," I said. "There's nothing else." Dawn, I knew would come in an hour or so, then morning classes. Sleep, now, would do more harm than good. We headed off toward the railroad tracks, intent on food. Until after a few steps, I threw my arm around Botanicos shoulders. Botanicos was amused. He had found it memorable - sort of like a movie.

We had reached a decline which would take us through a short tunnel under the rail trestle. I stopped and looked back at Pearl's. There was no sign of life. Suddenly I was dismayed by what I saw - a grey and destitute tenement, alone, enveloped by winter. How could that defeated place have been, so few minutes ago, a mother to my great joy? Was I a low traitor to my kin? I felt drawn, in my chest, near the center, to race back, to be the absurd man on the roof, to try to slay the winter with a pop gun. Then, an issue of smoke. Charred, paper cinders were fluttering from her stovepipe. I knew she was stoking it from a pile of newspapers and pieces of packing crates. I should bring her some decent wood tomorrow. Now she would be sitting back with her bleak eyes, raising her gin and milk, staring through the chinks in the grating at the dancing flames.

I watched the smoke abate. Here was a manifestation, an honest one, of an anguish with which, in the past, I had indulged my own heart. The pain in my chest was real but shame blunted its exquisiteness and its right. I remembered the glance from the daughter as she had left the room.

I turned away. I was back on my jaunt through the hinterland. My jeans were loose. I flexed my back and patted the cavity below my rib cage. Lines of box cars commuted overhead between great lakes like Erie to the Orange Blossom state. My dad had counted them as a boy and before that, a half mile west, the broad waked barges of the Hudson River trade; now, both eclipsed by the north south super highways. All those cities like Schenectady, clustered near the movement, nourished from it and essentially attached to it. Between the tracks and the river was the access avenue to the highway; a miracle mile, fluorescent at night with spectacular neon invitations. By day a dismal sight. I saw our destination - an all night diner that resembled a railroad car with a stainless steel fuselage, known commonly as the greasy spoon, famous for its all-the-ways, genuine flight food. That is to say the treat that was now making my mouth water as I advanced on that place: a chiffon pork dog pumped up with air and filler lying on a lighter than cloud bun all weighted down with a brown gruel of chili beans, morsels of red peppers, green onion dices, garlic and chunks of hamburger - a poor man's stew fried in animal fat, glistening with it. Glistening with slippery one cell drops that squirmed and danced when it was hot on the griddle and then gelled like dots of paste as it cooled. This was not a diet for the queasy. It brought beads of sweat to the brow, heartburn to older citizens. It was combustible food; not nutrition but fire for the engine and best washed down with Irish whiskey and Blue-Ribbon draughts.

The Making of a Story

I had my schedule, meant to keep some balance. The garbage men came. Five floors down before first light, they heaved the empty metal pails back onto the pavement. The day began. Not with the lion stretching under the warming sun but with routine anguish, the daily call for courage. No sir. No Zip-a-Dee-Doo-Dah here but instead the searching painfully in the dark for the switch. No instant hot spray here. A trickle of tepid. No big shopping bags either . . . filled with colorfast packages. Only a thin slip of plastic with the name of the charcuterie stenciled in black. Into which I put my cotton trunks. It was several levels below

33

the pavement. It was the familiar large clock with
the sweeping black hand, still over green water and
chlorine gasses. Over 20 meters with several of them
circling in each lane. I was always on someone's kick
or passing into oncoming traffic. The goggles leaked
and often needed emptying at lane ends. By the time
I was done the body felt as if it had been dipped in a
corrosive. Every pore scoured. I turned in my towel at
the cage and went back out into the dark. There were
rainbows around the streetlamps. This was the best of
the day. Zip-a-Dee-Doo-Dah. My muscles feeding, my
mind bright. I had two shots of Turkish at the corner
cafe and the day's first drag on a Gauloise. Anything
was possible. And of course, no food for the drag it
would put on the Turkish.

I sat behind the dead man's desk and looked
down on the synagogue where the dead children had
been memorialized. Day had arrived. I had heavy
furniture from the thirties. It had been a pleasant
little agent. He called his wife *mon chou*. He had
broken the red wax seal three weeks ago. The tenant
had been dead for weeks before he had been found.
There was only the bed, a chest, and the desk, all of
which I had bought. The deceased had been careless
about the pigeons living in the vent to the toilet.
I did love the furrow of the ball point on the soft

bond, the indigo on the cream. The rainbow around the bulb and the muscles feeding. As I said, I had my schedule. I was taking a second or two off the swim each successive day. They served the Turkish as I came through the café door. I had the pen resting near the bond ready to move as the Turkish kicked in, captivated by the rainbow around the bulb.

It had been a couple of weeks ago that I had begun again. I had my scribbling from some school papers, the piece from the cafe in Cala Ratjada a couple of months back and a large manila envelope stuffed with scraps of paper on which I had jotted good words or important advice from my graduation onward. Unlike before I was not now engaged formally to other temporary objectives—finishing college, or some ersatz romance.

So there I was, sitting in the nearly-empty room with my dog-eared copy of Cowley's *Exiles Return* and my writing materials. I knew I had scant reason to hope: that I had laid little down from which to take off. Equally, there was little left after this. Without, that is, becoming what I had hated almost since birth and which I swore was worse than death. Cowley helped. In a way, it was a godsend. It presented company, albeit mythical and legendary, but still some secret co-conspirators again. And that, with time, thank God, would help to put me on a first tear.

At the onset, however, I stayed tentative with my pen. I chose to ruminate: inspect further a few of the notorious books I had brought with me from school. But this time as a solitary man in a dramatic situation. No doubt, some of it was procrastination—getting as psyched as possible before hitting the water. It was still awkward. I feared early on that I couldn't compete with the technicians. The veterans of fine arts. This seemed confirmed as I recollected on the various cautions summoned up by professors from my past.

Then, one day on a walk across the river, I copied an author's address at Shakespeare and Co. and found his apartment. Like those pedants who could jerk me off my occasional spontaneous elocutions at college with their 'stank for stunk,' this man—who by day was handing his copy out on street corners while his wife clerked to bring in the rent—took to curling up on his divan while I anxiously searched for metaphors that would please him. Shamed but not yet defeated, I needed to believe I was more desperate, had greater dreams. Back down the stairs as I had in the past, I reminded myself that he had not slid, bloodied, through the mud to head it into the net late in the season. He had not stood there at nightfall on America's great plains with his thumb out.

I got stuck on words. One took you through to another. I enjoyed taking a word through its varieties of meanings and sounds. I was picking my way through the sentences. Making the slow tails of the y's and g's, spending an hour on the etymology of the word above nympholepsy. Throwing out, it seemed, thousands of strings toward what the Turkish couldn't spark. Nothing lovely, nothing terrible. There was depression at the trifle. I stuck my hand out the window and pulled in my container from the ledge. They sold sparrows at the charcuterie with green cherries in their beaks. I ate cheese and cold cuts and drank instant coffee thick as porridge.

But wasn't my folklore replete with them, I mused. They had never studied in little leagues. They had pitched at a tire behind the barn until their father's whistle brought them in. Till 60,000 stood as one, as men like Cy Young left the last batter in the top of the ninth swinging at air. Phenoms. How had the writers been? Was there some of that in me? I was a Cold War baby. Fat on the bone. Sticking my big toe across the states at seventeen and then ever so briefly into the Pacific, writing WHY on public buildings. Singing sweet nothings with my last senseless fling, Phyllis.

I would write of the forces that conspired to rob me of myth and of being mythical. The leveling of prosperity, the birth of suburbia, the end of great hardship and yearning. Comfort as the scourge of heroes. The future in the hands of technicians. The way once upon a time the world had come through to the pale boy from the Scottish borders. Mysteries receding. Huckleberry dead. Yes, the story of the Cold War baby. The end of the millenniums of hardship for the Aryans. The sucking of blood in the hold of a Japanese tanker. The years of awful winnowing. The heavy hand, the thick wrist, the hairy bodies. The blank faces on the daguerreotypes of children in mining camps, on the plains, on deck, were gone. Mental illness up. Slow dancing under the hydrogen lantern. Sweets for the sweet. Less flesh on flesh, bone to bone. Nature slipping beyond the pale. Technology as the great Homogene. Climate control. Festering discontent in the sunbelt. Dying inside. Cold War baby. Winter born. Kicking and poking, it sees some light after difficult times. It cozies its cover up next to the masterpiece on the shelf. Or is it—rubbing my eyeballs, scratching, the particles of dandruff floating down onto the pad—more accurately, the rest having failed, the time for revering Shaman? Propagator of myth as truth. From truth as what is hollered on the street corner—Extra, Extra—to truth as what gets on a publisher's jacket. The great love of Bosco Depasquale and Serafina Scaramuzza. Bringing the guest before the crackling fire. Standing on the crate in Jamal el-fnaa and competing with snake charmers for an ear. The drop of virulence slid down one coarse hair and amidst the upheaval and the uproar dropped unseen into the darkness of sheets and dresses. But how was what furrowed the forehead not to be confused by the ardent technicians? Like old medieval women who spent a lifetime on ambitious weaves. Who weighed every letter in each word, each word in every sentence, for weight and sound and symbol. Empirical wonder words. Three and seven as most favored numbers. But who turned the pages on such tricky matters? Nature almost beyond the pale. The first sounds. The first sounds. Wolfe's forgotten language. Wind and sea. Echoes from the beginning. The stories around the fire. The charcoal on the walls of the caves. What a life.

The sun leaves my window and I'm writing in a cold room. Writing on speed. On my cup of soupy instant. Coming down at night on booze. The rush between shots to jot it down. Tequila combusting inside me. In a chair with a regimen. Pulling up on doors, pushing off from floors. Scrubbing the toilet bowl, washing the horse mackerel from my new mustache. Garbage. Like hunting chickadees as a child with BB guns. I left for a long walk, down the hill. So then the cliché bobbed to the surface. You are what you do. No effusive contemplation would be the building block. Write. Like push-ups. Do 2000 words a day. Crap or not. The clerk who writes ads for dogfood is more the writer than the flâneur

So I embarked. Rolled over the cloth. Left, out of necessity, the world of careful construct—the monks laboring for a month on the vines for the 'A'—and pushed forward as if writing to a missed childhood friend. Covered the paper and once or twice toward the end made a nice pitch. Seemingly, not as a wrestler pitted in another's grip. Rather, forward, advancing through the magic, the funhouse, the house of horrors, as cut-out pop-ups suddenly appear. The wonderment described. All of them, concerning the heartfelt loves since childhood. For Jesus. Consumed by Jesus and/or His frightful strickening. Pursuing fair Hawthorne, down under, and his brilliant cat's eyes amidst the roots of the gum tree down by Rose Bay . . . or as a bare-assed boy in Connecticut with Dickie scampering over the thick banks in muddy brook with buttercups sprouting from our pee holes, with Big Bob lurking in the weeds, striking out at our child's bodies with his fishing line and barbed hooks. With Anne of Westphalia for whom I, at the back door of her tenement, suffered my first mutilation. Back to Jesus with Lennie who did more time in solitude pushing great weights heavenward than I was of age, and others of my youth that I loved . . . or hated for their shriveled souls. Swinging into view and then fading.

My room was large enough to pace but that didn't get the weight off. Lennie's eight black fifties on the stainless-steel bar gleaming in the prison yard became the molding on the entrance to the toilet whereby mid-afternoon my body needed to be used. I hung from the ledge and lifted, pulled my chin over the top, poking up at the imaginary Daphne. Hanging there naked, pulling myself up, she suspended in the clear water. Me hanging. Till my veins had burst: the shudder, the drool. Phyllis had been fascinated with the way it worked. Disheveled. The stare curious: my member quite stained with lip rouge. Eventually another shot of soupy coffee didn't help enough. The pen often stayed stuck.

I took more long walks, aimless, often down the hill to the river. I liked the warrior queens at Luxembourg, Gaul's stock, the good benches around Ugliano, a chair at the zoological gardens. Snooping, rewriting, more words jotted on scraps. Seeing the world fresh, I was coming down from ten days straight of writing. A baguette, a glass of wine in some unknown neighborhood. Miles I would travel as the observer. Inevitably past bookstores. I still loved the feel of them. The gift of a distant unknown's creations. Private thinking. Which eventually got my knees up against my chest on the mattress at night, back propped against the wall. A deep draw on my Gauloise and some piping instant and I would read until sleep overtook me. Not a word spoken to anyone all day long save the "merci" to the man who served me my first Turkish and to the woman who made my baguette. The tourists came. In droves. Banks of buses were everywhere. I walked farther afield to avoid this indignity. Absolutely no redeeming value, I accused, to bringing a busload of flapping suburbanites to ooh and aah at Notre Dame, scramble to memorialize the moment with a pic, and raise Holy Hell over the lack of comforts. "Did you see that toilet, dear?" America will surely be paid back one day for this invasion, I thought. This disgusting indignity. I sat on benches at Butte Chaumont and watched the poorer mothers wheel their babies by the water. In the background there were peeling, aspic-colored buildings with George Marchais posters slapped upon them and what must have been commie cafes down on the corner.

My back went. I was pushing hard against the big hand at the pool and something snapped or froze. I went to the American Hospital in the sixteenth arrondissement. These were shaded grounds. The swish of muslin in quiet corridors. A robed man in the courtyard learning to walk, a nurse by his side. Ernest convalescing, I thought. The doctor gave me an old-world syringe of Cortisone in the back. Back at the apartment I brought my writing pads off the desk and into the bedroom and there I began to drift. The wake-up was gone. At first the bed was better; it allowed me to be transported more easily, even get a couple of early images of life. I was perpetually starved for books and scribbled away frantically. Night and day became confused. I went in and out of dreams and Shakespeare and writing until I could not think outside of iambic pentameter. I was omnivorous for his work. Through the histories into vivid dreams and back to writing as I had not done since the clock at school had incited me to dash across pages in a mad scrawl to get it all in before the prof lifted the paper. I finished dreams with my pen.

Re-created on the pot with the pigeons warbling in my ear. The exhilaration was such that I wouldn't have pulled back for the world. Dust balls shifted like tumbleweeds across the floor. Shadows loomed like phantoms. My back was slow to heal. I was galloping through three of his plays a day and filling a dozen pages.

At the end of a week, grudgingly, I went down at dusk and bought enough tinned mackerel and Shakespeare for a month. I locked myself in. Twice I froze at persistent knocking. I had gotten to the point where I could not manage discussion. There was some swearing and they left. I was at my best. I was reading Shakespeare like the back of my hand and sometimes putting it down just right myself. Truthful stuff. Digging into my impoverished mind to try to see as clearly as the first man. But of course, as forewarned, such glimpses are not rare for nothing. They, like everything else, carry with them their own destruction. Spoil sets in. Brown soft spots. Something caught the corner of my eye. "The tail disappearing under the plinth," if you will, Mr. Joyce. A plate drops and you realize how taut you're drawn. You see the rat cleaning its fingernails in the moonlight. I pulled the sheet up to shield my face. Made a fist around my pen. Shadows of dust balls into rats. The phantom into Injun Joe leaning over with a rusty shiv.

The fall is precipitous. Within 48 hours my retreat had turned into a chamber of horrors. More Turkish for fewer pages. More Tequila to go to sleep. Puking in the bowl. Shooting pain behind the eyes. The exercise dwindles then stops. There is no end to the questions. Each one turns out upon another. Everything is involved. Everything is in question. It is, I had read, The Great Midway. The initial inspiration often gone. The cheers, as you pushed off, out of sight. Adrift, becalmed. What had begun as a thirty-page survey is now, can be, 100 pages of discourse on the yellow of my toenail. Weakness set in. I hid from more knocks on the door. I who strode through dark neighborhoods. Hawkeye vanishes along with his puzzlements. The upending of his enemy's canoe. The nightmares multiply. I could feel the cold nose of the barrel against the temple. Could see the farm girl, swinging on that gate I had passed in Kansas now in lavender floating up before my face, smiling, with her viper's tongue.

My boyhood orangutan is slamming around in a cage. Fear and hate as inseparable and indistinguishable. A magnetic pull. There came an insidious inclination to lay on my back and silently attack my Peggy, word by word in every conceivable way for presenting me one hopeful night with Fleurs du Mal only to allow her presumed assimilist father in Brooklyn, days later, to separate us so seamlessly. I grasping madly for revelations. Staring at the semen in my navel. Waiting for an out. Time to put bread on the table. But too trapped to move. Hopelessly lost in The Great Midway. Destined to be found, I feared, one day rolling back and forth, face down, in the crags. I was too scared to take my eyes off the page. Then I'd argue. Confront it. It doesn't exist. See how foolish. And I'd look at it straight on and there was nothing.

But as I returned to the page something moved on the periphery. Or once there was something warm next to my leg. I jumped up and back again as if I had landed on fire. I ran to the toilet and opened the door. I swear there was a pigeon there the size of a buffalo with sister Roo's head in its beak. I started snapping my head back and forth and chanting nonsense—in effect scrambling my senses so that nothing could come in. I thrashed down the stairs. I grabbed a note from the concierge and left before she could commit me to further inquiry.

So, I walked down the hill blinking incessantly and chanting. A mad exile for the tourists. I'd walk it to death. Same as I had done on the soccer field with the deceit of Peggy. Exhaust the wherewithal for destruction. Two hours at top speed around the Tuileries in the noonday sun and the rats had indeed receded to the shadows. I was able to sit by the pool and watch the children sail their boats. I was pale as chalk and had a scraggly orange beard like the hair under my father's arms. A woman seated across the water smiled at me lovingly. I must have blushed and looked away. Unless she had picked me up in her arms and carried me to her home it was no use. By the time I looked up again she was leaving. I imagined the apartment as rife with them now— nesting in my mattress, gnawing on my books. The beady eyes. The beady eyes over the beak seeing me as a worm bug. I couldn't go back.

The sun went down. The mothers took their children away. For me, madness had always meant loony. In another world. Unable to function on the street. Not the drill bit tearing through the tooth shredding the nerve. Which it is. You can't help but want to put a bullet through the brain to stop it. There's no fainting here to relieve it: no anesthesia. Only how long you can stand it before you stop it forever. I kept my head down and moved off the chair, trembling. To the extent I could think

of nothing, there was another respite. But I didn't
have the strength to sustain it. The thoughts on the
surface were submerged by the likes of pigeons and
rats. Always in the periphery of my vision. Always
menacing.

I sat in Le Bowling for three days, sweating
bullets, I think. Always dark, drinking rotgut, dozing
on the couch, peering circumspect as Francoise and
the Senegalese danced bone to bone. Buying a tab
off the pitiful Bulgarian boy. In my lair, yearning for
repair. At first talking. Talking to myself. To strangers.
Not letting them get away. Recounting to them how
it happened. I hung onto them, their disinterested
faces, even past their exit. I was trying to kill it by
putting it out in the light of day. Everyone including
the toilet woman knew what had happened. Left
alone, it became perpetual. The sharp fingernail
drawn slowly across the soft abdomen. Or taking it
on, foolishly. Pulling it out of the hole and eating
the goddamn tail. Pacing the dance floor and
bombarding the senses. Guzzling my wine. Now,
swallowing the tab. Anything to disappear from this
nightmare. Praying to my old congregational Jesus.
Talking to Him out loud in execrable French. In
iambic pentameter. By now an opinion was building

at the bar to get me out. To a hospital. They were bored with my situation.

Suicide was not uncommon in Paris. Life goes on. Abruptly, I fled downstairs. My imagined strength. My lump of concocted good health. Where I strode, I now quivered. The baby bawling. The son rocking with his father's dead head in his lap. I had almost succumbed. It was the clammy flesh of a drowned man. How, I cried, to be as rosy dumb as my only friend, the toilet woman, who only sees real rats sticking their noses up her drain holes. Succumb was intermittent visions of my body draining away. My finger on the porcelain and I've lost it up to my wrist. I direct my eyes elsewhere at the man pissing and his teeth are bared. And so I stumbled frantically on that thin surface. Big bum up, she was swabbing with those hairy arms and wart-afflicted face. I, too, took a brush and scrubbed. Babbling along with her about the work at hand. A cradle, this poor mama, until I could escape. Keeping me just shy of the padded cell. She was handing me the envelope that had fallen out while I had been washing so madly about the urinals. Half soaked. Ink smeared: "United States Armed Forces . . . August 15th . . . prosecuted and subject to imprisonment . . ." And my dad's scribble alongside: "this is serious. Please call immediately . . . It'll be OK."

I was going to war. The third and last notice, it seemed. Report or go to prison. "It'll be OK." Dad had meant a desk job. Rather, I imagined it was to be under a crescent moon with my childhood friend, Dickie. Never quite sure but, dare I hope, it seemed to drain. The pain slowly seeping away. Like a plug had dislodged. It took no more than to read it again and again to the toilet woman. For better or worse, I told her uncomprehending face, "I would ride with the brigade." Over and over until within hours the worst seemed over.

I was encouraged enough to leave, to say goodbye. The genie it seemed had been brought back into the bottle by the news of war. Certes, I could bring it up. But for the time being it wasn't insisting. Apparently, the concocted lump of health was being carefully restored. God, had I hugged that beating heart. Arms tight around all that lumpen mass, planting a huge kiss into her incredulous mouth and then emptying my pockets for her. I had left her thus: confused, counting her coins.

Still, that night, I had taken no chances. In one motion I had unlocked the door and had run through the dark for my passport, writing pads and wallet and then back in the hall without a breath, falling back and closing the door on them. Several hours later I was out on a night flight from Orly, with little beyond the clothes on my back, soon mouth open, deep in sleep.

NORTHBROOK, 1967

Since Roo was being oriented at her college in Southern California, oriented far away from the Yankee fastness, I had the parents to myself—full blast. "Men with your education can pick their assignments," said Henry. I had seen the advertisements. You give them the years and you get clean sheets at night. It would be a black porcelain panther on Major Rutherford's desk. Or it would be two years as a grunt. I couldn't pick anything in my present state. I needed to be swept along by what I described in my writings as a national movement, the most common denominator. Back on the bus to register—with my face to the window— with no personal commitment for the outcome of life around me.

I would go to basic like millions of Americans before me. Be privy to the details of men going to war, from Thermopylae to Pork Chop Hill. The stench of the battlefield. Of killing and dying, as described from Troy to the Ardennes. The primal ingredients of the human condition. The hands around his neck. Of slowly, with all your God-given strength, eye to eye, strangling the life out of your fellow man—watching him thrash and change color—or of lying, bowels cooking in the sun, face up to heaven, beyond pain. So drafted I was and drafted I'd be. My Aussie mother proud. She of such reverence for Tennyson and unwavering about better Dead than Red. She, who was genuinely grieved that she could not show us how it was done. This English settlement in the South Seas didn't give an inch at Tobruk or El Alamein. I told her my mind was not formed yet on whether to go or to return to Paris and miss the war. She stated, while Henry cringed, that if I did, the door to the house would be closed to me, forever. "I did not give birth to a coward." Was that the unspoken deal? The real marriage vow. Men went to war and women could accept the rest.

Henry, who had been spared a gun himself was less certain. As a booster there were some obligations to have a son serving. It rubbed off on him. As a businessman he knew war wasn't all his Swanie cracked it up to be. There was money involved and cannon fodder. But, as a photo taken of me at the time revealed, I was empty. I had nothing to lose.

I sat on the couch while the excitement swirled around, not mad anymore but dazed. Someone I was not attracted to. The type who slouched, moved with effort, picked his nose, unconcerned, in public. Uninterested by invitations for reunions in the city, preferring to watch reruns of *Father Knows Best* in the middle of the day. Ready to fall in step.

The drama returned on the eve of my induction. I knew that my life of skirting round the edges was finished. I was giving myself up voluntarily for man's periodic winnowing of the races. Man's breaking loose from unsatisfying peace. Only words when I hashed it out in school. What made it so academic eighteen months back was our inability to appreciate how little we had to lose. Through it all we had wallowed in how much we counted. Never thought of ourselves as some small pleasure: a bit of pain. You get up because you're not tired; you go to sleep when you are. If I stuck my toes past the covers, I could feel the teething marks on my old maple footboard. Through the window by my head I had crawled out and down the roof at night to fish for eels with Dickie. Imagine a pennant for Camp Sloan over the boy's desk where mom typed the final. Why do they bother? Why not just spawn and feed and fight? Little investments to take the gray off life. Across the hall Henry was snoring.

The next morning, I prevailed upon them. The instructions were explicit. I was to bring nothing with me save toothbrush and razor. Anything else would be sent home anyway. After breakfast they took me to the railroad station from whence I had made my forays to New York as a teenager. That same locomotive that had brought me on those exotic flights. The slivers of shower water on my face as I lay bundled in those last days before Montmartre, aside the tub with Phyllis, goose bumps in a dark bathroom in the city. Steps were put down. My father looked away. My mother was drawn, shadows under the eyes. Doubt apparently had crept in over the night. Sometime before dawn the advertisements for war had come under her closer scrutiny.

Imagine Rutherford of yore, of less than two years ago. Now I fairly whistled from the stop in New Haven to the induction center. Almost bemused amidst the rank and file as I raised my hand to swear allegiance and then joined the file to police the parking lot. "All I want to see is assholes and elbows," the sergeant bellowed. Even then, stooped, as we muttered our complaints, my health kept returning. The inherent glow returning. Shivering at attention before sunrise. The drone of the sergeant in the dark. Until we were right-turned, double-timed, thirty four of us moving to the same rhythm through the dew, steam rising off the body, breaths trailing. "Bo Diddley, Bo Diddley, have you heard..." Squeezing toward the sun in the bleachers while the sergeant took the rifle apart. "This is my rifle; this is my gun." He had grabbed his crotch. "One is for shooting and one is for fun."

The platoon double-timed off. The jolt of the stock against the shoulder. In the report, the smell of gunpowder. The making of an army—from Appalachia to South Bronx to Northbrook—the flesh, the smells and noises of us all packed into the back of a deuce and a half. My ear on the faint heart of the boy from West Virginia, on the rumbling bowels of the man from Chelsea, on the pig's snore from Georgia. The din of hundreds in the mess hall. Chowing down. Dark again. The lowering of the flag. Crapping knee to knee, ten in a line. Too-soft Hargraves low crawling outside in the ditch. Hick's foot long. Reading the orders to the illiterates. Swinging from the doorsill to the bunk. Muttering rebellion after lights out. Dreams of sugar and women. Hardly a thought stirring of the past.

VIETNAM, 1969

There was just this sliver of moon over the shithouse where this boy was tucked up inside. I guessed he was on "record" because he had started talking to his mother. A group behind us talked low. They were claiming to have called in the world on the hillside. Phosphorous, drums of high octane, a pissing down of orange tracers. We heard that some troop had been out there on the ridge line all night. Making those nightmarish screams until he had died just before daybreak. Someone in the group behind us said it was time to go and waste the Lieutenant. Flares hung up there like lanterns on the perimeter of the firebase. They were agreeing that they had wanted to pull the wounded back. The fucking officer had said he'd hang their ass. Behind me and Percy, fifty calibers raked the shadows. Earlier, the C.O. had appeared in starched fatigues and poured us a martini. Later, half full of bourbon, I had taken the amplifier from the showgirl and had tried to haul it back to her quarters. I had lost my footing and fallen down the incline and into the concertina wire. She called down "asshole." Toward the end it shook the senses as they might not have been shaken since childhood. More magical then: stunning now. A drop of water on the pane, a rainbow-colored jewel. A word passed now stayed with me. The world at war, as advertised: a world of original aspects.

I had known Percy since we both turned up at the Infantry officers' school in Benning. A Latvian, getting a chance after six years as an enlisted man. Me, because officers had always figured in my mother's stories. He, the soldier who had always known what was going on. How to bring the polish up. The natural bark for moving the men, swords gliding past the stand. A soldier's officer, and I who couldn't lead and refused to be led and hadn't thought of us together. But at the survival school in Panama we had shared the honors. After, at the Blue Goose, I had his woman and he had mine. I declined his invitation to have our women together. Percy had surprised me. And now again, the group moved off. Presumably to off the Lieutenant. We could still hear the boy going on to his mother. Percy told me he didn't want to go out tomorrow. How now, I thought. Here, on the eve . . . my friend, the lifer, trying to step back when it's too late. Too late, that is, without the chaplain or the stockade.

Hard to forget the face. The round Latvian face stopped in time under the flare. Seconds with the power of a lifetime. All else now seemed false and passing compared to that face. I would see a handful more in the days to come. Faces that still hang up there inside my mind. My corporal when he first came over and sat next to me after that time when I had lost my first man. That thin, blue-eyed point man, now beatified, that I lifted myself onto the chopper floor. Then, later, the corporal's face, like a mask lying in the weeds, next to the bowl of brains that was left. Percy wanted to know if I didn't feel the same. Since then I have often played it back and told him yes. I'm not sure where that would have taken us. Maybe better than what we got. But I didn't. I couldn't. "I want to get on with it," I said. On the next morning I got called first. A helicopter was ready to take me out to my platoon. I got my gear together. Percy was in the showers, a large tent, by himself. He didn't see me until I was almost on him. He was washing his groin. I stuck my hand in the water. I'm not sure where his mind was. He looked at me as if we didn't know each other real well and then he took it.

———✶———

The C 141 cargo plane was floating down on the air force base outside of San Francisco. Snub-nosed and barrel-belly, it lolled down the concrete until it was parked outside the ambulance pool. The ambulances had begun jockeying toward its tail.

Once set in the queue, the drivers got out on the runway to chat, quitting it only when the massive hydraulics on the tail-ramp began to whine. The plane's ass-end now slowly separating and dropping to the ground, leaving a gaping view into its strange inside, from whence blew an antiseptic wind.

For such a giant, its guts were unsubstantial: flimsy with straps and cords; I.V. bottles and plastic tubes; exhausted nurses and nylon stretchers. Three high they were filed: some complaining about last night's chow, others staring silently, being kept alive intravenously.

During the flight, I had rested and saved my strength in the dark; I knew I would be unloaded in the daylight and would be taken through traffic.

The stretcher bearers were in a routine now, and I guessed it wouldn't be long before they got me. I had been lying in my own stink since an hour out of Japan. An orderly came over, unhooked my intravenous bottle from the fuselage and laid it next to me along with my chart: what had become my infamous billboard. I tried to engage his eyes. I wanted to get by his sense of routine and let him know that this was I that he was hauling. But it didn't matter. As we approached the rectangle of light at the end of the plane, I could already see it hanging from the top of it. I tried to scream and the hole in my throat frothed up.

I jerked my shoulder and threw my dead right arm across my body till its fingers could grip the left wrist below the arm cast but above the burning palm. I commanded my brain to start hollering its half muted nonsense. "La di da, Da di da, Dah dah dah . . . " I was fighting, hand to hand, at the base of my cerebrum. A continuous holler that reverberated until the pain in my palm retreated.

The orderlies had put my stretcher down near the ramp and were trying to find a doctor. My body was curling around the palm till my face was within inches and staring wildly at it. Behind the fire, I was trying to throw my left leg up and over so that my whole body could surround it, now turning purple from the grip. My trach continued to froth.

One of the flight nurses was kneeling down and loosening the restraining straps on the stretcher. When she smelled the sheets, she told the orderly to get her some new ones.

"Take it easy, Lieutenant. How can I help you?"

She put her fingers over my trach hole and I rasped, "Cut it off. Cut off the fucking hand. I want a stump." She withdrew her fingers.

"They'll take care of you in the hospital. Just let us get you there."

I was rocking, still contracted around my palm. "La, la, la, Dah, dah, da, da, da, da, da, yaaaaa, yaaaaa." They were lifting me to a clean stretcher. The nurse leaned over me. "OK Lieutenant, we're going to bring you down to the ambulance now. I'm going to give you a shot to help."

Then the dart of Demerol in my shoulder and I closed my eyes. The orderlies were picking me up again. "Da, da, da, dada, dada, dada, daaa, daaa."

My mind took the drug. There was the "pop" again: the sound snapping fingers would make. The millisecond of horror before the roar of twisted metal. I was slammed down on all fours, and when the black was gone I gazed upon an eggshell, a bowlful of brains. My corporal's head. I looked up and cried, "Medic, medic, get this man a medic." My radio operator stood in front of me. "I think he's dead, sir." I stayed on all fours, staring at the dried weeds, his face and the scrub, the sand between my fingers, the brains, and the valley until the wind from the rotors were scattering debris over the head.

Two of my men dragged me over to the Huey and laid me on my back. When they released my head, it fell back and hung out over the lip of the open door. The helmet left my forehead and was held between the sill and the back of my skull. Then the pilot banked and raced for home, not more than twenty yards off the paddies. It was now inalterably in my head that my life depended upon whether the helmet would shake free and drop or stay with me. The helmet had nothing to do with my slashed arteries or my open gut. But in my mind, it was simple. If I lost it, I would die; I would release my grip and let it be over.

Then, the red moustache was over me, next to his thumb.

I was being pushed on a cart into a Quonset hut, where a doctor covered my bloodied neck and was asking:

"What's your religion?"

"Does that mean I'm going to die?"

"We have to ask it."

And, at last, she was there. Blurred, but there. She was, finally, the kindness, a full heart. I raised my head toward her and asked for a kiss. The nurse smiled, and then the pentothal hit.

The traffic in town had been smooth so far and I opened my eyes. I was still holding the palm, but the intense burning had ceased after the shot. I could hear the two punks, up front, jabbering about me.

For some time, I was chewing sections of the sheet around my face and then spitting them out. When I had wet a section the size of a facecloth, I jerked my shoulder and threw my right hand up. I clinched the top of the sheet with my working fingers and then, by flexing my chest and stomach muscles, I bounced the dead right arm and the trailing sheet down the cast of the left arm to the simmering palm. Slowly, I cooled it in the moist cloth.

I closed my eyes again and started to sail with the Demerol. I wanted the field nurse so fucking much: her kindness above all. The drivers had just turned off the engine and slammed the doors of the cab. I had a glimpse of them as they moved toward the back of the ambulance, and quickly, I began my chants. With my eyes shut and my head full of my own noise, I might make it through the joggling of the transfer to the hospital. They slid me out and carried me into the basement where they deposited me on the floor among two dozen other casualties. It was a temporary holding station—poorly lit and dank.

I felt my fear ease. A staff sergeant was orienting us: "Some of you will be permanently assigned to this hospital; others will only be here for a couple of days until we arrange flights nearer to your homes. Pay attention to the doctors and the permanent party here, and you'll get along fine. The doctors will be by in about one half hour to check you out, and then you'll be taken to the wards. Welcome home."

I had been through this before in Japan: a senior doctor and his residents surrounding me, passing the chart between them, and plugging my hole so I could whisper some answers. And the pronouncements: "Causalgia, Neuralgia, Neuropsychiatric, Traumatized—quite common with bomb victims during our own civil war, a fusion of the parasympathetic and sympathetic nervous systems." And the paralysis: "You've got some movement in the fingers; let's hope you get the leg back. We'll see about the arm. Let's get a look at that steel plate in your head Lieutenant. Hmm, neat job. I had a patient once with a plate like that. He told me that when he'd take a shower, he thought he was in a tin shack during a rainstorm." By this time I was recoiling onto my burning palm and incessantly beating out sound in my brain.

Some of the flesh-wounds in the basement were sitting up, joking about new canes and the services they could provide San Francisco's ladies. I turned my head to the wall. I had to keep my mind alive for a couple more days. I knew my last shot hadn't been recorded on the chart and I hoped I could get another before the doctors came. I wanted to return to the field nurse.

I had never had more than that one communion with her: the one smile after the rescue, before the pentothal had entered me. A day later I had woken up in an intensive care unit, bandaged like a mummy, in dreadful pain with tubes everywhere from my penis to my new trach. During the following days, there were only two thoughts: morphine and a wet sponge on my lips. There were no nights or days: just the four-hour cycle between shots and the hope someone would pass by to wet my lips.

There was no declaration of permanent nerve damage yet, but the advance signs were there. Except for my left leg and the fingers on my dead right arm, I was helpless. Nothing was foreseen. Staring straight at the ceiling, suddenly a team of doctors would be muttering over me; without warning, a nurse would be pricking my veins for blood; with no idea from where it came, a scream would startle me. Then to Japan, where I was left in a ward as big as a gym. The assault against my nerves was continuous: shuffling of patients, irregular pain shots, the critical housed with the malingerers. Card games on one bed and on the next, a moribund: million-dollar flesh wounds and basket cases.

During one of these nights it came. Someone bumped my bed or turned on the light, and I felt my palm burn—a fervent sting such as a child feels from a caning. It was beyond my comprehension. All I could do was determine what triggered the pain, and try to avoid it. The skein of sensors that had kept me afloat in the world was, it seemed, hopelessly confused. My spirit's adrenaline pumped indiscriminately. I came to believe I was at war with an antipathetical environment: a hostile, all-electric clinic. Glare, dryness, and definition made me squirm. I could not tolerate shrillness, traffic, or dry sheets. At day's end, when the ward lights were dimmed, I rested. I was calmed by the shadows, especially if I could convince the nurses to pour water on my hands. I yearned to become transmogrified. Under water in my parent's brook. During my last few days in Japan, the pain had completely left the rest of my body to gather and strike the soft center of my palm. In the swirl of the drugs and the pain, it became the hideous torch.

The team of military doctors had just entered the basement and was stirring up the room. In anticipation of their visit, the ceiling lights were turned on, and I was becoming increasingly anxious. When I saw a nurse doing a blood pressure on the man next to me, I dropped my right arm off the stretcher onto the floor, and with my shoulder jerking my arm, I beat the tile. I began shaking my head back and forth evincing as much hysteria as I could. But instead of approaching me, she left to join the doctors at the other end of the room. Meanwhile the play was becoming reality as I smashed my limp arm down with more vehemence.

The nurse's aides arrived. "Take it easy, sir, we're going to take you up to your ward now. The doctors will see you in the morning." They hoisted me up onto the litter and rolled me into the hallway traffic where dozens of gurneys were shuttling past each other. While the aides argued baseball during pileups around elevators, occasionally I would turn my head to the side and confront a kindred casualty. Where had he been, a quartermaster sergeant with hemorrhoids or an infantryman with no feet? What battles were raging in his head?

They pushed me off the elevator on the third floor—neuropsychiatric—through the commotion of the intercoms and the clanging of my IV bottle against its stainless-steel pole, and into a private room. I was thankful for the privacy, but when they shifted me to the bed, I cringed from the dryness of the sheets. After the aides left, I thrashed the sheet back and started spitting saliva down onto my hand.

I could hear the evening shift outside my room gossiping over my chart and soon one of them came in. She checked my vital signs and put a piss jug between my legs.

"Just a half quart tonight, Lieutenant?"

And, then, laughing, "But then again, this is imported stuff, isn't it?"

I didn't respond, and she leaned forward. I stretched my head back to show her my trach and when she covered it, I patiently conveyed my needs: "Wet towels and a shot."

"Hang on, Lieutenant. I'll be back in a couple of minutes."

Soon after, she returned to stick some dope into my shoulder and to bandage my hands with sopping towels. By the time she was done, my mind was already sucking in the Demerol. I leaned back and exposed my trach. She covered it and bent her head near my mouth. With only enough breath for a few words at a time, I labored to get it out: "Don't tell me . . . Teller . . . about the violence . . . in a flower . . . here is . . . one G.I. . . . who would like . . . to kick your . . . fucking head in." She straightened up and looked down curiously at me. Then she left.

She had given me a full shot and I knew I could be alone with my distant hope for hours. With dilated eyes, I went home with my nurse from Chu Lai—into the Village Green with its statue of a gaunt civil war soldier—stern with his rifle and greatcoat. Back to my home as it was in the time of Dickie.

Some shuffling and commotion was beginning in the hall outside my room. The morning shift. I swung my arm against the bed table, searched for some tissue, and then threw my arm back against my abdomen. I closed my eyes again and gave myself up to her. Afterward, I lay silently for a few minutes. Then I noticed the day's first light coming in under the shade. My fingers rolled it into a ball and dropped it on the floor.

The noise of the morning rounds and breakfast were accelerating outside and suddenly, it was as if a 155 shell had just taken down my door and was being followed by a Southwestern high school marching band. The head nurse strode in, and the torches were ignited.

"Good morning, Lieutenant. Hope you slept well. Let's get these shades up and let the day in."

She strutted over to the window, snapped up the cords, reared back, and with hands on hips, studied me. Then she reached over and snatched away the damp towel.

"God, Lieutenant, what are you trying to do to my bed? You'll have mold growing there before long."

I shut my eyes against her. I hated her. A close-cropped Major. Bilious. I wanted to stick a grenade down her and blow out her belly. She continued to glower over me as I began straining my head toward the palm.

"The doctor will be here in a minute. Try to act like an officer in front of him."

I hooked my left foot under my caste up right leg and kicked it up over behind the palm. The IV needle in my ankle vein ripped out, rattling the stand it hung from and trailing blood across the sheets. By now I had my teeth deep into the plaster cast above the pain and was silently demanding: "Cut it off . . . Cut it off . . . Cut it off . . . Cut it off . . . "

The doctor was gripping me under the chin and struggling to straighten me out. The head nurse had pinioned my plaster limb and was stripping away the fingers of the other dead arm. The torch now sent a thick flame drilling through my palm.

Later there were other hands and excited talk: a fool's face above me, an 8-inch needle, and a syringe full of Novocain. I felt the needle enter my neck close by the throat and tediously they shoved it through my flesh till its steel end was rummaging against my spinal cord.

With the confident extraction the half-dozen hands relaxed, I cocked my one good limb, my left leg, knee to chin, and shot it through the air striking the fool in his gut and sending him down on his ass.

Automatically I cocked again and let it fly till it smashed against the metal end of my bed and skidded the frame. Someone tackled the leg and quickly a half-dozen arms suffocated and hog-tied me. I felt the weight of no escape. They strung nylon straps across me till I was heaving to no avail. Then surrounding my bed, they stepped back for the victory stare. A few minutes later the doctor and his cortege departed.

"Give him some pain medication," he uttered at the door.

The head nurse followed them out and returned much later with the Demerol. I was humping autistically, my bed bouncing on the linoleum in time with my relentless internal chant: "Skip to the loo; skip to the loo; skip to the loo."

She held the needle up to the light and depressed the piston in the hypodermic until half the dose was wasted in a thin fountain. She stuck the rest in my shoulder, checked the metal teeth on the straps and headed for the door. Then her eye caught the ball of tissue by my bed. She carefully picked it off the floor, and, holding it in front of her like the pestilence, dispatched it into the waste can. With her back to me and talking to no one in particular, she gave her final indictment: "And this belongs in here." Then she was gone.

Under the straps I twisted and buried the burning palm in my sweaty groin. I put the fire of my hand to my damp testes. Slowly the Demerol was dissolving the cerebral struggle.

I had been able to smell bad weather coming. On the run from my enemies, I had shimmied trees and hid in their tall branches. The army had inducted a fighter and given me a universal shine. On helmets, buckles, boots, floors, rifles, and commodes. In place of stroking my instincts, I broke starch and shouted orders to lampposts until they obeyed me. It was a campaign to kill the hunt in me and in its place to accept an accommodation with the absurd.

We had moved out of the company perimeter about mid-morning; my platoon, dog-faced draftees from West Virginia, Brooklyn, and Cleveland. Far from the world where high-level strategies move easily across maps, my troops were bedecked with golden spangles and long hair. They lived on tins of fruit cocktail and sliced peaches and hunted "Charlie" with hoods made from G.I. issue towels and a tape cassette plug in their ear. They moved in a 110 degree "free fire zone" and still were downtown, slippin' and slidin' with James Brown.

I wanted to keep them moving for about four hours and then find some cover and shade during the afternoon blaze. A Barnum and Bailey parade. Confrontation eluded us: just an old farmer, who turned the wrong way and got bounced down a trail by an M60.

Later, my point man got wasted. Darting back and forth up front with his shotgun and, then: the poof, the roar, and finally the shouts of "Medic, Medic." He had tripped the bomb's invisible filament. The boy's bowels were hanging down to his knees, and the medic was trying hopelessly to gather them back into a hole as big as a basketball. When I laid him down inside the medivac I saw that the boy's blue eyes were beatified and surely dead.

The hill where we would take shelter was a kilometer in front of us. It rose up from the surrounding paddies about a hundred yards and was covered with sandy soil and knee-high weeds. On its crest was fifty square yards of shoulder-high scrub.

I requested artillery preparation on the hill, but the request was denied. "God damnit, Lieutenant. We don't want the whole world to know we're here." So we advanced to the scrub on top, searched it, and then dug in around it.

An hour later my third squad leader left his foxhole to talk with me. About six feet away from me: the filament, the poof, and another teenager, with his instincts intact, had ridiculed the plans of America's traveling circus.

I lay in my room, trussed on my side, full of hate for the nonsense behind my mutilation. Angrier still, that I was still tied to it in their hospitals.

The door opened and I felt a shock cut into my palm. I squeezed my sweating genitals and closed my eyes. I heard her breathing. There was no sound for several minutes until:

"Lieutenant, they've got a flight for you tonight."

I opened my eyes toward her and, pulling my head back, I showed my trach: rocking my neck to make her understand.

She covered the hole and I wheezed, "Shot and the straps."

"No, Lieutenant. The straps will stay on until you've learned to behave. As far as the shot goes, they'll give you one at the airbase before you get on the plane. I expect them to be in here to get you in about an hour."

Then she walked down to the foot of the bed, tapped the IV bottle a couple of times and went out.

My mind exalted in the news. Home. My kin. Some few friends and civilian doctors. Allies. And she'd come too—once she had heard my story and knew how to find me—to join me as I repaired. And to return with me. To smear black pitch on our faces and run close to the ground on moonless nights. To smell their fascist spoor and to wait silently for hours in the shadows of their barracks until reveille, when they stood before their young recruits, to hear their blasphemy: the drill sergeant puffed himself up with disdain and slapped the butt of his rifle on the ground.

"And Sergeant, what about women?"

"Pussy on the hoof," the Sergeant scoffed.

"And what about young ones, Sergeant, say thirteen-year-olds?"

And the response: "If they're old enough to bleed, they're old enough to butcher."

And to bring the sergeant's temple into the notch of our sights and slowly squeeze the triggers.

To wait till they've offered their guns and fifty cents to some Vietnamese, for a suck, and then, once again, to slowly squeeze the trigger.

In the late afternoon they came to deliver me to the airbase. The Demerol was nearly gone. I'd have no help.

Under the supervision of the head nurse, I was lifted to the litter. More straps. They transferred the IV bottle and chart. Finally, they wheeled me down the hall for the descent, and then the ambulance. From the beginning, I closed my eyes and tried to concentrate on her and home. Complete thoughts were impossible. I started my double-time chant to keep my mind protected: "Do it, Do it, Do it, Do it, Do it, Do it."

An hour later, they took me out of the ambulance and pushed me into a corrugated Quonset hut. I heard the high-powered resonance of the jets. I was at the airbase.

They brought me down a plywood hall under bare-wired 50 watt bulbs to a windowless plasterboard cubicle. There was no bed to move me to. I wouldn't be there long. They hung up my IV and checked the straps.

"The plane will be ready in a couple of hours, sir. One of the permanent staff here should be in to see you soon."

I lay there alone, stored and bound. I watched the IV bottle drain, drop by drop, into the plastic tube that fed my veins, and imagined the relief ahead, five miles high in the dark womb of the night flight home. Two more shots—one now and one over the Rockies—and I'd be there. Chelsea. My sharp chant had relaxed to a hum: "Up jumped the swagman with his jolly tucker-bag. You'll never catch me alive, cried he"—when the door swung open.

He was perhaps nineteen: skinny with an acne face. His pants were fastened high. He was carrying a transistor radio in one hand and a wash basin in the other, both of which he placed on the floor near my litter. When he stood up, I was already gesturing for my hole to be plugged. The orderly complied.

"A shot. No straps."

"I'm afraid I can't do that, Lieutenant. I'm here to wash you." I shook my head in absolute denial, but the orderly had bent down again and was turning on the radio. As brash noises rose from under me, my anguished cries for a "shot, no wash" were left to froth at my trach.

Then, in front of my eyes: the orderly's impatience, the pallor of his face draped by black hair. His persistent fingers pried my sheet past the straps down to my knees and I closed my eyes and tried to go back to my stream with her. I felt the warm water being spread over my stomach and groin and the gentle wash, and remembered her head above me with its nurse's cap and the loveliness of her eyes.

A hard tug had stopped my dream and my eyes broke open. The orderly's face was over my dick. They came long distances this time. The hand on my dead right arm crawled furiously, under the straps up my hip, poised for a second, and then slung my stiff forefinger into his eye.

The orderly whirled back, blinded, spinning in a crouch, knifed in his open socket. He flung his bony arms up and threw them down on my hand.

"Why you fucking prick."

And then he yanked the lifeless arm from my groin and jammed it up under my back.

The fire had come long distances this time . . . in a great arc to char my palm. New circuits were seared. I blacked out.

It must have been a good shot. I woke up with all this in my head at 25,000 feet in a cold sweat, midway to Chelsea. I was going home and none too soon.

Things didn't go anywhere in neuropsychiatric at Chelsea. They rolled me out and down every week or two to the basement to probe the ganglion with a needle. Face up I watched them push the needle through my neck until it reached the spine. The results continued to be hopeless. In the time between, I sailed on drugs. Except for another big nurse who threw away wet towels and snapped open shades, the others left me alone, wrapped in wet cloth in a dark room. Eventually, they had taken the casts off my right leg and left arm and while there was some regeneration – except of course in the dead right arm – it didn't matter anymore. The pain in the palm had completely crippled me.

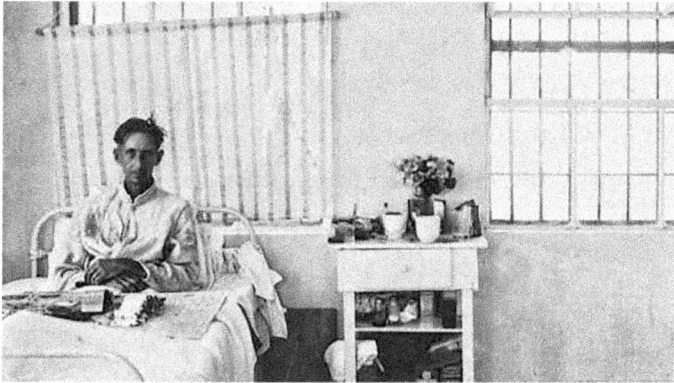

Chelsea Naval Hospital, 1970

I passed the time in my way. After the shot, I had learned how to push the needle with my thumb into the groove on my portable record player and whereby be, for the most part, asleep but conscious enough that I could control my dreams. In direction, pace and with great detail. I painted dreamlike scenes. Changed colors at will. Moderated the breeze – yet kept fantastic happenings. Angels descended. Hell boiled and bubbled. Faces were beatified. Fish spoke. No more torches appeared. The towels dried and I slept on, unaware of their dryness. The I.V. was changed and I slept on.

I took the prescribed CCs from one shot to the next. The bedsores multiplied and grew in circumference, from rashes to pulp. They had given up on trying to get me to walk. They said they had others who needed their time. Change the solutions, wet the towels, Demerol, clean up my mess. And as with the music I served myself in other ways. I used the fingers on my dead right arm to walk to the "on" button, to get the pack of cigarettes, the pieces of food, the lighter, the tissues. At night, I was happiest.

I stayed awake and smoked, my resting right hand just under my chin, my forefingers lifting the butt an inch for a drag, staring out the window at the Chelsea Bridge as the trucks moved under the lights.

I blew the ashes down the sheets and flicked the butt on the floor. I was not crazy, as many thought.

"He'll be well when he wants to be well," they had told my parents when they drove up. My father, unable to look at it; my mother, set to nursing the wounded. My mind had it all; I knew what was going on. The sympathetic and the parasympathetic were fused, and my left palm burned intolerably at the prospect of sound or light. Beyond that, there was the big nurse and the weekly practice on my neck in the dungeon that would, I knew, soon enough drive me crazy.

Finally, after months, they gave up. They gave me a refillable prescription for drugs and a permanent transfer out. Permanently disabled, I was called. Pensioned out, honorably.

They laid me across the back seat of the Ford, swaddled in the wet compresses. My father's meek attempt had followed. "Rutherford, just so I understand, how does the water help?" Silence. "I mean, what would happen without it?" I didn't bother answering. They had a war hero on their hands. So back off with the things-will-be-okay routine. My mother looked at Henry to drop it and pulled out another washcloth from the bucket she had put between her legs in the well of the car.

After some more words, they agreed to set up a bed for me in the basement. It had always been dank. The cement sweated. The floor was beneath the water table. There was one old cobwebby window at ground level which, when I reclined, gave me a limited view of the sky and, when the wind blew, of a branch of the cottonwood. There wasn't much else. My old set of barbells, the furnace, the oil tank.

My mother brought down a side table for my portable record player and a wastepaper basket. With time I was able to crawl and to stumble my way around. There was a rusted tap and a sink where I soaked my towels. I pissed in a sump hole and shit in a bucket. Three times a day she brought down cut-up food. Once a week she took the sheets. She informed me of visitors and callers and dutifully sent them away. With time she urged me to lift the hatch at night and to try to walk around a bit in the back yard. Which I did. Barefoot in the cold grass, ragged in my hospital bottoms, I took my first steps in months, with my grandfather's mahogany cane no less.

Except for an occasional bark or the light coming off a full moon on a cloudless night, it proved painless. By later in the year, I even took to running. The sores retracted. My mother was pleased with the progress. There were traces of something else on the bone beside skin and gristle. The bucket could be taken away; I shat in the woods. With the first snows, I wore slick black rubbers on my feet and draped a blanket over me.

Days were different. Darvon, even several, is not Demerol. I got my mother to bring down jug wine and washed them down. She disapproved, yet this kept me blissful until nightfall. Henry said he hoped she knew what she was doing. I heard his car pull in each evening. He'd stick his head down the stairwell and ask me how things were. I answered, "Okay."

"Any chance of you joining us tonight? It'd sure mean a lot to us." My palm burned at the thought. Silence. "If there's anything you need, call us, won't you, Rutherford?" Silence. "Won't you Rutherford?" A tinge of anger in the voice.

"Yes," I answered. The door closed. Sister Roo visited once, but I closed the door there, too. "I told you mom, no visitors. It's not their bloodline that determines burning. It's their noise. Is Roo noiseless?" My sister had brought a friend from California. They were sitting out where I walked at night. In Moroccan leather hats and lumberjack shirts, their hair braided in corn rows.

I didn't come up for Christmas, and there was nothing I could use anyway. I got a little drunker than usual and played "Adeste Fideles" on my portable. A couple of weeks later I moved my bed closer to the furnace and lost my limited view entirely. I spent the rest of the winter and spring like that: running— even in the snow—building my strength, actually putting a clock on myself as I ran, right arm still dangling dead like my old schoolmate, "polio Clem," through the forest to the field where Dickie and I had made a sort of love in our underground tunnels and back again. Down to the frozen swimming hole at muddy brook where fifteen years earlier we had danced around with flowers in our pee holes. Usually, outside by midnight, I was back before the first car lights in the morning came down the road. I didn't think beyond that. There was no one looking for me. My father had suffered as much as he could. His only boy, in his prime, living like a mole. A dark story alongside all the sales talk. His Swanie was nursing her child. Roo had her life. I had my woman in my mind, who came as she was imagined, and of course the faces of the dead soldiers hanging there.

By summer, my mother had effected another breakthrough, almost on the anniversary of my seclusion in the basement. I had had my hands in the sink, under water, gripping onto a towel when she had slipped on the last stair and the tray of lunch had gone clattering onto the cement. I had spun my head into my shoulder ready to take the inevitable burn. It never came. While she was bent over picking up the pieces and calling herself clumsy, she had unconsciously happened on a great discovery.

It seemed I could handle noises, and presumably light if I, my hands I mean, were in water, in contrast—and this was the discovery—to only being wet. I told her to scrape her shoes on the stairs. Nothing. Not the slightest burn. Asked her to turn on the lights: to rub her dry hands on her dress. Dry on dry, in glaring light. The worst. I looked down at my hands magnified in the water, one apparently doused, the other hanging by a deadline from my shoulder. I turned my palms up underwater. There was no pain.

In the beginning, I was tentative. I went out at twilight, my mother holding a pail of water with my hands in it. My father stood off to the side offering encouragement for the first steps, however fearful, in daylight. They phoned Roo to give her the good news. My father prevailed. The pool they bought was a temporary model—a Kool Pool it was called. A plastic tub four-feet deep and fourteen feet across.

"Don't be ridiculous Swanie. We are not spending ten thousand dollars on an in-ground pool for something that could be over tomorrow. Sometimes you amaze me. Is it that you want the boy to spend his life as a reptile?"

Of course, she didn't, she said. "Sometimes, Henry, you can be so cheap."

Now my life was topsy-turvy. In the blaze of the day with lawnmowers humming and children screaming, there I was lolling like an alligator in my pool, feeling none of it. My metal headplate warming like a pan. My body was shriveled like a pink prune, the sun burning my maze of scars scarlet.

Neighbors stopped by to converse. My father brought Rotarians by. I was interviewed for the local paper. Always with my hands way beneath the surface. Otherwise, I stared over the edge of the pool, took in the world at peace, and when I had had enough, dropped down underwater and pushed off across my pool, my hands fluttering like fins behind me. This was late June. By August I was propelling myself from both elbows down. The nerves definitely regenerating in the dead right arm, as the doctor Henry had brought poolside pronounced.

Life crept up to my shoulder. Muscle reappeared on the arm bones. And on one dramatic day, I took both my arms out for a stroke, dragging the right one along the surface, and letting it sink down. Late into the night, one became several, my body rolled in the rhythm of the crawl. Progress was swift. I pulled myself across. Back and forth in fourteen-foot laps. Then no legs, and finally by the cool days of autumn, with weights tied to the ankles. Emerging, at the end of the day, over the side in the dark. Purple and shriveled. And soon back under the light in the basement with my hands in the pail, my body now becoming a faded pink jigsaw. Now with the flush of health on the face and unkempt hair, I took the vanity of tailoring the beard. But not much more. Once I had overheard that Roo was looking for a solution. From November to April I reverted to running at night.

Only once in the second year—for my father' sake—did I let myself be taken out. Someone from the town. One of my former enemies from school, now a born-again Christian. I took several Darvons, drank a couple of quarts of wine, and soaked my socks and gloves beforehand. I donned sunglasses. I looked like a myth.

There I was, in the shadows at a corner table, overwhelmed by the glamour of the bar, alternately pouring water into my shoes and gloves. Girls had never been talked to as such by someone with a live coal in his hand putting words to them fearlessly. Throwing back glasses of whiskey without a wince. Dousing the dry in his shoes with table water. And they can tell when its real. No theatre by the piano at Saratoga from me this time.

Those glossy lips, the creamy skin, the sweeping lashes were getting more passion off me than in a lifetime. Nothing to do with legs in the air and a dick like a piston. A brilliant residue of war inches from their lips. Others, boyfriends, tugged at them even as they looked back to stay with me. The bar was closing. I put the rest of the water in my gloves and was driven home.

The Christian didn't call again, and anyway there was no future to the incident. How would the unprecedented passion hold up when they pulled the shirt apart onto a crisscross of scars, onto the black specks of shrapnel, now a year later rising to the surface? A lover who did them in his basement on wet sheets? Whose last remembrance was the pocked orderly's face over his dick?

On a night in April, my dad waited for me to come out and run. He sat on the stump of the willow perfectly still, as the whole family now knew how to do, save those hours when I was in the water. There was a specialist, Dr. Benjamin Whitcomb, who would see me. Roo would drive me there. I'd see him at his home tomorrow night. I said I thought I could stay as I was. Why confuse it?

For the last time, I prepared to go out, this time to an old Tudor home on Asylum in Hartford. I was led into the main room. Tapestries and hardwood. A great stone fireplace. I sat, Roo still, the sock drying, licking the palm of my glove. I would ask him to cut it off. A white-haired Yankee. The Healer. He talked to me before the fire. I described the pain, what had been done before Chelsea. "Could you take the glove off?" He saw me shaking. Inside I was chanting. Blinking my eyes. The doctor held my hand and with his other, he reached up to a table lamp. I chanted louder and looked past him. He pulled the switch and I could go no further. I yanked back my hand into my crotch and doubled up. The nonsense burst out. "Do dah, Do dah, Do dah, La, La, La."

Roo took me to the bathroom where she filled the sink over my hands and soaked the glove. Later she took me out and we met the doctor on a path through the front lawn. He told Roo to check me in the next day. He'd operate the day after. "Can you fix it, Doctor?" I asked.

"I think so," he said.

AFRICA, RECUPERATIVE WANDERINGS, 1970—1973

A resumption of boundless movement, it had been, for this apparition now resurrected from the cellar. Along the earth's equator, offering to my mind the requisite high velocity . . . RICKETY CLICKITY RICKETY . . . maybe in preparation, I wondered, for the eventual return to the would-be narratives of the smoking room at Suffield Academy which no longer existed.

Perpetual movement it was as a natural antidote for the legacy and residue of causalgia; moving faster—a din in my ears—than my fears could congregate and advance on me. A bombardment of the senses precluding insinuation and infection from inside. Not the "Do dah do dah" or the "La la la" for the burning in the palm, for that had disappeared the second Dr. Whitcomb had found the nerve in question and cut it. But rather the trauma's legacy—its dwelling in me regardless—the unconscious fear of light and noise, even though they could do my actual body, writ small, no harm.

So the "doo dah" ("gwine run all night") had soon enough become "I" standing in the corridor on that train from Cairo to Aswan, head stretched out the window of the rackety car as it jerked through the night, up the Nile, en route to the ferry terminus at Wadi Halfa and the descent into Nubia and across Africa. Exhilarated with the movement and once there at the next stop on my map, anxious to move again. Yes, Haraka Baraka, movement is a blessing, a tonic for neurosis.

Waking up on the planks of a rail car, the contrapuntal of the piston's cadence and the carriage clattering up the Nile, opening my eyes to the black balls of a Sudanese *fedayeen* as he sought to step over me in his *jellabiya*. Stepping off at the terminus in Khartoum where I and my mother in me searched to reconnoiter with the ghost of General Gordon in vain: where afterward I had a Christmas by myself in a Greek restaurant festooned in paper pastel banners. Off at dusk the next day, purchased for a pittance, a place on a flatbed billowing across the Hamada under crystalline skies toward Kassala on the edge of Eritrean highlands, past a stark mud and wattle cone, for worship, whose only call to Allah inside was two unadorned crossed spears. There had only been a splash of water from his bottle before the driver's forehead had been put down onto the earth: a smoke, a chai afterward, before he was once again billowing toward the border. While an

erstwhile Yankee companion took out his Jew's harp
and leaned into:

Banking off of the northeast winds

Sailing on a summer breeze

And skipping over the ocean like a stone

While the Arabs dug deeper into their burlap
amidst the sacks and slept on.

Into the thin air of Asmara by New Year's Eve,
just in time, by candle, to stare at a peeling plaster
ceiling while a girl's perfectly noble head (above her
bones and what flesh she had under her pink chiffon)
also stared at the ceiling, waiting for me to make a
move. I did finally—for the door as she chirped for
some dollars. It was all so sad.

Thus it went, under a bed in an Indian flop
house in Kampala as the strongman Idi Amin Da Da
stormed in, bathing my poor colon with ointments
at the headwaters of the Congo. I was put in a burlap
manger of sorts on the back of a Bedford covered
like a red Indian in laterite dust for the journey
back to Bunia port, fearing the damage I was doing
to what life I had left, through the always festering
vegetation, eventually to Nairobi. No skipping
over the ocean this time, I was recuperating finally,
skin and bones, in the manse of a stranded English
widow who would have me take her diamonds out

of Kenyatta's country in my asshole as a gesture of gratitude for her hospitality. All on a handshake.

It was a down-to-earth version of what the Demerol had incited, albeit with less control over pace and content.

All the while, as my Wolfe once whispered to me, "The old hunger for voyages fed at his heart, to go alone into strange cities; to meet strange people and to pass again before they could know him; to wander, like his own legend, across the earth—it seemed to him there could be no better thing than that."

Two years it had been like that, more or less: squatting on makeshift decks or in the back of dug outs, seemingly washed around the tributaries of the Nile and Congo rivers or eating dust on the back of cargo trucks as they thundered across desert pistes and slammed into flood-torn *wadis*, perched up high on their sacks of cargo behind the cab, a skinny red man on a dollar a day for all the fruit and gruel I could eat, all my earthly possessions in my old boy scout knapsack.

Long enough away in any case for the pink scars to fade, for my bowels to survive dangerous and exotic tastes and grow the great colonies of various microbes and worms, still in my guts as I write, to gain distance from my earlier reptilian life in the basement.

But, more importantly, and thanks be to God, I came to believe I had eliminated the possibility of a recurrence of that "hideous torch," though never convinced fully enough that I would not, under certain conditions, test myself for a relapse under my covers at night.

I came home to all the smells and sights of the modest Cape; to all the varied infusions therein since we had arrived from Australia, seventeen years earlier. And, truth be told, if I had stayed away much longer, the parasites would have eaten me to the bone, already getting too weak to hoist my backpack onto the Bedford, or pull myself up onto its freight.

And, notwithstanding the Philistine that I was and the "Up against the wall, mother fucker" that I was becoming—fueling my growing dissonance with both Victoria—as applied to the modest "cape"—and my dad as Babbitt, I could not help but feel for that awkward salesman and that very Victorian Swanie from Crosby shipping he had brought back to his world. Catching the flies off dad's bat, at dusk beneath the reach of the cottonwoods. Arrested for the moment after school as I walked in on Mum with her evening sherry in the same armchair that offered perspective of her Rose of Sharon outside, John Buchan resting in her lap.

You see, despite the dissonance, they were mine. In me, now and forever. Should a Big Bob or his ilk have hurt them, I would fester with my hate far into the future.

HARTFORD, CONNECTICUT, `1973-1980

Now I would sit in that central room, drawing in the small clan around my designs for a business success, to be supported by mostly unopened and unspent disability checks from the Army.

Yes, the fair-skinned mascandrogyne, targeted through my adolescence for my high voice, my shapeliness, my droop before the yawning appetite— now perforated with metal fragments—had come home from my self-imposed recuperative wanderings in Africa.

From my start in 400 sq. ft. and two phone lines in a renovated warehouse, I drove the baby hard in what quickly proved to be a high-volume, low-margin, easy access business. It was to be "travel-wholesale and retail." I stuck my nose in all the nooks and crannies of possibility. I mortgaged my house: a shack really, hidden away in the country, only feet from a stream that raged against its foundations each spring. I would sneak there after dark, leaping over puddles and mud, a cheese pizza protected under my black wool overcoat, searching the wall for the switch to illuminate my refuge. Now, laying it on the bed and shedding my Tweeds, then, stoking my Korean stove with wall vinyl and rug remnants stripped from the interior till the stove had burned red and I could lie beside my box of pizza, roll a joint and drift away, until the following dawn pushed me outside to the thirty-foot rope hanging from the Red Oak which I would climb twice—no feet—before I got myself transformed into pin stripes, regimental stripes, and the other accoutrements of Main Street.

And thus, I got started scrambling for nickels, personally, handling the smallest transactions. "Just keep the phones ringing," I told my staff. I held up my hands: "If it gets quiet, we're dead." Yellow pages, cold calls, ringing the bell for the Salvation Army at Christmas, steering the cash flow to within minutes of checks crossing desks. It was to become "I," incorporated. My sparkling women fanned out each morning in the city to make cold calls. "Just take the elevator to the top and work the doors till you hit the pavement," I told them, "and then work your way down the street." My long-legged skaters who dodged city traffic to deliver the tickets. My rendezvous in nightclubs to purchase volume. I, who taught the team to love the cacophony of ringing phones.

The ubiquitous sales charts. The shots I gave myself at the end of the week for success. The amber distillate of the mesquite plant alongside a draft and the generous sharing up and down the bar, all assigned to the corporate gold card. And so the once-college sensitive, the distraught warrior, now burned with his baby. Burned to the point of thinking about dark retaliations for the competition. Dreamed, in fact, as he stared into the rows of liquor opposite him, of a storefront door opened a crack on a sultry summer day, a grenade rolled down the aisle. But no woman sat on the stool next to him to share that dream. No women. No, all disappointing for years now. Just more bad food. Time and again. No cripples at evening tide, no likely partners in crime, no unsuspecting faith. All poor American porridge.

That is, except for sister Roo, for whom circumstances had conspired to create an unprecedented love. This little sister with the flaxen hair who had bumped. Who had rocked back and forth so furiously on the chairs and sofas that her head had begun to flatten. "Let's bump," she used to ask me on dreary days in our Australian winters, the two of us alone in a Victorian living room, flattening our heads on the upholstery.

Then, out of the night she was rushed to the emergency ward, where twice she died and twice revived. An infant finally in the iron lung, miraculously one day wheeled into the courtyard under the eucalyptus where I had donned my mother's hat, the broad brimmed hat with glass cherries in the band, and danced around trying to coax a smile from the pale flaxen head with the blue polio straw sticking out of her neck below.

Soon after, Henry and his Aussie love initiated a transfer from Down Under to New England where a corseted and atrophied Roo had made the march back, slowly completed, it seemed, by summer of her senior year, when she could be seen drifting through the hills of central Connecticut in a very cherry Corvette, with a very freckled and curly farm boy. But apparently, even as she glowed, she could not stand this for herself, not over the horizon in any case, and by the end of college in California she was gone, to surface in a 5th floor walkup in Florence. She, it turned out, was not to come home for a long while.

And so, since the polio in Sydney it had been Roo who accompanied me through the brutes and

Philistines, through the various degradations in boot camps, through this daily round with death in Vietnam. Even though we were oceans apart for some years at that point, there was the bond born of the two children in tow as the father moved around the world. I remember well that when I did rush out of the CH47 for the first time to establish a perimeter, it was Roo in the locket around my neck.

And now, a decade on, and other capitals gone by, she had come to marry a Dane. Something of a speculator from what I could tell. Thin and stoop-shouldered, shapely himself, blessed with an endearing wink. And in what was an eruption of joy and family embraces and empty bottles of Bola strewn about, they had agreed to come back to share the burden of what was now my seven locations, both wholesale and retail, as the prospectus indicated.

Well, the rest, I'm afraid, is cliché. The invitation of the new V.P. for finance into my baby only served to accelerate the intensity of the burn. Roo's lover became sequestered, with tails of calculator tape wrapped around the swivel chair, fingers tapping ever more intensely. Sales became the step and fetch it for Finance. And the logic to grow the whole works for future sale became inexorable. The Dane locked in, shifting monies by phone, streams of tape across his floor, with me, unbounded, ratcheting it up from marketing to acquisitions.

Roo mediating and insisting on Bola and midnight embraces, all intoxicated with the prospect of a future payoff. And Henry on the sideline, chewing his nails in trepidation over the furious rush of his children.

With the margins now razor thin and volume overwhelming capacity, and with my name all over it, I had found myself, this night once again, at my Friday night shots for success—by then quite far into that amber world—when she offered to serve me more.

God knows it had been the immediate and passionate courtship of cripples. With all the attendant costs, as time would reveal. Tethered so precariously at the time, as we were, to enterprise, in my case, and to beloved child, in hers, we cut the lines. For her, an unsuspecting faith in me—tears when she had read the medical reports of how the shrapnel had blown into my body, a pupil spellbound, at the knee while I recounted stories from the larger world. Holding hands, desperately in love at the Athenaeum while I, at her behest, described life in the awful hiatus after graduation until I got anchored in a rented room near Metro Cadet with some stacks of mackerel and books about my bed, in my so-called noiseless hunt for "His hem," until the ambition for the wonderful narrative made me very ill and afraid and caused me one day to flee those dust balls, transmogrified.

For me, she was the bravest of any mother's prolific issue, the primordial head and strong brow. Those wonderful slightly bucked teeth. Charmed for the time being by the unpunctuated narrative of her life in the foothills, by her apparent willingness to be consumed by someone who had never consumed. For her unsuspecting faith.

This became the wrack and ruin left in the wake of our flight. And while no one would be so foolish as to think that this was where the story began or even when the seeds were planted, it was when a different course was set, a course that would leave failure behind and produce new life. And the shame of it was—even as we had soon gathered in the living room for marriage, there was no one who could sense this, no one who could feel the force of the storm coming. Culminating in the autumn, so ingloriously, at the Greyhound station where I would board for an "employment orientation" in New York.

Henry and Helen had finally said goodbye, Henry no longer able to think straight, with the toll mounting by the hour and yet to crest. The family name so publicly sullied now. And this for a man who valued name; had spent a lifetime making a name. The dread of living amidst his son's growing carnage, the estrangement of Roo from her brother. Helen forlorn, incapable, for the sadness of it to look up at the bus window at the departing fugitive and neither of the parents getting any relief from the son's persistent argument that the family name would soon be resurrected—across the world—in many languages on the covers of his book. Yes, even as the bus pulled out, I was reaching out, pantomiming for them with imaginary pen and paper, the notion of fame around the corner, punctuated with a "thumbs-up"—an affirmation that victory would be ours. To include Pen and the embryonic "Hank," who would stay a while in Northbrook until I would signal that it was safe for them to join me in Beirut.

After all, it was Catholic. It was a culture I had had little to do with. I mean there were fish sticks on Fridays at elementary school and then later those hairy Polish boys at Junior High who crossed themselves before they took their "at bats." But not much more. And now I was being passed around the offices of the headquarters of the overseas relief and development arm of the Catholic Church in the Archdiocese of New York.

Indeed, it was a sorry place, which in a strange way accommodated me better. The key here was to get away and to get some, any, income coming in. It was part of the resurrection. Along with baby Hank and being married, it was meant to bring the family back to life. And this, it appeared to me, was a place which would serve but which I would not have to take too seriously. The book, the eventual book, lost in the midway as I might be, was still how I was defining myself.

I had appointments where no one showed up. And appointments where I was coddled by a Sister—who hadn't gotten past the Vietnam on my resume—and with old timers with no teeth and with a priest whose room, ceiling included, was painted vermilion.

And, in the end, no one was comparing notes, so I made it to the traditional picture with the Bishop who was in his C suite in the middle of watching a ballgame on his television. A young woman came in with a trickle of pimples running down her chest and popped the flash.

The next day, I remember, a few of us entry types spent the day around a conference table to learn about U.S. food assistance, P.L. 480 as it was called, referring to the huge transfers of agriculture surplus begun under Eisenhower. I recall it being, absent any overseas context, complicated as well as painfully tedious. Finally, at day's end we were all given a copy of the Law, public law 480, that is, and packed off for shots and tickets.

They knew I was a Protestant, a cultural one, in any case. I didn't advertise it, but I did check that box on the personnel form. But, as I was learning, with all that taxpayer subsidy at play, there apparently was some felt or perhaps regulatory obligation to hire on merit—such as it was, coming in off 1st avenue. From this first day on, there was to remain this disconnect between me and perhaps a handful others, and this "Overseas Arm." Not a Catholic-Protestant divide, strictly speaking. No, something more akin to heritage. There was no trace, not a hint, of Lawrence in the proceedings. Nothing of Speke or Baker or of Hawkeye, for that matter. No, for the most part, this was up from the Irish in America, the Irish after the famine, the Irish of the Northeastern ghettos, and only now the Irish of the middle classes.

In fairness, I noticed some khaki and cotton shirts rolled to the elbow, here and there. And war stories certainly circulated. Biafra, Cambodia. Airlifts, Malaria, Africa hands. It was evocative enough, I suppose, for most. But, as I said, there was no sense of the mysteries, in the sense of Conrad's mysteries. In the sense of the dark continent, I had roamed during my years of rehabilitation after Vietnam. No. What we entry types mostly took away was this heavy loose-leaf binder on P.L. 480 and the sense, from what the semi-retired "hands" at HQ told us: "Don't worry, the field is better. The field is where it happens."

I didn't care. It was overseas and paid a bit, and it was a fitting excitement for my wife and me. Warriors work, even—since people got wars for their first assignment. And war suited me well enough anyway. You might think that damaged as I had been, I would steer away from it. But, short as it had been before I had gotten hit in Vietnam, I knew well that there was an incandescence at a war zone that could elevate me beyond the mundane but was rarely found, elsewhere to the same extent, save for these few months in Paris, pre-Vietnam, when I was really moving in my confinement, up until the time when the transmutation of the dust balls darting about my bed had begun.

But there was more to it than that. Lessons I had picked up from my earlier brushes with war in Africa, under my bed in Kampala when Idi Amin Dada rode in, on mountain passes through an Eritrean insurgency, or on the back of a truck billowing dust on a Piste through the badlands—cultivating me as enthusiast—to get close enough for life to be revelatory but not so close as to end me up dead to the world. Of course, no guarantees—but nevertheless, there was a way. I was counting on it—as both the essence of the contract with my wife as well as with myself.

And so, I kept learning. That last few minutes to touchdown as you come in over the Mediterranean in a sleek MEA jetliner into the dark menace of a shuttered airport. The fog of tobacco smoke inside, the long dead pot plant, the shifting militias draped in their fire power, and the urine—always the smell of urine from a long-broken toilet.

Charity Overseas, 1981-1982

And out into the cacophony, into the thick smog and hot sun and Jack, the CRS veteran of thirty years, now welcoming me, welcoming "Dick" in fact, for which I corrected him. For which he seemed to think such correction inconsequential, as he waved it away and pointed to his BMW, the driver just then rearranging the crate of oranges to make room for my bag.

Now squeezing out of the chaos of the parking lot and then creeping along through the noise and fumes toward the city center and then along the corniche. Inching away, it seemed, through some sort of massive hijacking. Lanes, turns, checkpoints, and any and all real estate, down to the water's edge. I asked Jack about the various flags, flapping away in the mayhem—a safe enough inquiry I imagined, given his five years in the country—but he didn't know since for him, I gathered from the broad sweep of his hand, they all were more or less the same fact of life. He repeated the question for Khalil which I learned later was not his name either, but by now had become his name. Khalil began a recital which quickly had me lost.

That night, Jack had me over to his apartment for dinner, high up from the corniche into an Art Deco residence with marble floors and curtains lifting gently with the breezes off the sea. It was an amiable Jack at the door saying "Good, good," when he saw me, putting his fingers to his hearing aid to get more response. And then Sophia was by his side. I must have blushed. Very hard, at least for me, to be confronted by such unabashed glamour, face à face.

"Scotch?" Jack asked. Soon after, we were all around the brass table with some assortments of Lebanon's produce—principally, almonds, olives, and figs alongside a crystal glass—fully half filled with Chivas. "Ice?" he asked—always a bit loud.

There were photos, from those early days of their romance, I supposed: Corporal Jack in army khaki and Sophia as luminous as a movie star—a story similar, I imagined, to my own Henry and Helen. And then Corporal Jack must have said, "No need to go back to Detroit." Not I imagine, with that Italian beauty loving him and the dream surrounding him.

Meanwhile, his America, with fully 60% of the
world's GDP, was pumping assistance to a European
continent asunder—now, to millions of wandering
dislocated refugees, many from the Catholic
heartland. And Jack, soon to be cashiered, joined
Catholic War Relief to manage the shiploads around
the Mediterranean, transporting materials to Europe
and refugees to America.

Lebanon, he said, was his last stop.

Incipient paunch, thinning hair, he was refilling
his glass. I marveled at how they could put deaf
Jack and his beauty in the middle of all this killing.
Sophia and the Asian maid were spreading the table.
Imagine it. The best of Italian and Lebanese coming
my way after months of fast food in Hartford and
more recently, Mom's old standard—shepherd's pie.
Of course, I thought, Jack wasn't ever going back to
Detroit.

And then Jack brought up what he called "a
drink of water—a long drink of water," he corrected.
"Have you been told about your colleague?" he asked.

"No, why? I'm starting at zero," I told him.

"Well, don't get too close. He's got problems."
Which, as you can imagine, was kind of unsettling,
getting this advice from your boss of only a few hours
about your new associate.

But this was, as I learned later that week, how the man managed. Heaven knows it was easy enough to do in Lebanon. And, as I guessed, it wasn't just the flags of the militia which escaped Jack. Concerning the social, political, economic: he hadn't a clue. He knew only what he needed to know to get him and Sophia through this to retirement. He knew to arrive and depart the office without warning. To have an alarm hooked up under Farida's desk so he could go out the back whenever an unpleasant cleric arrived. To use a Telex service so far across town that New York was never in the loop. He knew the calm of his suite of rooms over the Mediterranean and the calm of his nap there in the afternoon. And given the ubiquitous death and deceit of the place—as much, as I was about to learn, in the office as out—he had concluded that his only hope to be responsible was to try to feed all his staff various and opposing "confidences."

Later that night, lying in bed at the Mayflower in Hamra, spread-eagled on the sheet with the ceiling fan slowly revolving above me, I was processing what I had just joined, when I heard the first whoosh. Quite close. And then at close intervals several more. I moved off my bed. My balls ascending. I looked sideways out my window. It was mortars down a tube in the next lot. And God only help me if anyone sought to return fire. I was already discombobulating.

It's one thing to be a grunt on a perimeter outside Chu Lai, a uniform among uniforms with a world of fire on call, and quite another to be a relief worker lying on a bed, belly up, in a capital city, waiting for a mortar to drop through the window. And you can be sure, I was now actively having second thoughts about whether to bring my wife and unborn baby into this.

But with no working phone—not anywhere in the country as far as I could gather—and certainly no inclination to go out into Hamra at this time of night, I went the way of avoidance. Which was to take some very deep, meaningful drags on my cigarette and then, despite the heat, pull the sheet over my head and hope by Christ for sleep.

The walk to work—from the Mayflower to Rue d'Amerique— could have been quite easy, even pleasant, a few years back. But now, six years into this civil war, it was not a walk for the sensible. It was again the absence of a "rear area" in which to stretch out under an umbrella with your book. No, even as the city crumbled and its sewers were exposed, and the rats were multiplying, you would step around amid this frantic bustle, blare, and fumes of business. And then there would be wheeling around a corner in a terrible instant, Nissan Patrols, with the militia standing up through the windows with their AKs on full automatic, screaming toward the hospital with their wounded. And for that instant shopkeepers disappeared, people hunched behind sandbags, and the sidewalks emptied—but only until the patrols had wheeled through the next turn. And then the commotion of business resumed as fast as the shopkeepers had stood up.

This too could take its toll on the average white boy in his seersucker. The mortars dropping around you at night and the scream of the Nissans at odd moments in the day. It got on my nerves, admittedly not the best to begin with. And then you turned into our street, immediately effecting that sense of the deliberate walk, the eyes down, trying to shrink your back as thin as a pencil. Those men there, on their sandbags, truly stopped your heart. True stone-faced men from Algiers or Afghanistan who killed people easily.

This was not to mention the parked cars. Impossible to say which: the burned-out Impala with no wheels or the deep black Mercedes catty-corner to us. But day after day there were the explosions and the fragments of metal which turned some of that bustling crowd into bloody flesh for the hospital or morgue.

On that first day, the office seemed like a sanctuary. At least there was chatter and some work and a stone wall. And no one in your immediate vicinity was fidgeting with a trigger mechanism or putting a cold barrel against your face.

Jack wasn't in yet, and so Farida, his scarlet-haired administrative assistant, took me in. "I'm so on fire," she had said. She noted my bewilderment. "You know, upset. Jack should have told me you were coming."

That office of CRS, as I was to see for myself over the months to come, was indeed upset. Jack stayed mostly absent, waiting out his time with Sophia in their suite of rooms high over the corniche. As for Farida, I never knew her not to be on fire. Mike and I often wondered whether all her fire (preceding fire) resulted in such stylish black for a dead husband. Then, on that morning, Farida took me down a hall to the back room and assigned me to Muriel's desk, crammed as it was next to George's and facing Toufic's. George, now rising as a suave little man with elf's ears, while Toufic stood in waiting at parade rest like some happy sailor out of a WWII musical.

George offered me a Dunhill—not what I was used to—and reached over to light it with a glittering gold instrument. Toufic was given some keys and dismissed on an errand. We talked. He was so pleased to see me. I would come to dinner soon. Yes, that pile of projects was mine. Yes, Muriel had been gone six months now. They all needed progress reports, for the donors. He reached across with another Dunhill just as a bent servant named Vache, with black hollows for eyes, entered with a tray of Turkish and very deferentially served George, then me. George's eyes twinkled. And I was wondering what the hell he did. No phone that worked, nothing on his desk: just his golden instrument that he toyed with and the packet of Dunhill's and then again, Toufic, who bounced in and out for orders.

He was giving me history. Taking my questions, pausing, inhaling, smiling very kindly. Of course, I was also fixed on the tower of projects before me, guessing that it represented six months' work—the nature of which was a mystery—and not knowing for sure but suspecting that George might work for me, but also being too interested, during these introductory hours, to ask if he was to do anything with me or, at my direction, to the pile. Others came into George's court: the accountant, Mike's engineer, the cleaning lady. Toufic arrived, spread napkins around and served us a delightful welcome feast of labneh, baba ghanoush, unleavened bread, pickles, olives and honey cakes. More Turkish came in on the tray, and I became quite voluble, to include a few forays into French. I was, however, still waiting for some shoe or another to drop. I presumed I got paid for something, though I didn't really object that at every twist and turn CRS seemed such a joke. It was giving my family breathing space, and that was all that mattered, as long as I didn't get wounded too badly again.

Taken otherwise, it would have been quite humiliating. This infantry officer, this Chamber of Commerce key man, this presumed creator, jammed into a little desk in a back room. Thank God my wife wasn't a witness to such belittlement.

"You know about Jim," George asked me after the others had trailed out.

"No," I said.

"He was before Muriel," George went on, "but died."

I shuddered. Despite the explosions and the careening to hospitals, I was hoping that maybe ex-pats might have some kind of exceptional immunity. "How?" I asked. I corrected myself, "I mean, I'm so sorry." George maintained his kindly aspect. "But how?" I repeated. He held the packet of Dunhills and offered me one. And still more silence as he extended his lighter.

He inhaled, "Mike had an accident, and Jim died."

"What kind of accident," I asked. George now had his hands together like a little chapel with the fingertips to his brow. He brought them down. "At night, he hit an Army jeep." He could see I had more to ask. He waved the smoke away and said, "but you better ask him."

Then I could hear Farida advancing, telling me that Jack had turned up and wanted me in his office. But by the time I got up front, Jack was at the door, beckoning me to follow him out. "Tell you on the way," he said as we got in the backseat of his BMW. He tapped the driver on the shoulder. "Port," he told him.

"Museum?" the driver asked.

"No, no, no," Jack said, wagging his finger.

Actually, as I learned later, museum was right for today, but Jack had his habits, and whenever the odious task of visiting the Maronite Bishop on the other side came due, he took the Port road.

After thirty years in the business, Jack knew the essentials. Keep the U.S. government grant clean, and for that, he had been sent the long drink of water (yet, on my first day, to materialize from the South); keep the local Catholic hierarchy happy enough, short of cohabitations; and whatever else, no public vice, or at minimum, nothing that could ever turn up in the Western press.

And so now we three were going to the East to try to please the Maronites. He turned to me. "How's your French?" I stammered something about "rusty" and immediately could feel the sweat trickling down my ribs. I hadn't done French in Paris. I had done English on legal pads and Shakespeare in print. Before that it had been as a teenager in Dordogne teaching swimming to eight-year-olds at a Colonie des Vacances.

Despite my opinion that not much since that pop of the flash at HQ could be taken seriously, I hated to fail and was now imagining failing in the midst of both my boss of twenty-four hours and the majesty of the Maronite hierarchy. "Your CV stated French," said Jack. I acknowledged he was correct and started talking French. Anything that came to mind as rapidly as possible.

Then Jack patted my knee. We were slowing to a stop right there on the eastern edge of that bustle and blare and fumes referred to earlier, right on the far edge of that commerce. Directly ahead were the carcasses of buildings: acres of them reduced by the horrible combat of the Maronites and Fatah, locked in a death struggle before Syria had intervened. Now, except for a Syrian lookout, the multiplying vermin and a few lunatics bereft of senses, it was dead, but oddly, was still called green for the shade on the map. And then, with as little ado as bending over to change a fuse, Jack was down and with two fingers on my lapel tugging at me to join him in the well. Khalil lit a smoke, jacked up his "Eye of the Tiger," and gunned it. We took a half-dozen sharp turns, then flew down a straightaway until (in less than five minutes) we were in the business, so to speak, on the other side.

To some extent that was what the Bishop had wanted to tell us. The majesty I had imagined in the car was not exaggerated. He was elevated in an ornate chair and dripping in gold. It was medieval.

"Come back, come back," he was telling Jack, the archetypal Italian American from Detroit.

Jack was "Excellencing" this and that at every opportunity, but still standing firm on keeping the office in Ras Beirut (that is to say, not in Maronite land), while the Bishop was offering offices next to him—every Catholic accommodation—frankly presenting a nightmare to Jack, a certain death to the uninterrupted sea breezes shifting over him and Sophia at sunset.

Fortunately, for ecclesiastical reasons, this was not a bed the Bishops of America cared to be in. Or in any case to be insistent on. For, as I would learn that night from Mike, also sharing that bed was Israel, and that certainly posed some issues, particularly with respect to Palestinian Christians.

So far, so good for me as interpreter. Jack had been spared using one of his office Maronites, and this initial dialogue, stripped away from all the courtesies, was really no more than an invitation refused.

Then it got a bit dicier—not from the Bishop to Jack but rather in the other direction—as Jack, for probably the umpteenth time, was explaining how the large transfers to Lebanon from the U.S. government, via CRS, were not strictly speaking Catholic in origin but taxpayer in origin and, as such, could not be just handed over to the Bishop, but really had to be divided in some rough equivalency to the varied confessional strengths. And yes, he acknowledged it must have been difficult for His Excellence, not to mention the Patriarch, to watch the ceremonies on TV as the official overseas arm of the Catholics of America presented millions in gifts to Shiites and Sunnis. But also, Jack kept reminding, a full third was also going to his people.

There were enough subtleties here that I got quite flummoxed on a couple of occasions as they related to church-state relations in the States but barged ahead, regardless, with false aplomb, guessing that this was not a new subject for either party.

I was really spinning by now. Imagine my first day: from the mortars being fired in the middle of the night from right under my window, to racing across the green line and jetlagged as I was anyway, now with about twelve demitasses of the high-octane sludge in my veins, stumbling along at quite a precipitous speed in my childish French before the majesty of the Bishop.

I declined a refill, with due courtesy of course. Was it winding down? It was a familiar dance to which Jack was hardly new. Some more pleasantries. Yes, Jack confirmed to the Bishop: George was doing well. And yes, he did not forget. Jack reached into his breast pocket and drew out a check. For 20,000 USD, it appeared.

The alabaster hand, with the remarkable long nail on the pinky and the wad of gold on the ring finger, took the check and placed it away from him on the desk.

Jack pointed at me. "He will be back, Excellence, to write a report." The Excellence looked at Jack without expression. It seemed Jack had just put himself in some hot water and he knew it. "He will need to see receipts." This last word, unavailable in French to my saturated mind, caused me to use "preuve" (proof) as a substitute in my translation. The Bishop placed his pinky with its fine pointer of a nail on the check and slid it back across the desk toward Jack, who was now wiping his brow with a handkerchief.

"You told me last time that this gift," and he emphasized this word, "was from the Catholics of America." He was staring directly at Jack, right through his rimless specs.

"It is," said Jack. "It's why I can do this—but they too expect receipts."

His Excellence pushed it across the edge of the desk, and Jack was forced to snatch at it before it would have fluttered to the floor. "I am shocked to hear that the Catholics of America demand proof from me." He paused, obviously quite agitated. "Tell me, sir what they want. Do they want 'proof' that we are dying for our faith? Yes, young Catholic boys are dying every day. Catholic families are being destroyed by the Muslim terrorists. Churches desecrated. No," he concluded, shaking his head. "I will not accept it."

Jack sat there at an obvious loss, with the check still in his hand, now sweating profusely.

I felt inadequate and complicit in my boss' dilemma. I sensed a better vocabulary could have avoided this. Now there was dead silence, only the tick tock of the golden clock on the mantle. Jack just kept looking at the check, and the Bishop looked away.

And then Jack tried again.

I began translating that perhaps I could just take pictures of the well instead. The Bishop seemed somewhat eased by that and leaned forward again to address us. "Yes, you may have some pictures. That is not the issue. Yes, you might have some proof, as you call it. You are my guests. Maybe, even, I personally will see to it."

Jack placed the check back on the desk. The Bishop left it there. "But I will not. No, not ever, accept a demand—an exigency—that we who are suffering for our faith are required to give proof. I thank you. I thank the American Catholics for their generosity. They may have their pictures."

"Air," Jack said, too loudly. Khalil looked back over the seat, puzzled. Jack reached forward pointing at the console and turning his fingers in midair. "Air conditioning," he repeated. "So, what happens now?" I asked him as we pushed back down the slope toward the green line. "Not much. You go out to the Beka'a and talk to Kluiters. Get some pictures."

"What about the receipt?"

Jack smiled. "Oh, I don't know. Maybe, maybe not. If you're nice they may give you some sort of receipt." Jesus, I was thinking, this whole job just goes from one disgrace to another.

"It's just one pot," Jack was saying. "One big Maronite pot and when the money goes into the pot, only God knows where it ends up. Marble for the residence, M16s for the Kataeb or, perhaps for Kluiters' well."

"Great," I responded.

Khalil was wedged into a bottleneck with horns blaring all around us. A crazy mix, I thought. Chic salons and tailored women lined the street behind high walls of sandbags. Soldiers with gold necklaces had Mother Mary taped on the stocks of their M16s.

"And what was his salutation for George about?" I asked, then quickly added, "By the way, is he supposed to work for me?" Jack was smiling and smoking. Still locked up as we were in our capsule, and, still unequivocally, stuck in traffic.

"George was the deal," Jack said. "The compromise."

"What do you mean?" I asked.

"Well," he paused to inhale. And then put his finger, now surrounded in exhale, to his pursed lips and then pointing behind the seat at Khalil, he said, "Come closer." Then, with his mouth to my ear, "George was a Seminarian. You know"—he looked over at me— "they're all connected up there on the mountain, just one tribe. He's the Bishop's man. So," he continued, "we keep our office in the West, and George crosses over each day. He and his Maronite pals. That and the occasional donation keep the balance."

I was trying to digest this, still just inching along in our capsule. As for Jack, well, he was eyeing me. Probably wondering how many beans to spill. Not much choice, I was guessing. Surrounded by Maronites in the office, obviously some sort of problem with the drink of water that was Mike. I mean, who's left.

"I want you to go up to Tripoli next week and find out what George is up to."

"You see," he continued, "we put a lot of US grant money up there while Mike was out of commission. You know about the accident?"

"Yes," I said.

"Well, there's about a half million in U.S. government money up there, and I want you to find out where it went."

The coffee was wearing off, my gut was growling, and quite suddenly I felt the burden of too little sleep. You really want this new dick, no Arabic, white Anglo-Saxon Protestant to motor up to Tripoli in my maroon Chevette and do undercover work on the Bishop's man? I thought to myself.

"Does he work for me," I repeated.

"Who knows," said Jack, so close to my ear, I could feel his lips.

Jack dropped me off at the office and then was driven home. Inside there was a bustle and imperative, of which no hint had been given earlier. Not that there was much to put in order. A pencil here, some car keys there. The only effort of any significance— clearing the ashtrays and coffee cups—was left to Vache's mother, a diminutive Armenian who, I was told later, had decades earlier, at the beginning of the century, made the trek down from the slaughter in Turkey. She would finish her days, I feared, in the middle of another horror.

Then they filed out, quite intent on their imminent race home across the green line.

Amid this exodus, Mike arrived. He was indeed the long drink of water as described by Jack. The first representation, I sensed upon seeing him come up the steps, of what I had imagined the relief type to look like. The khakis, the sandals, the cotton broadcloth rolled to the elbows. Sunburnt with a haystack of brown hair.

And painfully thin. I mean, I am thin, not so much genetically but more so from the loss of a meter of lower bowel left on the floor of a Quonset hut in I corps. But still, seen from the back I do fan out some around the shoulders. Not him. Not from what I could see, as I followed him to his office. He was the pencil I had hoped to be, walking up from the checkpoint that morning. He put up two fingers to Madame Vache. Then looked back. "Without sugar?" he asked. I nodded.

"Bidoun Sukar."

Ah, I thought, a small first trace of Lawrence, as we sat at his "battleship gray."

"Madame Vache?" I asked.

"Yeah." Mike said. "Jack is from the beginning: Christmas '75. He just named them all when he hired them. Some with their right names, and others with what he could remember the next day."

"He calls me Dick," I said.

Evidently Mike liked that one, laughing and bending like a praying mantis and getting flushed in the face. He took the cups off her tray and handed me mine, still laughing. "Here you go, Dick."

"Hey," I asked, "how do you rate?"

"You mean, my gray metal ensemble."

"Yeah, that and the private room."

He pointed at me, grinning. "1651," he said, "And don't forget it. It pays for everything in this place, right down to the cat food."

"You mean the U.S. Government grant?"

"You don't think CRS would put its own money in this hellhole, do you?"

"They put their money in worse hellholes," I said.

"Yes, but those hellholes are comprehensible. People understand famine. This," he said, pointing out the window, "is inscrutable." He could see I was too new to argue. "No way," he continued. "My grant is political money, 15 million of it, and CRS has the contract with a nice thick slice of it staying in HQ. Hell, I figure, I support most of the 12th floor. This is

127

to placate," he went on. "A little something for the Lebanese Americans, something for the Iraqi Bath, something for Armenian Americans. Something for the Greek lobby and so on. And frankly it keeps Washington's hand in a region it will never leave— not as long as there are Jews in America."

I sat at Mike's knee in the gray office until dusk.

He was quite animated by now, sucking on his smoke, one minute hunching down, cradling his demitasse, the next snapping up straight, emphatically extending his long neck to introduce me to the complexities.

"You'll see tomorrow," he said. "Fatah sets up its command in an old age home. The Israelis bomb it, we repair it and the whole cycle, one way or another, is paid for by Uncle Sam."

"Except for the old people," I said, "who get wasted."

"Believe me," he shot back, "most of them are already wasted."

"And so what do you do?" Mike laughed. The mantis, rising from his desk.

"I get paid to make sure they don't put too much sand in the cement. Let's go."

An odd, man, Mike. I knew what dark thoughts my own shapeliness had produced at prep school. The dread of facing the taunts each morning from the bullies. It was not difficult to imagine what had been the fate of someone who must have been topping 6'4 by age 16 and yet was little more than 120 lbs. And who, by some cruel trick of inheritance, had never been able to shoot a basket or hit a ball to save his life.

You could see it anyway. There was no grace. He was all bones and sharp angles. Either pulling in around a cup or ashtray or jerking up like a lollipop to make a statement. Prone to breaking up into laughter, his face aglow with it. "No," I was exclaiming, incredulous, as he recounted the Widow Farida's recent visit to the kitchen, her entry coinciding with poor Vache's ejaculation.

"Jack was going to fire him," Mike recounted, "but I told Jack if Vache goes, I go. So Vache now hangs around me like a puppy and his mother brings me Armenian sweets, and Farida is disgusted and now refuses to type my reports."

Mike had a subterranean room and a half in the same apartment building as Jack. Outside, we sat around a bamboo table in his sunken terrace, like a well between his furnishings inside and the hedge alongside the public sidewalk: the only view was straight up at a sky full of stars. Now, I learned about the Levant from my Arabist friend. He would explain, I would make extrapolations, and he would say, "No," refusing to let me conclude anything, arguing that understanding lay somewhere in the midst of the confusion. "Nothing linear here," he told me, "except for the bullet at your head."

I asked him about my assignment as a spy, and he laughed. "Look it," he said, "you can spend the rest of your life up there and still come back with nothing."

"I doubt it would be nothing," I said, slighted. He was pressing the cold can of beer to his forehead.

"So what are you looking for?"

"A bridge that we paid a half million for," I answered.

"Well, have no doubt, they will show you a bridge. Just like the one in the text. And the whole village will turn out and thank you and load up that pathetic Chevette of yours with gifts—some quite beautiful—and then Franjiha or one of his family will motorcade in and whisk you away to his palace and put you next to him at the Majlis and pat your knee as the tribe files by and strokes your hand. And just in case you don't get it, you will also get to see some of your stone-faced characters outside, armed to the teeth, as they take you back to the Chevette."

After that he took a long hard drag. I took some more nuts. My stomach growled. Thirteen coffees by now, half-dozen beers and as many bowls of nuts. All of it proscribed by every doctor who had ever tended to me.

"So, who's that?" I asked. An artillery exchange had begun a mile or two south of us.

"Amal and Fatah," Mike answered, without pausing. Jack's long drink was standing up. "Come on."

That isn't very smart, I thought to myself. Not for two gringos at that time of night. But I trailed behind him anyway without protest. He seemed quite unconcerned and, as it turned out, we only walked across the road to the sea wall. Most of the day's earlier commotion had died down with just a few stragglers left out there with us on the corniche along with a couple of vendors with their pushcarts. We bought some beer and Za'atar and sat up on the wall like two pop-ups, I feared, against the horizon. A sea of garbage swelled and smashed against the rocks and then fell back. Mike pointed out a rat. And then I was able to spot more. Certainly, one species that had grown fat off the war.

"Don't underestimate them," Mike said. "They're bold. They'll take that bread right out of your hand."

"So, what's tomorrow?" I asked.

"Got to get you out of here ASAP."

"What do you mean?"

"Well before I got here, no one went South. The staff terrified the ex-pats. Basically, told them they'd never come back alive. Which basically meant more money for Maronite land or more bridges that were built twice . . . if you get my drift." I got his drift. The liberals' instinct to snuggle up to whatever confronted Israel and its allies. "Anyway," he continued, "you should meet Latif Zayne and Haddad. Fish around in that pile on your desk till you find the Tyre project." He smiled. "And don't forget your Brownie. Photos, we want. Photos we need," he corrected, "to keep those old ladies back home putting their change in the collection." I took a swig, peering down at all the multicolored plastic bobbing up and down beneath me.

"On average, twenty-five cents per Catholic per year. And that's why—" he was sticking his finger into his chest, a bit deep in his drinks at this point—"my 1651 rules, and you, with your pitiful parishioner monies, well, you drool," he said, extending the vowels for his own amusement.

By now the nuts had done their worst. My gut was inflating, and I wanted to go to bed. The hotel was straight up the hill from where I was sitting. Earlier fears about being carried forth by a malevolent current returned. I felt ignorant. I had been around the block a few times, and even blown once, as we used to say. And admittedly, forty-eight hours is not much of an acquaintance. But, I thought, is this really where I want to make a stand? I slid off the wall and put my hand on Mike's shoulder. "Got to go," I said. He shot his finger up in the air, head erect with a foolish grin.

"Say good night to Jumblatt," he said, somewhat imploringly. As Helen used to say, "his slip was showing." He started walking across the street on a diagonal, heading south. I hesitated but, at last, felt I couldn't let him go off into the night. I suspected this was the problem that Jack had referred to. In any case, he wasn't the mentor now, rather the scarecrow disappearing, and so I went after him.

When I came up alongside, he had that same fool's grin. "Weren't sure, were you?" We were headed right at a sandbag bunker with some militia outside. Over them was another flag and a large Kamal Jumblatt emerging from out of what I took to be a red poppy. They knew Mike already. He was going back and forth in Arabic, getting assistance with a word from them from time to time but generally doing ok. I was Abu Hank, he told them, referring to my unborn child. They were not the stone-faced sort, up by our office. They were, Mike explained, university students before the war had interrupted their studies. One of them handed me a political tract by Jumblatt in English. "Yes," Mike said. "They agree that your wife and baby will be safe in the Chouf."

One of them started in English. "Our guests in the Chouf," he said, but I needed to disengage, and so I thanked them and started to walk up the hill. But Mike would have none of it. He would escort me to the Mayflower. Better yet, we would have a nightcap. He could sense my reluctance. "To celebrate your first day of work," he argued.

What could I say? At least I would be where I would sleep. But the notion of more drinks, and Mike descending the hill by himself frightened me. We were already alone, with the artillery still resonating and all that daytime bustle and blare now locked up inside. Alone on these eerie medieval streets, we had walked the way by starlight, mostly in silence, passing one or two street vendors packing up, debris shifting with the night breeze, amid the screech of an assassin's car.

We ducked in, past the sandbags into an unseen box of light and life, into all the excitement of ex-pats trying to wind down, a din of chatter and long arms reaching over people for pints.

Mike sidled in, as I had seen him do before in the office when he had first met me, sidling down the hall to his office. And now again he sidled into this din, moving from the door along the wall looking apologetic—quite another Mike from the one who had earlier engaged the Druze.

"On me," I said and began to work my way into the crowd to get our drinks. I had left Mike with a couple of relief workers from SAVE, who seemed to know him quite well. I sensed from the greeting that Mike, in general, was well known within this small relief community. He was still against the wall when I got back. Alternately bent over or jerking up emphatically to make a point, most of which, as well as I could hear in the din, involved his insistence that something or another was his fault despite what appeared to be their willingness to forget it. I wanted to lean over and whisper to him to drop it. How many times did the three of us have to listen to his unequivocal insistence that he was totally to blame for something? Finally, one of the SAVE workers laughed and said, "Well, I guess we'll just have to disappear you."

Not long after, I found an opportunity to sneak out and up to my room. There was the rather critical imperative of relieving my growling gut, and I longed for the moment when I would drop my head into the pillow.

I got to the office early the next morning, where I was met by Madame Vache—my first saint, I suspected—who soon after had her disabled boy bring me coffee. I have to admit I did now see him, still stooped and hollow-eyed, in a somewhat different light.

I found the Tyre project and had begun reading it by the time George and the rest of the clan had arrived from the East. Dapper George with the elf ears and the smell of talc arranged his Dunhill's and his gold instrument. Almost on cue, as he took his seat, Vache was there with coffee, while Toufic bobbed on the other side.

He must have known what had gone on last night. He was sipping his Turkish and smiling at me. I kept my head down, trying to decipher the project text, the various "project identification" boxes. It must have seemed amusing.

"Sabah al Khair," George said softly, a twinkle in his eye. I looked confused. "Morning of the light. Sabah el Yasmin. Morning of the Jasmine," and he went on describing all the beautiful ways of greeting the day, so reduced in my world to the prefix "good." He was opening an exotic world to me just a crack, as if I had been allowed to peek in and glimpse Ali Baba's treasure. Thus began an aspect of our relationship: I had taken the lure, swallowed it in fact, to the extent that within a few days I would be pulling pieces of paper out of my pocket over the morning coffee, onto which I had copied some calligraphy or jotted a transliteration, ever anxious for more glimpses from George of this so-called cradle of civilization.

Often, he reminded me of the dinner invitation from him and his wife Aurora. He reached into his blazer and took out his billfold, from which he produced a photo. These were, for me, the greatest Arabian treasures. Milk white and coal black. Pure bred. In such contrast to the mongrels of America. Shia or Maronite, it didn't matter. I couldn't help but stare.

"Prohibitive maintenance," Mike responded when I had broached the subject. "And don't you in your wildest dreams even think of putting your finger on them. Or you'll find yourself with no hand, if you're lucky. They're chimera," he continued. "For you and me, they're chimera. Raised from birth to be chimera."

We had been stuck for most of an hour at that point trying to leave Beirut, near what was called the Beaches. A few years back it had been cocktails and parasols at the water's edge, now a makeshift maze of discarded planking, cinderblock and cardboard—another expropriation to accommodate the inexorable spread of the Shia spillover from the South.

I asked how long we could expect to be jammed up there. He reached over the seat and held up a very thick paperback. "Those are your choices," he said. "If you've got air—I do and you don't—" he interjected, "then you roll up the windows and read. Sometimes as much as 100 pages before you budge." I thought back to my Poli sci professors describing democracy as an acceptance of give and take. The traffic light as a symbol of such. Well here, it appeared, there was no trace of give. Just horns blaring and clouds of dust and gridlock.

"Or?" I asked.

"Or," Mike said, you better have some Nissans, some AKs and a few RPGs, and then you break through."

Outside, it was a wild scene: ragtag teenagers sporting their fire power; a donkey trotting along, laden with a TV, winding through innumerable well-worn Mercedes amidst old trucks with Shia furnishings piled up in back. Waiters now running through the mess with trays of water and Turkish. And everywhere, gigantic holes in the road with re-rod sticking out of them. While off to the side, stands of gorgeous oranges and strawberries were being set right up on collapsed slabs. And everyone, it seemed, packing revolvers, except Mike and me. All this, of course, transpiring amidst a swirl of diesel fumes and dust, and as the sun rose, I felt increasingly as if I had been dropped on a crowded griddle.

"Seventy-four kilometers and twenty-four checkpoints," Mike was saying.

"So why did we leave so late," I asked.

"Because we have to avoid lunch." I thought on this awhile. "You'll see," Mike explained. "It's all a question of debts here. Back home we build savings accounts or equity investments. Here you accumulate debts. That's the only wealth that counts. They don't quit," Mike said. "From the elite to the peasant they agonize on how they can do you a favor. You'll see—they empty their kitchen for you. They put the women to work and they spread the table so thick with delicacies that sometimes there's several stories of them, and then there are various embroideries and crates of fruits, branches of figs, and on up to silver and gold mementos and couplets from Damascus." This was sounding all very wonderful to me.

"But there's always the knock on the door afterward. Never isn't. After all, they figure, it's not our money, and if a well has to be built, it may as well water their crops as those of the confession down the road." Here he started laughing. "Of course with the little pot of monies in your hands, I'd advise you not to dream of much more than napkins."

"So I take it . . . no lunch."

"Exactly," Mike answered. "First rule: always arrive at an hour which allows you the best excuse for missing the hospitality."

"So I am always to show up in late afternoon?" I asked. Christ, I was thinking, what a good man to check for sand in the cement.

We didn't stop in Sidon but just continued South toward Tyre. Now into checkpoints decorated with the revered Moussa Sadr or Chairman Arafat, with Syrian tanks in the mountains behind them. Actually, I was thinking, there it was: a very compact political trilogy. The three symbols: for Syrian hegemony, for the refugee's war for Liberation, and for the emergence of an insistent Shia ownership.

"Remember that TOTAL sign," Mike said as he turned his Chevy Caprice away from the coast. And I would. For the rest of my life. For this was where you left the witness of the relatively populated coast road for the lonely drive into the Shia Heartland, Nabatiyeh. This was the moment when Mike became serious, driving at unsafe speeds past hills covered in scrub. "Don't stop for nothing," he said. "This is where AMAL and the PLO kill each other."

I felt as if I was back making the dash across the green line, but this time it went on for a half hour, and while I didn't say anything, it seemed crazy to me that we were now climbing up over eighty-five miles an hour in his mid-size sedan, risking life and limb on narrow rutted roads, as if we would be harder to hit by whoever thought to make a name by taking out a couple of Americans.

Nonsense, I kept thinking. He may know flags, but the only thing he is assuring now is that if we get hit we will die by the crash afterward. My right hand clutched the arm rest. I wondered if this was how his partner was killed. I thought to distract him from his race to Nabatiyeh with small talk. I mentioned what I called the unusual management style of Jack. Mike found that funny, and the needle actually came down a bit.

"Oh, Jack's okay," Mike said.

"Okay?" I responded. "You mean never there, still calls me Dick, asks me to spy on staff, can't tell me who works for me. Christ, what does okay mean, that he hasn't joined a militia yet?" Mike found that funny too. There was a minaret and village not far ahead. "Look it, he and Sophia nursed me for about three months after the accident." I didn't say anything. He looked over at me. "I'm sure George must have mentioned it."

We turned a bend and were suddenly facing a funeral coming right toward us. Flanked by Fatah warriors, the professional variety. "Don't mention Zayne," Mike said under his breath.

We pulled over, out of the way. And thank God, no one confronted us. Five caskets went by. "AMAL," Mike said. "They're tired of the PLO acting like they own the place. They don't give a shit about the Palestine's cause and vice versa. The Shia just want their share of Lebanon. Which, if their women keep producing at current rates, in fifty years that share will be most of Lebanon. Think about it. It's all demographics here, and any Sunnite or Palestinian or Maronite with brains will soon enough be practicing dentistry in Houston or some such place. All Fatah means to the Shia is killers strolling about eyeballing their girls—that and getting rained on by Israeli fighter bombers every time the PLO lobs a rocket over the border."

"Where is Syria in all this?" I asked.

"Where is Syria? Hell, they're in the Golan, and in their relationship with Iraq, or with Khomeini. This is just where it plays out. Basically, on the benighted head of the ever-multiplying Shiite peasant who is pushed from his land to South Beirut and back, depending on events outside his control. Becoming," he added, "more radicalized in the process, more ready to die for Allah."

Abdul Latif Zayne was impeccable. Silver-haired, silk-robed, sitting in an ornate chair beneath a magnificent shade tree, his plantation before him, lush in this season with citrus and grapes. Behind him, a French colonial stone farmhouse, and around him in a rectangle, his council, the Majlis.

To me it was obvious we were being welcomed in. A chair next to him was being vacated, and Zayne was asking a servant to do something. I proceeded, while behind me I heard Mike telling me, "No," and saw him circling some fig trees on his way toward the farmhouse. "We'll wait there," he was telling me. But I was too far committed by now, and clearly places were being freed for us.

As I approached, Zayne started patting the chair next to him. "Here, here, my friend," he said in King's English. Another chair was being freed for Mike who, by now, was reluctantly coming in, all the while protesting that one of the more distant, empty chairs was fine. Finally, Zayne put his arm around his friend, sat him on his other side and said, "Now, Mike, why don't you introduce your colleague?" Mike sat up straight, and in Arabic told the council who we were and why we were there.

Zayne questioned me for a while, making clear his debt to CRS and Mike for the new clinic. He was so eloquent in his thanks that I felt compelled to ask how I could help, with the small pot I had. Zayne didn't do that type of conversation, I soon learned, and said I should talk to so-and-so, one of other men in the rectangle.

I told him about the funeral.

"Yes," he confirmed. "Fifty-six dead on both sides this month. Tragic when this happens between brothers." Some others, who had understood the English, were nodding. Then Zayne repeated it in Arabic himself for everyone. More assent.

"You know, my friend," he said, patting my knee. "They are our guests. This should not have happened." He paused. "But then, guests must also show respect." Again, he spoke in Arabic. Again, heads bent, hands sifting through their beads, with more murmured assent. Then he smiled. "When you're done with your good work here, you go back to America and tell them they need to open their ears more. Listen to other voices here. Not just Israel." He looked me in the eye. "You know it's in your interest to do so."

Afterward, some supplicants came into the rectangle and told their story. There was a spat of animated discussion surrounding the requests. After a while, one of the elders indicated it was over. They paid their respects to Zayne and left. I noticed Mike was fidgeting with the folder he had brought. In due course Zayne obliged him.

"You have something for me to sign?" he asked.

Mike turned red and stiffened. The mantis erectus, I thought.

"Here," Mike said.

"Why not, my friend," Zayne responded. Mike laid the folder in his lap while Zayne was handed a fountain pen by one of his faithful.

"Contracts," Mike told me later in the car. "Just acknowledging receipt. He doesn't like doing it much more than your Maronite Bishop. It's not the way business is done here. But he understands. He was educated in England." I told him it all seemed very much like an empty exercise: legal contracts in a land where there were no courts, no police and no jails. Mike shrugged. "I guess we're banking on the day when all that returns."

I informed Mike I had made a date with Zayne's assistant to come back and discuss a project. Medicines for the clinic had been mentioned.

"Just make sure you buy them," Mike said. "You'll probably pay three times as much, but at least you'll be sure the Catholics in Connecticut"—he winked at me—"aren't buying bad medicine. Look," he continued, "it's all smuggled anyway, and in that sense it doesn't matter. But what does count is that your hand stays on the spigot. You turn it off and you turn it on."

"Are we partners or cops?" I asked him.

"Both," he answered.

"I don't see how a partner can be a cop," I said.

"Try not being one for a while and you'll see soon enough."

It wasn't far to Tyre. In fact, all the distances here were short; it was the checkpoints and traffic jams that took all day. On the way out I related to Mike my opinion about speed as a liability on the road to the coast. He scoffed, but slowed down anyway. We had just enough time to pay our respects to the Greek Bishop, Haddad, he said, and then take a look at the nets we had purchased for the fisherman. "Yes, sir," Mike said, "Muriel always liked the idea of helping fisherman in the Holy Land."

I laid back on the car seat, still enchanted by the picture in my mind of Zayne under the tree as I had approached. Unchanged, I thought, for a thousand years. "But about to," Mike said when I had confided my enchantment to him. "There's a new generation growing up amidst the mess of South Beirut that will no longer cede decisions to gentlemen like Zayne."

"Et voilà," Mike said with a flourish of his hand. "Unspoiled by tourism." We passed more antiquities, Roman ruins serving as a sheep pen. "There's no respect there," Mike went on. "For them it is just another one of the Western invasions. Greek, Roman, Christendom, France, England and now Israel. Folks here think nothing of hauling those blocks off for bunkers."

Haddad, as a Greek-Melkite minority and humble servant of God, was unique in Tyre. He met us with a bear hug, a soutane with his silver pectoral a bit askew. A gregarious cleric. A man grown useful to all who were party to the conflict. The day we visited, he was accepting into his rectangle some swashbuckler from the SLA, Israel's surrogate in South Lebanon. And then, a Swedish colonel from UNIFIL (United Nations Interim Force In Lebanon) and an emissary from the sister of Moussa Sadr. Along with the more mundane: a young soldier and his 'intended' asking permission to get married. It was there where messages passed, prisoners got traded, wounded were brought back—where the common good was attempted. Unlike Zayne, he was less tied to his chair. Three times while we were there, he left the rectangle to "find" something, as he described it. Like Henry, I mused: always busy. Mike looked at me and tapped his watch. We made our excuses to Haddad and left our privileged seats beside him, and soon were off to see the nets.

Like Zayne in Nabatiyeh, Haddad in Tyre was to be my mentor, my protector. This was how Mike was setting me up. "It's how you will survive down here," Mike had told me as we walked down to the port. He pointed at my folder and camera. "We don't do projects. The American donors think we do, CRS/New York thinks we do, but we don't. What we do is invest in the only influences for moderation we can find and just hope that the money we run through them extends their influence."

"That's it?" I asked.

"Just about," he said. "I mean, what the fuck do we know? A couple of dicks from the American suburbs. Anyway, don't consider for a minute the alternative of wandering around like Johnny Appleseed, dropping unsanctioned little dollops of cash as you please. Within a week you'd be drawn and quartered by every pretender in town. And you'd end up running to Haddad to be rescued anyway. No, you take his list." Here Mike laughed. "And don't worry, he always has a list. And pick the one you like. As I said, for Muriel it was fishing nets and sunflowers."

"Sunflowers?"

Mike raised his finger in the air. "Ah, but that's another story. A Beka'a story. Something for you to look forward to."

"What else," I asked.

"Well, as I said earlier, hand on the spigot and then, if you're inclined toward the quixotic, you can always push for investments which seek to avoid patronizing the poor. I mean, empowerment is the word in the Western textbooks but don't push too hard or you won't get asked back. In general," Mike warned, "they like their poor just as they are. Totally dependent."

Haddad had sent a messenger ahead who had managed to find a few of the beneficiaries to translate for me. I took their photo on the sea wall with the new, blue nylon nets spread out behind them. Not exactly in keeping with the grandeur which was Phoenicia and which, I was told, lay sunken, not many feet under just where I was gazing.

"How do you like them," I asked. They said they did. Somehow, I had been expecting a greater show of enthusiasm and gratitude. After all, wasn't that supposed to be one of the benefits of my job, along with no taxes: getting thanked a lot?

The Bishop's man told me they had been sleeping. That there wasn't much work now. "How come?" I asked, which turned out to be a stupid question. They pointed out to sea.

"Israel," the messenger said. "They can't leave the coast or Israel will capture them and sink their boats."

I looked at Mike, who was fingering the nets.

"Oh," I said, not really knowing where to take this interview except that the money was already spent and I had to send something to the donor. The fishermen looked bored. "Do they use the nets on the coast?" The messenger translated. They nodded in the affirmative. "How do they like them?" I asked again. They said they did.

"Are they better than the old nets?"

"They're lighter," one of them said.

I waited for some other tidbit of success to be recounted, something to fill the page. But that was it. A dead end. I looked at Mike; he looked away.

I asked the messenger to ask them what else could help them in their situation. A refrigerated truck, one of them said.

"Why?" I asked.

"Because then they could take their fish to Beirut where prices allow some profit."

"What do they do now?"

The messenger didn't bother asking them since apparently everyone except me knew that they sold it to middlemen who had refrigerated trucks.

"Oh," I said, now on familiar ground. "Cut out the middlemen." We shook hands and walked back to the car. I was shaking my head: just one more confirmation for me that I had truly landed in the world of the absurd. I looked across the seat at Mike. "Translation, please?"

"What do you mean," he laughed. A sort of prelude, I guessed, to a much longer explanation.

Which got me to thinking that Mike had done this for too long by himself and was now thoroughly needing the company, especially of a new dick about his age upon whom he could unload his hard-won lessons.

"What do I mean, you ask!" I was raising my voice, tapping my head with my fingers like something was loose up there.

"We buy nets for fishermen who can't fish? Was this on Haddad's list?"

"They can fish," Mike said, "as long as they stick to the coast."

"But they said—"

"Did you see our nets?" Mike interrupted.

"What do you mean? Of course I saw them."

"Up close, I mean."

I didn't answer, so Mike continued. "Because up close you can tell these nets have never been dipped in the sea."

I groaned. "Tell me, professor, what the hell is happening here. Take the cover off, will you please?"

"They dynamite," Mike answered. "Except they use concussion grenades, which around here are about a dime a dozen."

"Ah ha," I said.

"So, yeah, on any one day you can watch them ply the coast, occasionally flipping out a grenade, and then there is a boom and soon after the water bubbles up and so does most everything else in the vicinity, belly up."

"Gotcha," I said. "That explains the refrigerator truck."

"Sure," Mike answered, "but I'd be careful with that one. Cutting out the middleman is basically rearranging power and well, that is definitely one you should pass by Haddad."

"And so," I put both hands on the dash and had raised my voice for effect, "please help me to understand, why Muriel got the nets."

"Oh," Mike answered, "that part's simple. For all the right reasons. That grenades would eventually ruin the fishing forever and much more, should it go on. And of course, Haddad couldn't argue with that. Nor with the proposition that the new nets might, someday, under different circumstances, increase benefits."

"Muriel," I mused. "An aging dreamer from the West befriending a few tolerant patrons with her little pocketbook of greenbacks."

The beauty was, as they say, uplifting. The sun was not far off the water, and with its light refracted and made brilliant by the clouds of fumes hanging over Sidon, it was but a short leap to seeing Queen Dido and her kin sailing on that same horizon.

By now we were somewhat talked out and both falling into periods of silence. I, quite snug, was still feeling transported by the myths of this place, when Mike reached over to click on the car radio. And then instantly filling the interior was a Bible Belt Evangelist, so close he could have been in the back seat. Praising Christ and introducing Southern Lebanon to "Little Bitty Pretty One." Except for one interruption to inform me that we were now enjoying songs of the 60's, courtesy of the SLA radio franchise in the Israel buffer zone, the ride back was without benefit of more lessons. Less traffic and no jams, and for half the way good ole rock & roll, same as if I had been driving back on some Friday night from the office in Hartford to where I'd get my shots for success. And, of course, during certain songs I thought of my wife, wishing I was going home to her tonight, and wondering about baby Hank.

And then the brilliance finally dropped under the horizon, and Mike asked me to find the flashlight in the glove compartment, which he flicked on and put under his chin as we stopped at yet another check point. It was for the illumination of the haystack overhead accompanied by Mike's characteristic "Howdy," which he had told me earlier so befuddles them that they wave him by.

This one was a teenager, wearing only parts of a uniform. Much more dangerous, I decided, than the regulars at the Syrian or PLO barricades: 120 lbs. soaking wet and probably couldn't find America on a map, and here he decides to look at a license he can't read while his muzzle is resting on the windowsill about a foot from Mike's haystack and his finger is fidgeting on the trigger.

A couple more howdies, some more perplexity from the boy, and then we were passed. I mean, for someone like me who had personal knowledge of what that haystack would look like after a round had entered into it: well, to wit, the dance I was just having with my wife quickly disappeared.

By the end of my first week, a pattern was established which, with the exception of those times when cataclysms shook the country, I was to maintain during most of my stay there. Lebanon was a small country and either way—toward Tyre, Baalbek or Tripoli—I could do my *visite de courtoisie*, my interview at site, snap a photo, and, at least in the summer, still be home not much after dark.

After the first week, I took leave of my apprenticeship since, by then, I was starting to sense I could do better on my own. The project or progress report, as they were called, was nothing. God knows I could write down anything I wanted and soon enough get a refill from the donors. One thing was for sure: no one anytime soon was going to go where I went to look for the truth.

It became mostly a matter of my own pride and my own sense, which I discovered during my apprenticeship was not nearly as American as Mike's, which, put otherwise, meant allowing more slack for the locals. Once I was convinced of the essential absurdity of everything that happened to me since the pop of the flash in the Bishop's room, it was impossible for me, intellectually, to dig my heels in on matters of principle when "principle" just didn't apply.

Quite apart from that, but also contributing to some distance between Mike and me, was my strong intent not to flaunt the odds. Of course, in a way, I lived for the sparkle that a couple of rounds on the green line will add to life, and "lived" is probably the right word here, but I had spent too long with a catheter up my dick (as payment for the last sparkle) to seek that sparkle again at any cost, not to mention wanting to be around for the sparkle baby Hank would provide when she finally saw the light of day.

Thus, I continued my mornings studying Arabic with George as he began to open up the Levant for me, particularly the divinity of the language, the presence of Mohammed in each syllable. Odd, I supposed, to be getting all this from a descendant of St. Maron.

Vache lurked, ever at the ready with his tray to inject me with more rocket fuel, as I called it. Seemingly also, like Toufic, at George's beck and call, this hairy little servant with his twisted vertebrae was undoubtedly his mother's cross to bear.

And of course, Farida, now two years widowed and still wearing black, more (I guessed) because it suited her than from any remembrance. Now, mostly, she was Jack's, which also suited her, since it effectively protected her from other assignments.

"On fire today?" I would ask her with a grin. To which she answered, "Thank God, not yet but—," and then she would go down a trail of discontent about someone or something. And, if I expected any help with the typing, I'd commiserate as genuinely as I could, even allowing for some occasional meaningful looks at what, actually, were quite fine features, despoiled unfortunately by her relentless personality.

And then one day, not long after our trip South, Mike had what George had described to me in confidence as his weekly fit, which, George continued, often coincided with pouch day, a day that apparently signified the only certainty in Jack's schedule. The day on which he could be found behind his desk quite early, fresh from his shower, signing checks for suppliers and staff and the cover letters for Mike's, and now my, reports.

It began with Mike asking Farida to pick up some photos for inclusion in his report. Exquisite representations, I chided him, since they were usually of engineers standing next to cement mixers. The day was apt to be stressful anyway, since Jack always took this weekly opportunity to change a sentence or two, which in turn would send Mike (and me) back to the typewriter, dabbing the mistakes with white-out and blowing on them ever so insistently, knowing that DHL and the plane it would be on waited for no one.

When Mike saw Farida, unmoved, cool as a cucumber, polishing her nails outside Jack's office, the long drink, quite agitated by now over the as-yet undelivered photos, went at her and demanded an explanation. The task, she cooed, as head of administration, had been delegated. Since no

158

one, Mike knew, touched Jack's driver Khalil, the delegate had to be Vache who, Mike also knew, once out of the office, was notorious for getting distracted. At which point Mike had begun shouting, the core of it being that headquarters would only get narrative. So much commotion that all the way down in our back room we could sense the storm. George slowly shook his head. I thought to go up front to calm Mike down.

Jack, I could hear as I approached, had also felt it necessary to poke his head out, giving you some idea of the ruckus going on, seeing his secretary not at all on fire and his expatriate assistant in full rant. Mike flew by me, disappearing into his room, and Jack retracted his head. Farida looked up from her nails at me: "You see, Mister Dick. You see we have a crazy man here."

Then there was a bang, and I dropped half to my knees, right before Farida who, unmoved as before, now looked down from her desk at me and laughed. She pointed in the direction of Mike's room and then, very composed, got up from behind her desk, walked over to her waste basket and made an imitation of kicking it, intermittently pointing at Mike's room. After about the second imitation she stopped. I think she was noticing that I was lingering on her flawless kicking leg, causing her to give me her best shot, albeit somewhat pathetic, with an intriguing little smile, which soon enough got snapped back into her traditional purse, as she had reconfigured it to what was appropriate for a widow.

I went back to making my corrections, with George watching the process like some kind of anthropologist studying the work habits of a Yankee, a pastime of his which I was feeling could get quite old with time. Other than dispatch Toufic on errands and be gracious toward my general ignorance as well as a willing contributor to its reduction, work for him was a place not an activity, not an uncommon characteristic, I was learning, of this, my new "living."

Eventually Jack signed my cover, in its corrected form. I don't think he read my report on Tyre fisherman, or Saida dispensary, or the others I had visited the few days earlier: a negligence for which I was thankful, not knowing for sure about what standard he might apply, and being fully conscious and ashamed by what I had been led to do: take some very slim pickings—as far as verifiable facts were concerned—and dress them up with every adjective and adverb I could find till I had filled the pages. God only knows, I told myself, what type of reception this crap will get in New York.

The next week was one of anticipation for me. The return pouch, I was told, would carry "feedback." An interesting expression, I thought. It would be an exciting day, occasional to the office. And this time Farida drove both of us crazy. There it was, the fat manila envelope, sitting on her desk, her two very sculptured hands, glorified with a brilliant polish, protecting it. She looked up at Mike and me, saying, "You can't see what's inside until Mr. Jack opens it first."

Now this was screwing with some very sensitive emotions. Wrapped up in her own conceit as she was, she risked going too far. These were war-weary Americans suffering from too many incoming at night and muzzles in the face, and in general trying to make our backs small, and inside that fat manila were undoubtedly letters—undoubtedly, some affection from home that would be taken off to somewhere private, certainly not in front of George, and be read and re-read, probably each day, until the next pouch arrived.

And those sculptured hands lay across the pouch, the pursed lips before our stare. Surely, I was hoping, she had to see that Mike was only one wrong word away from "going crazy," and I was not too far behind him. Finally, his long thin arms went skyward, like a ref at a football game calling a foul, and they sort of paused up there, just under the ceiling fan, and I saw fright in Farida's eyes. Mike's hands fluttered up there and then, like a guillotine, they came down on the pouch, barely missing her hands, giving Farida barely a split second to snatch them away. And so now it was Mike's bony hands on the manila as he stared hard at Farida and said in a tremulous voice, "Don't fuck with me!" And she pushed her chair back and emitted such a heart-rending gasp that the staff now entering must have thought that Mike had exposed himself or something.

The scene is frozen in memory: Mike leaning over her desk with his hands on the pouch, she with her hand covering her mouth giving the appearance of a woman in shock, with the semi-circle of staff around us. And then she put both hands on her face and began sobbing. Mike remained unmoved. The staff did not budge.

He ripped open the envelope, fished in and brought out a few letters, took one, handed me a couple, and dropped the pouch on her desk. Then he walked out.

After a while George went over to Farida, who was still sobbing, albeit less dramatically, and handed her a box of tissues. He said something to her in Arabic, and she responded with shaking hands and an extended outburst, interrupting this wail from time to time to quite carefully pronounce the word *fuck*.

George put the box of tissues, now half gone, beside her and left (the others taking his lead), but I remained there, quite confused about my next step. Only a few minutes earlier I too had stood, looming over her. As a new dick, I certainly had no interest in getting on the wrong side of the gatekeeper, so to speak. But it was more than that. Anyone could see she was a poor show, a rather little person with a small life, punctuated each day for six years now by her daily gauntlet across the green line. I gathered up the discarded tissues and put them in the wastebasket, then returned and put my hand on her shoulder.

Her eyes were red, her makeup smeared. At that instant, looking up at me, she was very much the aging widow. "Jack will hear of this," she whispered, before wiping her eyes and nodding as if in confirmation of what she was about to say. I leaned in. "Fuck," she said. "He said 'fuck' to me. No one can say 'fuck' to me."

A half hour later, Jack had yet to materialize, so I left early for lunch with the precious missives folded in my front pocket and headed toward, as far as I knew, the only sanctuary left in Ras Beirut, the American University green; it remarkedly unmarked as yet by craters or smashed walls, still somehow maintaining a calm.

These are the precious missives that one absconds with and escapes into. Here there is no impatience for message. It is rather the prolonged savoring, the turning over of each word in your mind, the increasingly worn folds of the envelope as it leaves and returns to your pocket over the week: in the bed at night, on the pot at work.

But also, unfortunately, and notwithstanding the letter as affection, other news also got embedded there. Discordant news that amidst the affection would trouble you.

Henry was changed—permanently, Pen wrote. "He hasn't shaved since you left and looks, I'm sorry to tell you this, like a bum. He has put a lawn chair in the driveway. At the end, near the road, and sits there all day in the same Hawaiian shirt and shorts and waves at all the cars passing by. Not a normal wave, however. He stands up and bows with his arms outstretched like the movies depict the slaves doing for Sultans. And," she went on, "he doesn't come in to pee. He just turns around and goes on the driveway with the stream running against his shoes and out onto the road. My love, I know how difficult it must be in Beirut and we hear about it on television all the time, but I guess I feel you should know about your father. It's not good, my love. Yesterday, Helen had to go out and get him to zip up his fly—which he had forgotten to do . . . and he called her a bitch".

I could imagine my mother, probably haunted by the advice, a generation back, from her mother about the bad sense—not to mention bad taste—in marrying this little salesman from the Bronx. She, of Crosby Shipping. She, of the great schooners which had plied the Pacific, marrying the boy whose divorced mother made ends meet by clerking at the County Trust. She who, dressed for dinner: he who pasted stamps of faraway places while his mother relieved her swelling feet in a bowl of hot water.

I put the pages down. I imagined my mother as stoic. She would, I knew, not be ashamed. She had been brought up never to be ashamed. I could hear her: "No, of course not. He doesn't know what he's doing." And then, always, the assertion: "He was a good man, your father. He lived for you children."

She went on, writing about some practical matters. She was "doing her best" with the bills, but Henry had been in another world, and Helen, frankly, doesn't have a clue. "I think They are okay"—and here, in her inimitable way, she had capitalized "they." "The lawyer says, given Henry's condition, it is unlikely the courts would support action against him and Helen, but technically or legally or whatever (he doesn't talk so as I can understand it all, my love) if the suppliers can't get everything from us, then they can go after officers—and as you know somewhere along the line Helen was made an officer. As for us, well I guess you know the worst. I call the lawyer—it seems like every other day—but it seems he's out most of the time or that he really wants to talk to you, but I explained that the phones where you work are all out of order.

"Our house did get sold by the bank but it seems they took a big chunk of it so there isn't too much left over. The lawyer said he'd write you about this. And then I paid the lawyer with your Army disability check and we'll just keep handing this over to him, unless you say otherwise. And I guess that's about it. Your paycheck didn't get deposited yet so I called them at N.Y.C. They seem nice but still no deposit," and here she had put in a big exclamation mark.

"Don't worry about me and baby Hank. The
doctor says we are both doing well. Of course, I don't
tell him that we are going to Lebanon soon. I don't
really tell anyone since I've already had a couple of
calls here—one from someone who used to work
for you, who yelled at me and said she knew damn
well that you and your sister had cooked this whole
bankruptcy up just to make a bundle and that if she
didn't get every cent coming to her she was going
to the police. So you see my love I'm staying pretty
mum about leaving.

"That's about it. I miss you so much with that
war all around you and pray at night you will stay
safe. We love you and trust you know how to take
care of yourself. The way you survived Vietnam and
then those horrible hospitals, I just know you will
be okay.

"That really is all. Since I have to get to the
post office before it closes so this can get to New
York for the pouch. I love you so much and just don't
want any more scars on you, and will be there next
to you the minute you tell me."

It was the devil throughout, I thought. As in
Paris, at my favorite refuge during the time I was
struggling with "the great midway." That small park
behind the Rodin Museum. Ugolino was there. Here

too, I thought, there was a type of cannibalism going on. My brother-in-law was feeding from Roo, now exiled, and Roo from Henry, now half-crazy, and Henry from Helen, now martyred, who would feed off me, now fugitive, who was feeding off my wife, now isolated amidst the carnage. I mean, it seemed as if each of us had our needs buried into their next of kin.

I was where I had to be. Not exactly this war, but some rough equivalent. Another day or two next to the willow in the back yard, stoned and indecisive, would have meant both my mother and wife at my throat. Here, as related to them by local television, I was being heroic, which is such a condemnation. All that garbage after Vietnam, the various get-well letters from third graders. The shit about "our boys in Vietnam," when over there we all knew that most of those boys were shoveling shit in some rear area or playing volleyball. The few who were really out there were either craving the opportunity to kill some dinks or doing everything possible to get home.

Anyway, if the news anchors said I was heroic then that was that. Christ.

Her letter certainly kept me longing to be the object of her adoration. She was, in her words, "always there for me." Alive still. The cripple's love for the cripple and amplified surely by the surfeit of war-induced hormones, and the "coal black and milk white" mysteries of Lebanon. Sometimes a helpless gawk, I'm afraid, also for their beauty.

Such thoughts kept me close company. The pages lying next to me on the mattress while I blew smoke rings toward the ceiling, on the seat beside me at traffic jams, and on my bench in the University green.

It wasn't a letter I could respond to quickly. I kept going over it and eventually got pen to paper, but only hours before our pouch went out. It was, by then, necessarily short. Absent tracing my desire onto the page à la Henry Miller, what else was there? Some small advice about dealing with the lawyer which I knew to be futile given the distance between his wiles and her disposition. Some more hard words for my former partners who, as my several accomplices, had abetted my reduction of my dad. A rearticulation of my several dreams for baby Hank.

And always scratching my head to put down something positive—seeds of hope, as CRS called their small investments in godforsaken places, one such seed being the evident remission of those earlier illnesses associated with Paris and Vietnam. No, thank God, it seemed from the instant that the conception of Baby Hank was announced, the memories of those particular devils receded. So now I also mentioned that, along with my advices and threats and dreams.

As for her coming here, I wasn't ready for a decision. Constrained as they sometimes were, hers were the only eyes and ears—the only faithful eyes and ears, I should say—available to report in from that front. And then there was the issue of safety for a pregnant expat. I had nightmares about one of those sharpshooters on the green line putting a round right through her belly. I suspected that for most American heads of household, this would not have even been discussed. But for me, for us— including Baby Hank—there was the contract for myth hanging over us. At the end of the day this was and would be the compelling force. That ambition that refused "plain," that insisted on heroic as the only response to life as we found it.

And to be specific, myth now, maybe not this week, but soon, demanded they come to Lebanon. Baby Hank would not be born amidst the rather grimy story of family ruin in a Connecticut village. She would be born amidst the defining drama in the Holy Land. This was the understanding.

There also had been that other letter, fished out of the pouch that day by my enraged friend, the official one from my desk officer in New York and my first such letter. This also got more than one reading. Overall it was kind, not at all like the letters circulating in the marketplace where I had been. Most of the words seemed aimed at the pat on the back. Even what I took to be "corrections" were approached on tiptoe. The letter closed "with sentiments of esteem."

As for substance, beyond some quibbling about how to calculate beneficiaries (throwing their families into the count as well), there was only a suggestion that the value of the separation between Church and State need not be included in the text. "Inappropriate" was the word, and an encouragement for me to look deeper into the virtues of the Maronite Church and what Saint Maron had brought to the equation when he emerged from the neighboring Taurus mountains in the 4th century. This encouragement was followed by a hint about what I might find, should I look deeper: " . . . a rationalism which would cost the Middle East a great deal were it to disappear."

We discussed this amply on Mike's terrace during our beer and nut colloquy. I was having a hard time fully grasping the remark. The ferocity and ruthlessness of the Phalange/Kataeb was well-known.

Its league with Franco and others of a Fascist bent were documented. The stone-faced killers from Fatah notwithstanding, the Kataeb killed with unequaled relish. "Rational"—was this in reference to the traffic lights, casinos, marinas and the host of other Western establishments on their side?

Mike shook his head. "No," he said. "To the extent that the desk thought about this and I wouldn't put too much faith in that, there are some modern aspects"—he paused to take a drag and now on the exhale, he resumed—"its ambivalence for the secular for example, its allowance for argument in its schools. Its allowance for some women in its governance, some wine with its meal. Let's face it," Mike said, "we just don't like them because they're enough like us not to be exotic but not enough like us to see life our way. That and the fact that they are inestimably richer than the Shiites and the Palestinian refugees and shouldn't be getting any of our money, but as gilded as they are, the bastards still can't help reaching for it."

I asked him about news from home. After all it was he, not I, who had ripped that manila pouch open. I was curious about his love life: not more than curious, mind you, not with my own liabilities. For sure, already I had noticed that he was not entranced

the way I was by Arab beauty. Not caught, at least
not by me, appreciating those other parts forbidden.
I suspected that his occasional lack of self-esteem
must have made it difficult.

"Look it," he had said to me one night during
our solitary nightcaps out on the corniche. He had
been quite unsteady from drink, and he had pulled
off his shirt and then with his elbow on his knee had
strained to make a muscle. In the middle of this show
he had pointed at his bicep. "See," he said, looking
wild-eyed at me, "not much. Right?" He resumed his
straining and looked back at me, a bit threateningly.
"Not much, right?"

"Well, ok Mike," I laughed. I mean what else
could I do, since in fact it was not much. He wouldn't
be mollified. He shifted off the seawall and started
off toward the Druze.

"Goddamnit," he said, "I'll ask them."

I jumped off the wall and restrained him,
looking him in the face very seriously. "Okay, Mike,
not much."

He sat back down on the wall. "I knew you were
lying."

It wasn't as if I weren't drinking too. I was. Step
for step with him, but my sense was that after about
eighteen months of heavy-duty drugs in the wake

of Vietnam, my system needed more to transport it. And I at least had somewhere for the alcohol to go, compared to Mike's bones and brain.

I'd guessed Mike and women had been a tentative affair, and logic would indicate that he probably sidled into these encounters same as he would a room, very apologetic from the start. The one exception I allowed was perhaps along the lines of his tantrum over the pouch. If I closed my eyes, I could possibly see him, so passionately extended that those same long arms fluttering for a second above him would descend instead on some lover whom he would take and then leave, about the same as he had done to the pouch.

The only other reference he had allowed me was that time at his place when he had reached behind himself to his makeshift bookcase of bricks and boards and lifted a photo off the top. It was a Polaroid, somewhat blurred, of a girl in pastel shorts and blouse with short red hair and a mass of freckles. If Aurora, George's wife, was descendant to Arab black and white—to purebred—then this was the mottled orange offspring of those fleeing the Great Irish Potato Famine.

"So, is she coming?" I asked.

"Nah. She opted for graduate school," he said, fiddling with the photo. He laughed. "Tough choice, I imagine. Straight road to success or sort of festering alongside me as Lebanon goes down the drain."

Pen came as it turned out about ten weeks after my arrival, and now obviously pregnant. The situation back home, as she had been writing, was really no different; Henry remained abusive toward Helen. "Gutter language," as Helen had always called it. Now giving vent to words that had never been allowed in their home and certainly not the currency in his old business circles. But as for Pen's own kin, they were now more accommodating as our marriage looked less "hit and run" with each week. It was hard to argue with the news anchors, as to the bravery of the new in-law.

In some respects, it was a reunion similar to the fantasies that I had had during all those nights up on the ward in Chelsea: my longing as I waited by the entrance, then the leap of my heart as I first saw the unsuspecting faith of those hazel eyes and the slightly bucked teeth breaking into a smile, almost phosphorescent in that shadowy place.

Then followed unpunctuated chatter about the flight, the meal, the tray, and the stewardess, until you might have thought she had just got off at Dayton not Beirut. All that she did not understand—the calligraphy, the flags, the flattened buildings, the squats—did not trouble her. She was at peace with what she did recognize. The innumerable banged-up Mercedes, the abundance of wares being hawked in the streets, the ads for Fanta.

I took her to the furnished flat Sophia had found for us. Just two rooms, but if you turned your chair right on the balcony, a view of the sea. Cost considerations had overridden more space. We were building again: an offshore, unattachable savings account. "Rising from the ashes," we toasted from our balcony with our first two shots of Tio Pepe, a bootlegged tequila.

"No dearth of ashes here," I said, as I directed her attention to tracer rounds in the distance.

There was a wonderful reunion with her various accounts of the personalities back home and my soliloquy on life in the Levant, increasingly broken up with intimacies.

We were quite unrestrained, given the absence and Tio Pepe, leading to my inquiry afterwards about the possible impact on the embryonic Baby Hank. Not to be vulgar, but it is something that takes getting past.

Now, for the first time since we met, she began making a home. Finding the various stores, figuring out the currency, and learning the names of the principal foods and numbers. Initially under the wings of Sophia and Aurora, she was then left to her own devices which, from what I witnessed, meant spending a large part of her effort developing the public presentation of her demands alongside a brave effort to build vocabulary.

Not to worry, I consoled myself. Soon enough she had plants and watercolors in place and full cupboards and had begun work on a crib for Hank, an oil canvas depicting the astrology for Aquarius, wrapped and pasted to a soap box. If you could close your eyes to the war for a moment, the way we had done to the mess back home, then the morning kiss at the door from breadwinner to homemaker appeared almost suburban.

Except, of course, in this instance, my maroon Chevette and I would be braving the road to the Beka'a and not Hartford for an inspection of our "Investments." Amidst the other feedback from the desk, there had been a simple capitalization of "Investment" with a string of question marks after it. I had suspected the word would make the good hearts back at HQ feel uncomfortable, given its other associations, but investments were, in my mind, what we ought to do, and the sooner CRS started looking at them like that, the sooner we'd have something worth the paper it was typed on. Which meant the sooner we'd venture beyond the age-old gift from rich to poor. I recalled a news clip of Papa Doc, flipping coins out of his limo at the street urchins in Port au Prince. Well, with a few more bells and whistles, that was our state of the art in 1981. So, yes, I intended to keep nudging HQ to say it, despite that string of question marks.

Of course, I knew damn well that this was only a small first step for them. Once the word is said then they have to figure out what they are investing in, and as far as I could tell, that mystery, even in my own mind, often defied understanding. Yes, once you get past the nickel flipped out the window, then the issue of "to what end" becomes the bone in the craw.

The road from the coast of ancient Phoenicia, up over the mountain to the valley beyond, was not so threatening in the morning. Not to minimize: the switchbacks, barricades, and crumbling shoulders existed just as surely in the morning sun, but the pace was more accommodating. Trucks chugged up as opposed to careening down. Drivers stopped at roadside cafés. You could see wildflowers along the way. And then instead of descending into the cauldron that was Beirut, here, once over the ridge, you now settled into great plots of chocolate-colored topsoil, amid vast fields.

Revelatory it was, even for my tired eyes: Lebanon's amber waves of hash. Mike had apparently intended this to be a surprise for me. For a generation like mine, preoccupied with where to hide the roach, that panorama of hash, like corn in Kansas, was such that I had to stop the car to fully fathom it. I had read Muriel's text. Hash was one of the reasons I was making the trip. But either because of my old mindset or Muriel's reluctance to sketch the extent of the cultivation in all its glory, I still imagined hidden production in isolated patches.

"Yes," Father Kluiters told me. "Shia planted and Shia picked, Syrian processed and Maronite shipped. Quite a coming together of tribes," he said. We were in his room, picking at lunch. "I came seven years before the war," he said. I asked him how much longer he expected to stay: the question seemed irrelevant to him.

"Usually," he answered, "we are where we are, forever."

So different, I thought, while he chatted in Arabic with a couple of friends from the village, from our tours. Hopping around the globe every three years. After all, he is certainly into investments also. This indeed was quite an adventure for me. Here he was: unshaven, fluent the way Mike could only dream of, open work shirt, tangled hair. Mike had called them the Green Berets for God. He began ladling a stew onto our plates. His friends were grinning.

"Eat it. You'll like it," he said, ladling some more onto my plate. I bit into what looked like giblets in gravy, chewing away without comment until Kluiters stood up and grabbed his genitals, as they all broke into laughter.

A priest of a different color, I thought. A color naturally appealing to me. The Society of Jesus. After lunch, he took me around and reported on the investments. First, he laid his arm on my shoulder. I was to forget about the sunflowers. Earlier I had read parts of the project text to him: the idea of substituting one corrupting crop with one wholesome crop. The project holder, as listed on the cover sheet, apparently had skipped town a few months back as a result of some personal entanglement with the Syrians—who, on that day, to my eyes, seemed to be dug in at nearly every crossroad in the valley, battalions of them—clear to the eye as the hash.

"Well," I said to Kluiters, "I can't just tell HQ to forget it. I have to send them something."

"Then send them some hash, because that's all you'll find here now." I laughed, imagining the Bishop watching football in the corner office in a cloud of hash.

I broached the investment in the well, recounting Jack's conversation with the Bishop on my first day of work. I asked for his cost estimate, and after I made the deduction, concluded that a significant balance was left. Kluiters allowed that maybe the Bishop had more than just this one well in mind. It was now midafternoon, and except for the pleasure of his company, I was going in circles. No sunflowers (abandoned), and project costs for the well that represented only a fraction of the allowed budget.

We stood on the site of proposed well with some boys standing around, giving me Sir Richard Burton's famous "stare curious" until Kluiters ran after them, playfully, with a willow branch. "It's meant to get them together," he said, "them" being the two villages which needed the water: one Maronite on its last legs and the other Shia, in full stride. "I make them do everything together. Plan it, provide labor, work up a schedule for its use"—he frowned and looked away—"that is, if we ever get water."

I could see the well was only half-finished, with our pump and bags of cement lying under some plastic sheeting nearby.

"It's hard," he said. "The people in the villages are okay. They want it. But they get visited—the Shia—by political leaders, and are told to stop. They were told last week that they'd have their own private well if they stopped working with me."

"What political leaders?" I asked.

Kluiters looked up. "The Iranians are in Baalbek. And the Syrians don't lift a finger."

"So should I put an X through this one?" I asked.

"No, not yet. These people have been neighbors for generations. Before the French, under the Ottomans. They are Lebanese. They have nothing to do with those zealots in Baalbek. But now, look," he said, gesturing toward a Shia girl on the road. "Now they're all covered. And the young men, now all trying to grow beards and help themselves to Maronite land. They scare the family off, and then they take it and the Syrians just watch." He shook his head wearily. Not the same man who had grabbed his balls at the table. "Come on," he said climbing back into his pickup. "You can't go back without a look at Baalbek."

"Next time," I said. I was looking at the sun and scared about the descent down the mountain. I had paid keen attention coming over to the various wrecks scattered along the road.

"Come on," he said, smiling. "You development types have never objected to tourism in the past." By now he had the key in the ignition, and I felt intimidated. A Jesuit sitting right in the middle of an emerging firefight, and I'm balking at road conditions.

The Palmyra was a monument from the past, the watering hole midway on the Damascus to Beirut road, for colonists and idle rich alike. It was one of the classics like Hotel Saint George in Algiers or the La Mamounia in Marrakech: colonial history in every corner but, given the time and place, no clients. Its grand mahogany bar had been closed since 1979 by the men in black with red armbands, the same uniforms as those who now guarded the entrance.

Kluiters grabbed my elbow and strolled by them. Boys, anxious to end up their mother's martyrs. Quite scary for me to be face to face with the rank and file of the Iranian revolution. And, as I imagined it, ready at the first provocation to "win one for Khomeini."

Just as we were passing, Kluiters stopped, his face less than a foot from the guard, and winked, as if they were sharing a joke.

"Jesus Christ," I said, both an exclamation of disbelief and prayer for protection.

The guard swayed back and raised his AK to Kluiters' chest. They stared, one at another. Kluiters now holding steady with a wry grin, the boy with so much faith in his eyes that I couldn't see how it could be resolved short of him squeezing the trigger. Then Kluiters turned up the steps, and I followed. Talk about the small back response. Never had I ever wished to be so thin. The muscles in my legs were still twitching as Kluiters showed me around the common rooms. An old man in a striped vest was now attending to us.

"Refreshment, sir?" he asked.

"Yes," I replied. "A triple helping of your best scotch." He looked at me blankly for a moment. I remained expressionless.

"I'm sorry sir, not in these times." I put my hand on his shoulder.

"Water is fine."

On the way out, Kluiters refrained from a continuation of his game, maybe because he could see he had already scared me to death. He drove me over to the ruins.

From the time I crossed over the summit, I had had a series of epiphanies: those freeze frames that remain indelible until the mortal coil gets cast off. An old man, brother to the waiter at the Palmyra, was sitting on a Roman pedestal, bent over fingering his beads. He had a small cash box and a roll of tickets. Behind him lay the might of the greatest empire known to man, a colossus of stone: a myriad of temples constructed in a time and place when every man lived in huts and hovels. He actually handed me a ticket as proof of purchase. Kluiters and I were the only souls around wandering in this late afternoon amidst the columns and the shadows, with rays of light coming off the sun, just then starting to touch the peaks in the West.

Once parted from Kluiters, I drove hard, intending to get up the East Side before the sun disappeared behind the mountains and down the West Side, before it dropped under the horizon.

I had no protection. Talk about thin skin and brittle bones. This was a fucking Chevette, and thanks to Kluiters I was now about to join a late afternoon race down to Beirut on one of the most treacherous runs in the world, bumping noses along the way with everything from tanks to mules. "God help me," I pleaded.

"No governance," I repeated several times later on the balcony, that evening, to Mike and Pen. But not before I had those three "helpings," which I had missed at the Palmyra.

"There are crashes just left in the middle of the road," I recounted, "until they get hit so many times that they eventually fall off and down the cliff. And here I am forced to hurtle"—I turned to Pen—"And you know how I hate to hurtle. Damnit, am forced to hurtle." I took another shot of Tio Pepe, rapid fire, and stuffed some humus in my mouth. "And hurtling down because I have a battered Mercedes on my rear bumper and I am sandwiched between, and you won't believe this Mike," I said, while he cracked up, "between it and a fucking dump truck on my left which has a faulty trap and is now spewing garbage in its wake and, God love me, someone—and only in Lebanon, some sheeting is blowing out of the dump truck, visible from my rearview mirror—and is now plastered on the Mercedes windshield. God help me, the guy in the Mercedes now has his arm out his window and is shooting at the back of the dumpster.

And then emerging on my right, since we are now taking up the whole road—I'd say lanes but there are none—is a deuce-and-a-half carrying Syrian soldiers on benches in the back and they are all laughing, while the fog starts to infiltrate, triggering my greatest fear, the dark, because I know these cars don't have lights that work. Then suddenly, like a reverse Kamikaze, in the sense that they went down, this guy appears, in the only worse car in the whole country than mine—a fucking Deux Chevaux—and he's coming out of the fog, up and at me. When he sees the three of us abreast coming down on him, he veers off into a ditch, thanks be to God, on the mountain side and not on the cliff side, and the Syrians swerve and just manage to miss him and then pull in front of me to a stop, I guess to help him, which forces me to stop too. And the poor guy is now actually weeping and thanking Allah and alternately the soldiers, who then decide to block the whole road off, this major artery between Damascus and Beirut, so that, with many comic mishaps, they can finally push him out on the road to continue his journey toward actually meeting Allah, probably that night.

"And the cars behind the Syrians are now a wild cacophony of horns, except for the first two rows, which can clearly see the Syrians and their weapons, and are meek as can be, and then I, or rather they, spot me, trying now to edge around the deuce-and-a-half. Here my heart sinks, since they ask me to get out and are highly amused that an American would be driving around the Beka'a making investments, which I don't think they believed, or at least not the one who had some English, and so he calls over a captain. Here, I remembered what you told me, Mike: in situations like this, officers are good. So I tell him my story, dropping names fast and furious of every notable we've ever helped, from Sarkis on down. And he just keeps me standing in front of him with his troops watching very appreciatively how he is controlling this 'American' situation, and I am watching equally appreciatively the position of the sun, knowing that I definitely don't want to make the run across the green line in dark. And then, I guess, he figures he has toyed with me enough but wants to give his men a little more, so he waves over the guys who initially approached me, and asks them whether they'd like to trade the benches in the back of the truck for some seats in my car. They answer affirmatively, and I'm determined not to add to this absurdity by adhering to the agency policy against picking up hitchhikers. So before long, five of us are smushed into the Chevette, with my seat pushed all the way up, and the soldier next to me quite expansive. I am now once more hurtling, but with my knees up against the steering wheel and my arms pressed to my side while the English speaker has his muzzle pointed in the direction of my ribs, and the Syrian in back has his aimed at the nape of my neck. I am one"—I spoke quietly now to Pen and Mike, out of reverence—"I am someone who carries no illusions about what that muzzle velocity does to flesh and blood, and very much in fear's grasp. And this English speaker is telling me about how he is related to several important officers in the Syrian army, swaggering like this all the rest of the way down the mountain and into that cloud of fumes now hiding the city and then into it, dimming the failing light.

"The guy next to me gives me directions, and at this point I am helpless since I don't know where they might be taking me—under orders or not—and frankly I am just praying, such as I pray. Then abruptly he says 'Here,' and I stop: they get out without even an acknowledgement for the ride. There I am left feeling like the luckiest guy ever as I face the dash home across the line." I paused, drank more tequila and gathered my thoughts. "I felt more serene after making that race down that mountain, maybe how

I had felt on the road at sixteen when Ski, the old teamster, and I had sailed through a tempest into Chicago at dawn in his 18-wheeler. Afterward, I ran the green line quite cool, singing "six days on the road and I am coming on home tonight."

I then collapsed, what often happened after a tear like that. The story, I could tell, endeared me very much to Pen, since this seemed to be not far from what she had wanted to marry. As for Mike, it had also made him quite happy and had caused him to echo most of the tale with sympathetic laughter. Quite happy, in fact, because he had been alone with this type of fear for a long time after his friend had been killed and before we had arrived, and now it was just what the doctor ordered for him to be sharing hummus and shots, limes and labneh and flat bread: all of us, for the moment, quite safe and sound.

That special place was where, on most nights, by dark, the three of us came together. Sitting on our balcony, with the same array of Lebanese dishes circling the bottle of Tio Pepe and the amber shot glasses, recounting our various brushes with war. The art, of "incandescence without the catheter."

We moved into winter, and the rains came down hard on the city. With the sewers clogged or broken, the torrents streamed down the streets toward the bay, which now in the downpour churned with silt and the city's garbage. That was our view of the world, the three of us bundled up in wool sweaters observing the neighborhood from our high perch. The eventual yellowing of the hash fence around the little tin café across the street, the comings and goings at the Friday nights debauches at the U.S. Embassy. And once, during that wild jubilation when Sadat was killed, we ducked inside, thankful we had a roof over our head with so much lead falling from the sky.

Actually, it was quite a shock for me. All around us, the near- hysterical broadcasts shrieked, followed instantly by the people pouring out onto the streets under our balcony in celebration. Such a disconnect, we thought, between what we imagined at that moment to be the solemn mourning in Washington, with all the Americans, including Helen, glued to what they believed was a tragedy.

Mike thought the mood was shifting. He put his finger in the wind. Even for Beirut, he had said, the partying was more desperate. We felt that too. Even among the staid, the university professors and those businessmen too tied to their investments to leave, there was little if any small talk. People exhaled right off the bat, or proclaimed, or danced their hearts out, particularly in the unseen subterranean boxes, where militia and relief workers mingled amidst laser lights and deafening repetitions of "Eye of the Tiger."

During daylight, more frequently now in the afternoon, as if shot from the sun, the Israeli jets flew in. Low and fast, their sound shattered windows across the city, with particular effect on the babies and children who, for some time after the flyover, could still be heard wailing. Then there would follow the useless peppering of the skies by anti-aircraft guns or the occasional dreamer with an AK.

The Israelis owned the air just as completely as the sea.

Inexorably, Pen was getting bigger, and when we got into striking distance of her due date, we began to make more serious contingency plans. Despite the entreaties from Aurora and George, we would stay put in the West. Perhaps not the wisest choice, but we feared being captive to the Maronite hospitality. That and the fact that the American University of Beirut Hospital (AUBH), even as it was increasingly resembling the city's MASH unit, was where the best and brightest still practiced. It was less than a kilometer up the hill.

What we worried about most was making the connection when the time came. God only knew what would be happening during the second week of February. And the doctor, a Maronite, usually slept in the East, where he also had a practice. We liked him. Young like us, but more confident about good outcomes. He soothed us; he had yet to miss a birth, he told us.

Thus we waited for baby Hank. And for her as deliverance: unequivocal deliverance from the miserable happenings back home. We filled our letters with our progress toward deliverance, with "up from the ashes" talk. Helen, we were told, related the good news to a Henry who, as she said, despite being preoccupied with his immediate concerns (like his Giants cap which somehow had gone missing) was aware of the consequences of our marriage and apparently, not unhappy.

As far as our lawyer—our "mean dog," as he was called in the trade—Helen had heard nothing. Which was as it should be. For these several months now we had been pouching his recompense. Presumably allowing him to weave enough challenges into our situation, for those who would pursue us, causing them to have second thoughts. But this was only presumption, since I was getting precious little back from him. Some few gratuitous comments about how he shared my distress for Henry, and how the thoughts of the other Rotarians were with him.

He acknowledged receipt of the payment which, for reasons of his and Henry's mutual Rotarianess, he would accept despite it being, "As you know, significantly less than what I would normally expect." Finally, there was nothing in response to my request for the details. All I was getting was a monthly summary of hours he had dedicated to the task, each hour attached to a preposterous dollar amount, followed at the bottom by a generous reduction in fees which still was sufficient to swallow up my disability check in its entirety. And for all this, I still received no details about the case. Only a scribbled note once, with a reference to sleeping dogs.

As for Pen, unreal as it may seem, she remained my slightly bucked-tooth caricature. Which I knew were not supposed to exist, except in celluloid—but peering in, I could not detect the complexities which surely had to be there. She walked with me, belly out, on the corniche on weekends, did her shopping each morning, had tea with Sophia, and even entertained a delegation of Shiite ladies from my project in South Beirut. Without discretion, she had no inclination to retire from public during the final weeks. No. The navy-blue Shetland just stretched tighter as she went about her business.

Our evenings on the balcony continued without much modification. She had stopped drinking toward the last months of her pregnancy, leaving Mike and me alone out there to finish the bottle after she retired, drinking more definitively as the general terror, especially the car bombs, grew worse, producing an idiocy of the gallants, when in the early morning hours, I would insist on escorting him home. He would accept, only to insist, once we reached his door, that he would do the same for me. And so we headed back and forth, two drunken souls in a city where, at that hour, no one stirred except in those unseen boxes of light and music, where the occupants stayed until dawn. Eventually, in a grand finale, we would come to agreement halfway between our respective beds, near the embassy, each of us looking back several times to be assured that the other had not been silently offed or (more likely) fallen into an open sewer.

Only once as I remember it, did both Pen and I go to his place, on his sunken terrace with a view of the heavens: his fledgling experiment in hospitality. There were others there when we arrived. Two female Brits from Oxfam, and a woman from the U.S. embassy: Mike's grant liaison. Mike was in and out of his kitchen, apologizing for what we were about to eat, for fewer knives than necessary, and for paper napkins, which often left me with his three guests and Pen.

From the start, the guests were very comfortable with their erudition, lounging on Mike's oriental cushions and creating a localized version of *The New York Times Book Review*. As a habitué of such alternative haunts as the West End Bar and Café, I assumed a natural antagonism to those pale foils for "rough and ready," their abnegation of the Beats, and knew how to puncture their Vassar-groomed well-being, whether I had read any of their references or not: that is, as long as I could take the conversation to other more indelicate authors or issues.

But poor Pen had none of these experiences, and just smiled, with her chestnut hair braided up on her head like those early French Queens I had seen in the Luxembourg Gardens, and her belly like a big, navy-blue balloon. She was perhaps a discomfort to these others, whom I sensed would not be quite as apt producers of human life. Pen would just jump into the talk, and of course got side-eyed, as if to say, "Where did she come from?" The women were engulfed in "literary talk," and Pen was interrupting at will, to ground them. Pen loved to chat and skipped easily from one subject to another similar anecdote—tales from her town—which had the three erudites pushing the peanuts around in the dishes in front of them wondering, as I said, who was this woman.

While Pen's chatter did at times test me, I had no affection for these lettuce eaters, who would always exist in my mind as lying about with non-compliant pussies, telling me to hold on while they reached over to their night table and plied themselves with yet another handful of spermicides. And, frankly, at that time and place I was loving Pen even more, ever since I had gotten that sight of her, phosphorescent, coming through the destruction at the airport.

Quite instinctively, since the two Brits had excused themselves from listening and were talking to each other *sotto voce*, I let the Embassy-type take the heat, explaining to her where my balcony was and how as anyone could see it was a straight road downhill from above my building, 100 meters to the entrance of the Embassy before it turned a sharp right toward the corniche. Any fool could load a VW bus up with explosives, tie the steering wheel

down, and blow the U.S. mission to kingdom come,
I said, and if I, who paid scant attention to such shit,
could see the possibility, surely the martyrs in town
must be onto it.

The two Brits stopped their conversation and
were very much focused on me. I stopped there,
seeing that the "official" American was hating me at
that point. This was confirmed when a few moments
later, she got up and went into the kitchen where
Mike was washing dishes and soon after was at the
front door with Mike, who afterward came over to us
with the dishtowel still on his arm, red-faced.

"Jesus Christ," he said. "What the hell did you
say to her?" I put my hands up in a mock plea of
innocence.

One of the Brits volunteered: "Oh, not much,
Mike. Just told her she would probably be blown
to kingdom come." Mike looked back at me, only
half-serious, I could see.

"You shithead. She's the one who approves my
disbursements."

"Shithead nothing, everyone in Ain el
Mraseh has been saying what I said long before
I even got here." But I was sorry. I felt sorry the
moment she had removed herself from her pillow.
Antagonist-fonctionnaire notwithstanding, she was

one of those ubiquitous American mongrels who are fastened together all wrong, especially at their joints. Probably more kin than not to Mike or me.

One of the Brits looked over at Pen and then down at her belly. "Gee," she said, "aren't you afraid to have the baby here?" Pen put her hands on her belly.

"Well, you know what I always say?" She was looking around to see if anyone could guess. She now had everyone's attention. "Well, what I always say is if my friends from South Beirut can have children here, then so can I."

Life at the office, that is, on those days when my Chevette and I were not touring Lebanon and tilting at windmills, was constant—that is, in its reflection of life outside it. The previous week it had once again been Farida, waiting for me when I got back from Tripoli. The rest had already left on the basis of intelligence about shooting at the museum crossing. Intelligence was what Toufic mostly did: he visited people George knew, and got information about "events." That day, I had come in weary and wet from driving through another one of the winter tempests, and she was sitting straight in her tailored black, very thin-lipped, obviously "on fire."

"Did you hear?" she asked me.

"Did I hear what, Farida," I asked.

"Am I good, Mr. Dick?"

"Well yes, Farida. Why?"

"You know I am very religious," she continued, quite obviously holding something inside her that wanted out. I nodded.

"It's about Vache," she said.

"Go on," I told her.

"Well, I think maybe it's more kind," she looked around and lowered her voice, "if he goes to God now."

I stood for a second and stared at her. Even for Farida, this was over the top. But her lips were twitching, and I could see she was feeling very righteous. I slumped down into the chair opposite her and covered my eyes with my hands. I stayed like that for at some time before I parted two fingers—like lifting the shade a crack—but seeing her still unwavering, I reclosed the crack.

She reached across the desk and took my hands away. "Mr. Dick, they will kill him anyway. Meanwhile, he is killing us." She began to cry. "His poor mother," she said. "She can't take it longer."

"What do you mean. Where is she?"

She pointed at the kitchen, and I stood up. "No, don't go. She doesn't want us to see her like that."

"Farida," I said, addressing her very sternly. "From what I understand, you are saying that we should put Vache to sleep."

She didn't look up. I leaned over and put my hands on her shoulders. Her face was a mess. "Listen very carefully, Farida. I'm only going to say this once but, please, for your sake, don't forget it." I was speaking very deliberately now, in a remedial way. "This is"— I pointed to the Pope's photo on the wall—"this is Catholic Relief Services. You"—I shifted my finger from his Holiness to her—"work for Catholic Relief Services." I paused to let that sink in. "Catholic Relief Services does not, by policy or principle, kill people on purpose." I lifted my hands up. "Do you understand that?" She choked back some more sobs, but eventually she said she did and then rather abruptly set to tidying up and, frankly, I was quite surprised at how fast afterward she dried her eyes. Then she prepared to leave, almost as if we had been discussing office supplies.

The next day it got clearer. As George told it, Vache had grabbed some woman's crotch, while she was coming down the steps by AUB. "A Brit," George explained, "a student there, and Vache was coming up the steps and according to her, he just reached out, as they were passing, and grabbed her crotch. And she had screamed while he had taken off up the steps as fast as he could go. And then she dropped her books and went after him. A fast runner, I think," said George. "In any case she chased him all the way up to the office and was just about ready to get him when he rushed in the door past Farida and hid in the kitchen. And the British woman started yelling at Farida to tell her where he was and where was the boss and who was this 'miscreant.' I think that was the word she used. I immediately went up front, but she was already in the kitchen, so I followed her and by the time I got there she was turning in circles and hitting one hand against the other, repeating, 'I don't believe this fucking place.'

Right in front of her was Vache's mother, and Vache was on his knees clinging to her with his head under her apron. So then she comes out with me to the front, collects herself, and asks me if I am in charge, and I tell her I am since the Americans are out, and she asks, 'What kind of business this is?' and I tell her, and she starts shaking her head again, asking me how we can have such a miscreant working for us, after she had explained what happened. And I tell her, pointing to my head, that he is not all there, as you say. She wanted to talk to Jack. She said in

Britain she would press criminal charges for assault against him, but she knows that will go nowhere here and therefore she wants to speak with Jack, and when can that be.

Which, as you know, Mr. Dick, is always difficult to predict. But I take a chance and say this afternoon, since I know the pouch goes out then."

"You did well, George," I said, which pleased George. He took a long pull on his Dunhill and said, "Well, what else could I do?"

Well, the afternoon was a beaut, as my mother would say. Jack did arrive for the pouch and any thought he might have had of blowing off the Brit was soon dispelled. She had been planted since lunch in front of Farida, who was quite sympathetic and went into the kitchen herself to make them coffee, since Vache was now in hiding, and his mother was far too distraught.

I'm not sure what the Brit told Jack, but given his subsequent action, it must have been an ultimatum to fire Vache or else she would write to the Pope or some other powerful figure in the Church, which I imagine was enough to get Jack quaking. I assume he made the appropriate assurances, which he communicated to Vache's mother, whose anguish caught the attention of Mike, returning that moment, still in the process of trying to get his reports ready for the pouch.

The next thing I knew, Mike was storming past Farida and me, slamming the doors of Jack's office behind him, and this, as opposed to the earlier, closed-door discussions, could probably have been heard out in the street. And predictably, the more Mike boiled over, the more Farida became totally pert and professional, sealing envelopes, licking stamps, and preparing the covers for signature.

Finally the office was treated to Mike's concluding words: "No Vache, no me." Which I knew must have torn Mike up inside, since he allowed Jack and Sophia all their shortcomings out of the debt he felt for the kindness they extended while he was healing from the car accident. But, further, Mike must also have known that without him, there was no movement on 1651, and that no movement on 1651 meant no wherewithal to support the office, unless Jack moved me into Mike's place—a thought that had me feeling very uneasy.

Mike came out in the same fury by which he had entered, right past me and out the door. Absent also, I might add, from our balcony that night.

As it turned out, thanks be to God, baby Hank arrived on time. It was also the same time that an

RPG had just gone through the front door of an AMAL command post. By the time Mike had dropped us off at the entrance, a dozen fighters were running down the corridors bearing their wounded on stretchers, showing no hesitation to expropriate what they weren't immediately offered.

This was not, I knew, an unusual occurrence those days at A.U.B.H. At first, I concentrated on staying as inconspicuous as possible, sneaking past the wild commotion and into maternity. There were some anxious moments when access seemed denied, principally by some half-crazed militia who was waving his AK around wildly and motioning for everyone, us included, to get away. At that moment, I was prepared for him to start firing over our heads.

But a doctor appeared and told him to get out of the way or no one would get helped—and said it with such authority that I assume he had been there before and by now had a well-honed sense of who held the power. Pen and I went by in his wake and past a couple of holding rooms which were packed with AMAL militia, leaning over their bloody comrades. Very crazy, with IV stands clattering around us and nurses pleading for the warriors to wait outside.

By this point, I was acting quite aggressive, pushing us into the elevator and affecting the air of someone important. It usually worked and did here. People made space. I kept checking on Pen, on her attitude. But the unsuspecting faith just stayed in her. She smiled, even excused herself in Arabic when she left. She remembered where the nurses' station was and less than five minutes later was in her room getting prepped. I was left with nothing to do but squeeze her hand and dry her forehead. Shortly thereafter, the doctor stuck his head in and repeated his assurances.

Hank wanted out: no inducements were necessary. One last heave from Pen and Hank was into the light of day, soon enough getting her cord tied and then sponged off. A live birth in Lebanon. Pen was sobbing. She told me they were "tears of happiness."

Later that day, Mike took the family photo. Pen was sitting up in her bed in a cotton gown, her hair disheveled, cradling white-haired baby Hank. And in the background was the afternoon sea, Homer's sea, quiet except for that one Turkish Dhow moving South. "Those quiet Kampuchean girls who dared not stir the earth as they proceeded. Morsels now." Something I had scribbled earlier, while Pen slept, in the margins of an article I was reading on that war. Pen found it after I left the room, tore it out, and it later turned up in the same shoebox as the photo: with the humidity, the photo had gotten pasted to the article like a caption. Part of the family photo if you will.

The nursery where Hank was put, between her visits to mom, was a glassed-in pen, a rectangle in the middle of the floor around which family and relatives crowded to guess which one was theirs and then to seek first evidence of both its uniqueness and its inheritance. When I left Pen's side for my first experience at the holding station, I walked into a group squeezing in on each other—with women putting their hands to their mouths in astonishment and men nodding and confirming "albino." Apparently, Hank was the cause of this commotion around me while, in contrast to a certain liveliness in neighboring cribs, she rested serenely in sleep, so deeply that I got anxious for a thumb twitch or some other small sign of life. I was forced to stand on tiptoe in the back of this crowd, fascinated as well with my albino.

I spent the better part of the day like that. Up on my toes when necessary and back on my heels when possible, becoming increasingly anxious at what I imagined to be the thin thread between baby Hank and me. This grew on me. There were just numbers on these carts—not much different from Safeway carts. When you wanted to see your baby, a nurse looked at a list, read a number across from a name, then an orderly went in and wheeled out the cart.

Not to be xenophobic (especially now that I presume to break the back of such practices), but even after fewer than seven months in Lebanon, I knew about "lists." God knows my project had lists, and I knew just how authentic they could be. Wrong number across from wrong name, and the wrong baby gets carted out with the wrong family. And I had few doubts that there were Gulf Arabs who had slaves, and who know damn well that albinos do not have sky blue eyes and who would pay dearly to have baby Hank in their compound. Given no governance, as the euphemism goes, I got so worked up that I refused to leave the rectangle, and so in time had a front row position against the glass. Finally, when baby Hank got carted out, I followed, and then of course everyone knew the albino was mine. Then she was pushed into Pen's room, lifted out and put into her arms for feeding.

Of course, Pen was oblivious to what went on at the rectangle and about the uncertainty of lists in Lebanon, and I didn't want her to get shaken by what was scaring me. But I did persist, more than I would have, in gathering an assessment of her strength and her concurrence about the benefits of going home.

In the end, it became too nerve-wracking for me, and so I signed them out, after first swaddling baby Hank in layers of old sweaters and putting the whole bundle of her under my overcoat. We walked the kilometer home like that: Pen, with one arm in mine for balance, and I, with both arms around the bundle inside my coat, leaving only a small fold open for air.

I was quite irrational. Maybe it had been too much Tio Pepe for too long or the fear I had always laid on myself as infertile, now wonderfully disproved, or what I knew about the dark side of this war. All I knew was that I was very anxious to get baby Hank home, accelerating my steps and even looking behind me, so much so that Pen must have noticed something "funny," as she would say.

Finally, we made the turn at what we called the engineer's house. A retired engineer, he had a stipend from the defunct Lebanese R.R. and was somewhat feeble now and a bit strange, to the extent that at dusk he would walk in circles around the small, fenced garden in front of his house. We greeted him and, as was customary, he approached the grate and said, "Like a monkey in a cage": if you stayed there, he would repeat it. He was the first to see baby Hank outside the hospital.

I felt an overwhelming pride as I edged toward the grate, opened the fold a bit more and said, "My daughter." He peered down the fold, with his beak of a nose almost in my coat, and then he drew back and put his hand through the grate into the fold and smoothed her hair.

"Beautiful!" he said.

Fifty meters later, we brought Hank into her home. It was a cold, bright evening: February 11th, a day after the anniversary of Saint Maron. Pen fed her and then laid her down in the Aquarius crib which I had already put in the bathtub.

We sat out alone on the balcony with Tio Pepe, and felt blessed. The myth was real. I tapped the sliding glass door behind us: "If anything does happen, Pen, at least in there, she can't get hurt by any flying glass." And then I went quiet for the first time ever since we had been taking our nights on the balcony.

The first few weeks after the birth of baby Hank, we laid low. The war was moving toward another one of its intermittent crescendos. Israeli fighter bombers were becoming an almost daily occurrence, dropping their ordnance farther and farther north. George and

Aurora were more persistent about us moving over to the East. Soldiers at the checkpoints were more thorough. The interiors of our cars were regularly searched. I spent two hours being interrogated by a Fatah commander and this time not a chat, either, but an hour alone on the floor in a windowless room with three soldiers oiling their automatics. Afterward, I sat on the edge of a straight-backed chair having my scars examined and getting asked over and over about why an American soldier from Vietnam would be in Lebanon, if not to spy for Israel. Which was plausible enough, I told him, except it wasn't true. I went through my references as I had done so many times before, but since CRS did not have the "refugee account," my references only pertained to Lebanese. I knew no PLO notables. Frankly, in his place, I wouldn't have believed me, but in the end, he did. I'll never be sure, but when I opened the wallet on the photo of baby Hank in her mother's arms with the Dhow going by—I think that saved me.

It was the same in the Beka'a and Chouf. Bulldozers were hard at work building berms for artillery and tanks. In Beirut, sandbags were piled higher in front of doors and windows. Pen now stayed mostly at home and received. Aurora braved the green line and visited. Sophia brought home-cooked meals and store-bought delicacies. The Shia ladies from South Beirut—all of them—trooped in one afternoon with a colorful array of handmade clothes for the newborn, including one lavender dress so beautiful that it eventually got locked away in one of our trunks for posterity. And, of course, as Pen described it, there was the constant stroking. One after the other, she said, visitors would take turns touching her hair.

"Habibe," they would say, then reach for baby Hank.

"Crippies," Pen said. "Good thing she's asleep most of the time. She could get a complex."

"An easy baby," Pen said. Blissful, even, I thought. I hoped so anyway. I knew that war, tequila, and ardent love are not prescribed for "easy" or "blissful," and maybe there was still a price to be paid. Irrelevant, I consoled myself. Without Pen's and my bent for life at the edge, there would've been no conception in the first place.

As for care and nurturing, I did almost nothing. From the start, it was Pen who washed and clothed her, put the rattles in her box, and strolled with her in the living room on nights when Hank couldn't sleep. I loved the baby from a distance. I showed

The Water Above

her photo to all, picked her up in the air when I got home, and stared at her on the mat by my feet and told her about "carrying moonbeams home in a jar." Every night in fact, with tequila dissolving some of the fear I had felt on the road that day, I sang to her: "Would you like to swing on a star, carry moonbeams home in a jar."

Even as preparations for total war went, as Mike had called it, "from simmer to boil," or perhaps because of them, Pen and I decided to get out of our two rooms, where the two of them had laid low for almost a month, and to strike out while we still could. It was springtime in the mountains, and Pen, I was learning, had her own great erudition in such places: an almost encyclopedic knowledge of whatever could push up from the earth and blossom. I marveled all the more because while my sense for nominative and accusative might be above average, I mostly knew flowers by their color. "There's a red flower," or "There's a blue one," I would say.

I watched her that day in the Chouf. It was sort of the horticultural version of tough love. Obviously in her element, bent over, evoking a bit of Latin here and there, she would lay her hands on the plant and improve its circumstances or alternately pinch off a blossom and stick it under Hank's nose, or lifting up a leaf and expose an infection. She moved through the garden for twenty minutes like that. I was surprised this hadn't come up before. That after ten months of marriage, I was only now a witness to her gift. I asked her, and she slapped the dirt off her hands, placed them on her hips, and gazed over the hillside.

"Believe me," she laughed, "if you knew enough to tell a lily from a daisy, you'd know I'm just a gardener."

The grandmother approached us then, walking slowly from the ridgeline through a field of wildflowers. I explained in what was still a very crude Arabic that maybe we could live in the stone cottage. "With the garden," I added.

She looked at Pen, who had just taken baby Hank off my arm. My guess was that this old woman in black had spent most of her life working these fields and was surprised to see a European getting her hands dirty. She raised her knotted hand and touched Hank's head. "Habibe," she said.

According to Mike, now after six years of civil war, the Chouf of the Druze was the only place in Lebanon that had not yet been wasted. It was, by now, an old balcony conversation. Around in circles we had gone about where was safest, what would be spared. The idea evolved to put Pen and baby Hank up in a cottage where they could get fresh mountain air.

"You know," Mike said, "Flowers in jelly jars, baby Hank discovering beetles."

I talked more with the grandmother. Price was certainly no issue, and life with the Druze: well, it would be educational, to say the least. But I worried about me and my Chevette getting cut off and blocked, then facing the worst. That fear as it was argued, stacked against the fear of baby Hank and Pen spending the war, as it went from simmer to boil, huddled together in the bathtub.

Finally, I told the old woman we'd get back to her.

The following weekend, sensing the last trip, myth as truth began in earnest, skyrocketing from a few refrains of "moonbeams in a jar" to driving at dusk into the snows of Mount Lebanon.

"The flag," I said to Pen as our Chevette pushed its way up the mountain. "She has to see the cedars before you leave. You'll see Pen, there's an imprint there, even for a two-month-old. For scents and tastes, the wind on your face. I'm telling you; she'll never lose it. When she's ninety, if she's clear enough, she'll still stir to those trees." Pen was leaning over the seat and checking on the straps we had fastened around the Aquarius crib.

"She'll probably smell soap for the rest of her life," Pen said. "And Winstons and Tio Pepe."

"Fine," I said, wondering if this was a precursor to the baring of the teeth. "Now she can smell cedar too." I touched her leg. "All right?" She nodded. But I knew inside her she thought that dragging Hank up into the snow-covered mountains in a worsening war, in a car with no snow tires, was not me at my best.

That was to be first of several disputes we had that weekend. Sad. Really the first dispute since I was languishing, indecisive, in the lawn chair in my parents' backyard. And of course, I dug in. I insisted on taking Hank down the piste in the little sled far more times than I enjoyed, and then risking a chill in what was now nearly nightfall, I insisted again on walking over to the cedar grove and poking her little nose next to the bark, so as to assure imprint of the scent. Back at the lodge we both ate in silence—pass this and pass that—breaking that wonderful spell we had been under for those many months. And then a tall Swedish soldier with UNIFIL came over and asked if she wanted to dance, which had me about one millisecond from jumping up, regardless of the results, when Pen told him, "No."

The next morning, our plans were decided for us. Since we had arrived there in Lebanon, almost every Lebanese we met had advertised the wonders of skiing in mountains in the morning and swimming in the Mediterranean the same afternoon, and while we couldn't quite follow that prescription, I intended to be swimming by the time the sun got hot. We packed up and sped down to the coast, and were registered by 11 a.m. in a three-story hotel by the sea, a couple of kilometers south of Tripoli. It was a semicircle of rooms with balconies overlooking a pool in the shape of Lebanon with a fieldstone terrace spread around it.

However, I soon found out that there was no beach there worth the name, but rather a rocky breakwater paved with cement, which Pen thought was for couples to stroll along at evening, but which I insisted was equally good as a platform for swimming. I affected a teacher's tone: "The advertisements were for skiing in cedars by morning and swimming in the Mediterranean by afternoon. No one ever said anything about swimming in a goddamn pool."

"You go ahead and swim," said Pen. "Hank and I are going inside. She can't take this sun." So we went back in, and I changed into my suit and grabbed a towel while Pen and baby Hank lay down. I was, at this point, getting fed up with her resistance to my belief.

Once on the breakwater, I managed to pick my way out to a rock ledge and then, suspecting and hoping Pen was watching through the sliding glass, dove into the cold swirl below. It was a terrific shock, instantly submerging my doldrums in a threatening situation. For pride's sake, I got washed about in that cold little pocket longer than I wanted, fighting most of the time to stay off the rocks, at last emerging quite purple followed by toweling off with the requisite conspicuous vigor, eventually to lie down on the pavement. But there, salted as I was, with each few minutes of a stronger sun, I could begin to feel that this pale boy lying on Lebanese cement was becoming like a once-cold fish in a frying pan, for which I would burn. But I refused to return for a shirt, since the original issue of Hank and the myth already had been dashed by the strength of the sun. And the more I fried, the less I reflected, and the more I ached to see Hank in that sea before dinner.

And so now, I figured, I had nothing to do but sit by the sea with the towel over my shoulder, peering off into the horizon, as if this trip was all I hoped for, especially concerning myth and reflection, and wait for Pen to soften as the sun set and come back out with Hank. Which, thank God, she did: at about the same time that my legs had begun to turn as red as Farida's hair.

"Let's stop this," she said.

"Stop what?" I asked. She sighed and sat next to me, looking at my burn, and asked if I wanted her to go get the cream.

"No, it doesn't hurt," I said. "Isn't it beautiful out here?"

Hank was in a cotton frock and sun hat, captivated by the swirling water below. Then it had come together in my head, and I immediately lifted off the edge and dove into the cold swirl again. Hank cooed as I held the rocks at arm's length, trying not to get smashed against them. I knew I couldn't hold this up for long. At the ebb, I reached one arm out to Pen. "Give her to me," I said. Pen refused.

"You must be crazy," she said. "It's too dangerous."

She must have noticed the desperation in my eyes, because she became evidently very nervous about what I might do next.

"Give the damn kid to me now," I said. And so, tentatively, she leaned over, holding baby Hank very tightly around the wrist.

"You better know what you're doing," she said. And then lowered the normally blissful Hank, who was now bawling bloody murder, into my grasp. A

swell had just hit my back and my sustaining elbow
was torn against the rocks. I showed no pain. And
when it ebbed again, I grabbed Hank.

"Let go," I shouted.

"The hell," she yelled back. "She's in, she's
wet, what more do you want?" She was in. In and
hysterical. And, by now, I had little left to give. I
pushed her back up the rocks from her baptism in
the sea and handed her back to Pen.

A couple of hours later, we were sitting out on
our balcony where I was now swigging my tequila
straight from the bottle to ease the pain from my cuts
and burns. "Same waters as where," I said, pausing,
"Alexander, Aeneas, Caesar, Jesus." Pen looked over
at me.

"God, you're a mess. Does the arm hurt?"

"I'm okay. Do you understand what I was saying?
It's not that she was in the water; it is that we can
tell her she was in it and be honest when we do, and
she will have to put that into the mosaic of where
she came from." Pen threw back a shot.

"Okay, it's over. Let's drop it," she said.

"But I don't want to drop it," I replied.

She was getting up. "Let me get you some more
cream." And as she stepped beside me, she bent over
and kissed my poor head.

Beneath us, around a sparkling pool, waiters had begun assembling tables, snapping linen over them, and smoothing the folds. Others were shuttling around with trays of various delicacies. Electrical cord was getting strung out and amplifiers put in place. Then, last, shimmering gold and silver tassels and other glitter were twined around the gaslights.

The party came at sunset. The women here lived for it. Slender creatures, coal black hair and eyes, nude under simple black Parisian creations. Gold bracelets and sculptured hands. They were in the company of their thick-maned men with open collars and gold chains. Broad waists and white linen trousers. And when they sat, conspicuous balls.

Up on the second floor above the semicircle, baby Hank slept while Pen and I nibbled on crackers and drank tequila, my legs and face becoming brilliant red, which I knew showed my blue eyes off to advantage. Pen declared how stunning I looked.

The party was circulating now around the gaslight, sipping on cocktails or serving themselves a delicacy. Charles Aznavour had begun to croon. Then suddenly, from the north, came a burst of 50 caliber. Orange tracers arcing out into the black Mediterranean. Instinctively I ducked down and pushed the crib back into our bedroom, yelling at

Pen (who was straining her long neck to watch another burst) to "get the hell inside."

Then I noticed the party. They were so graceful with it. With the bursts of the 50 caliber, I mean. They would just tap the serving spoon of tabbouleh on the dish or finish sipping and then, without haste, gravitate toward the restaurant inside. This happened twice more. The bursts of gunfire, just south of Tripoli, and the party swaying back and forth from the terrace to the restaurant depending on its intensity and direction.

Huddled inside the sill of our room, at my insistence, I told Pen to get smart. "Do you know what a 50 caliber round would do to you? How about a hole as big as my fist."

And then, as if to enlighten us further, directly in front of us now, up and down those rocks lining the shore, we saw the ripples in his long brown legs. Seemingly unconcerned by either the 50 caliber or the slender creatures, his lamp swung back and forth across his legs. In his other hand he held his bucket and crabbing pail. We watched him, speechless, for a long time like that, heading south through the rocks. We could only see his legs, really—and the lamp moving across them like a pendulum.

The next morning, I needed nursing. Unrested, for fear of the firefight, hungover, and feverish from my burns. I just wanted to get back to our apartment as soon as possible, to spread out on the sheets in the dark, drink, moan, and cover myself with ointments.

We drove fast on the coast road, me doing my best to bear it, and soon enough found ourselves stopped and taking stock before the race across the Port. Even though this was no longer new to me, I was always scared. Like the Nabatiyeh road after the Total sign, there is one stretch at the Port where you are totally exposed: a flat expanse as you race toward those carcasses of buildings, from which they can shoot you, just for fun. Pen got into the back seat with baby Hank while I got my resolve up, and then it was pedal down, screeching, as much as that Chevette could, across the flats.

In retrospect, that trip was the beginning of the end. I believed we had made another crossing unharmed, past the carcasses and into the traffic of the West. But when I got out at our building to pull out the crib from the back, there it was: a jagged hole. Clean through the fender and into the shocks. It was getting increasingly difficult for me to carry my own fear. I could see it happening. I was needing more

Tio at night and then more Turkish in the morning. And now carrying extra fear: more each day for baby Hank and Pen.

As I lay there in the dark, picturing that jagged hole a foot or so higher, slowly rubbing the ointment into my thighs, I decided I needed them to be gone.

That evening, very mantis-like, Mike—all hands and elbows—was describing the buildings collapse for us on the balcony. "They end up drooping," he said. "Like a mushroom. With the slabs bending the re-rod down." He was discussing Damour, where one of his buildings had been re-damaged by an Israeli air strike. Pen then told him about my decision: the next time they hit Damour, she and baby Hank were gone.

"It's too close, Mike," I said. "Next stop is the airport and South Beirut, and then we are indeed like monkeys in a cage." I pointed in the direction of the bathroom. "I mean, she's nothing Mike. A morsel, a whisp. You tell me how she hunkers down." He didn't respond. Both he and I felt defeated, looking down at our shoes. The silence lasted for a while, before finally he broke it.

"By the way, Charlebois is coming."

"Him, I remember," I replied. "The priest with the vermilion walls. God, I thought my dad was bad with name-dropping, but I had only been in his office

for ten minutes, and it was Cookie this and Teddy
that, and especially Rose. Shit, Rose popped up in
every other sentence. How does he get away with it?
I'm a total stranger, and a Cardinal is Cookie."

"Vietnam," Mike answered. "I think we may
even have a news copy of it in the files. Later on,
we got raked over the coals. The U.S. Army was
clearing villages and CRS was coming right in
behind them with foodstuffs for the 'pacified.' Talk
about being in bed. We rode their planes, used their
commo, went to their clubs, and then there was
all that other intrigue, since made public, between
the Archdiocese of New York and Diem. Anyway,
Charlebois got dropped into all that and landed on
his feet. He went way beyond dispensing Mass and
signing waybills. He got to be a player."

"And Rose and Teddy?" I asked.

"I don't know all the details, except that when
the end came Charlebois brought some planeloads
of orphans out. At least I think they were orphans.
The Kennedy family got involved in their care."
Mike laughed. "Ask him. He's not bashful. He'll tell
you more than you could ever want to know about
him and Rose. And Imelda, and . . . look, he's a priest
confessor for selected Catholic wives of the rich and
famous and that, along with his willingness to invoke

the Catholic Church for his own ambitions—and to be protected enough by Cookie to pull it off—well, all together, this has served to elevate him. Him, the poor Canuck from Quebec. Make no mistake," Mike went on. "He signs off on all U.S. government funding and that, right now, is 70% of CRS's annual take. He does what he wants at HQ, including papering his office in vermilion."

"And his interest here?" I asked.

"Well, certainly not your piddly, privately-funded projects," Mike laughed.

"They might be more interesting than all your collapsed buildings for the aged and infirm," I countered.

"He's not here for those either," Mike replied. "He's here for the President of Lebanon, the USAID director, a hotel room with a view and some carpets from Damascus."

"So how do we benefit?" I asked.

Mike smiled. "We, new dick, tell him what we need from the president, ambassador, patriarch, whatever."

"You know, Mike, somehow I am having a very hard time imagining Jack making all this happen."

"He won't have to," Mike said. "We will. Correction, George and we will. All Jack has to do is let Sophia do her magic over dinner and to make sure he has the right ingredients for Charlebois' martini. George will get Sarkis; the woman you terrorized at my apartment will assure the USAID director, and Toufic will acquire the carpets."

"So what are we?" I asked, pointing to Pen, who had just returned from nursing Hank.

Mike threw back another shot and snorted. "You guys?" he said, springing up. "Let me find the right word for mixed company. How does 'fawning sycophants' sound? That and keep Pen in front of you. At least she's Catholic."

What Charlebois had, as I discovered in the years to come, was a talent for getting your number. Or alternatively erasing your number. There he was—the six-footer with the aristocrat's nose, tending, I could see, toward bad skin, dandruff, and ashes on his pants. The poor boy from the Canuck family. Yes, from the moment he walked through customs, you understood that he no longer carried things, nor, for that matter, money, nor telephone numbers or addresses. Nor, evidently, did he ride in front seats. And, as I had been warned, he did not accept rooms without a view of the sea.

After check-in at the Commodore, he stepped into the elevator with me: "Let's see what we paid for." Which meant me helping the bellhop, and then digging into my own wallet to furnish the tip. He, meanwhile, went straight to the view, sliding open the glass. "Jesus, get a whiff of this stuff, will you." He was pointing at the abundance of fruit and flowers, sent up by Farida. "The place smells like a friggin' fruit stall."

Being new to this envoy from HQ, I just stood there for a moment. Were we talking about calling room service, or was that too tedious? Or should I just dump them out the window? He noticed my perplexity. "Just take them down with you," he said. "Give them to those gypsies in the parking lot."

Actually, they were Shia, but I got the idea.

He motioned for me to sit down while he studied his itinerary. Then he motioned for a pen. Luckily, I had one, which he was now using to put an X through roughly the first half of the afternoon. He looked up. "We'll save this for another time." I couldn't believe it. All of them were now in Jack's apartment, having risked the green line to have lunch with the big boss, the Reverend from New York. Half of them had probably bought new clothes for the affair.

"Ah," I said, tentatively, "I think they're already over there." He acted like he didn't hear me.

"Look, tell Jack to come over here. I need to talk with him." He looked at his watch. "Give me an hour. I need to crash. Tell those jokers down at the desk to wake me in an hour. Okay?" I nodded. And with that he started to remove his shoes. I started toward the door, imagining the disappointment ahead, when he interrupted my departure, pointing at the fruit.

"The gypsies," he said.

For the next forty-eight hours, this was to be the swath he cut. An hour later Jack was given an offer he couldn't refuse. Then he led this Catholic delegation into the Embassy, and in the midst of the USAID director's diagnoses of the war—in other words, taking time to teach us, as USAID is wont to do—Charlebois put his cigarette butt out in his coffee cup and asked an astonished director whether he wouldn't just prefer to tie a red ribbon on the whole project and be done with it. 1651 was what he meant.

That caused Mike to share some very anxious glances with his Embassy liaison: such suggestion for the red ribbon having been couched in several references to persons of influence at State. At which point, this normally cocky little man, with his brush cut, bow tie, and Ivy League signet on his pinky, stopped thinking about teaching, saying that he didn't think that would be appropriate, then continued in that vein with more AidSpeak.

"Listen," Charlebois interrupted. He pointed to Mike and me. "Who else in their right mind would run around this hellhole looking out for the American tax payer? If you want to put all this bureaucracy in their way, then we'll tie the ribbon on it," he said, dropping another butt into the cup. "But be prepared. President Sarkis and his friends in Washington will holler hard, not to mention the Patriarch."

Then the director dared to mention that there were other agencies which could do it. Charlebois was already getting up—terminating the meeting— just as the orange juice arrived. He smiled. "My man, we're bad enough. But you start putting a secular in here to dispense U.S. assistance, and I guarantee you every Maronite there is, on both sides of the Atlantic, will be coming out of the woodwork." And so, as fast as we were led in, he was leading us out, with Mike a few steps back in great distress, pleading with his liaison to believe him that he certainly had not wanted this, only a temporary release from the bidding requirements, since contractors were just not crossing lines these days.

She was just shaking her head as they followed us down the hall, looking at Mike and saying, "I certainly hope not."

Talk about killing a fly with a cannon. That was what I was thinking when Charlebois, in his first act of friendship, put his arm around me and said, "I know where I know that USAID guy from."

"Where?" I asked.

"He's Howdy Doody." I wasn't sure what to say.

"He is. Look carefully the next time you meet him."

Next stop. And George had done it up brown, as you might imagine. Once we got over the green line, he had the Maronite militia pick up the BMW and escort us with sirens wailing all the way up to Baabda, where, by Charlebois's earlier insistence, the rest of our Maronite staff were waiting. We proceeded through the palace with Charlebois admiring the art, quite at peace, as if this was just as it should be. Inside, with Sarkis, he did most of the talking, briefly acknowledging the support CRS received from his government and asking him for assurance it would continue, referencing some presumably powerful clergy in New York. Then, he asked the president if he could bring in the staff: "those who are doing the Lord's work," or something to that effect.

In they came: George, the accountant, Toufic and Farida, now erasing any earlier disappointment for his absence at lunch. They shook their president's hand (he certainly wasn't anyone else's president), and then Sarkis called in the palace photographer and had him take individual shots. It made their day. This snapshot of the governor of Baabda looking very much, these days, the sallow frog. They left and then there were some prolonged courtesies with the final shots being of Charlebois and Sarkis, which all of us got to see on the front pages the next day.

Then we trailed out, marveling at more presidential grandeur, leaving Mike still sunk in consternation. "My God, she'll hate me. I told Charlebois there weren't issues, but then he asked me why the hell he bothered to come and so I told him about the bidding problem." He was really depressed. "She'll kill me," he repeated.

That was it for the first day. This was, according to Mike, usually the time when he sought out his corner table. Jack was excused, presumably to discuss his transfer with Sophia, and his acolytes were invited to join him, in the recesses.

Charlebois was to remain, the several years I knew him, distinctly uneasy while outdoors. Apparently, he did not like weather, almost any kind, except perhaps a mild evening on a terrace. Now he was where he most wanted to be: in a dark mahogany bar with his almonds and dry martinis, surrounded by eager staff. There he would expatiate, almost always either self-flattering or spouting grand designs, sucking on a Camel so long and hard that I assumed the smoke got way up into his sinuses and beyond. And then he'd laugh and then we'd laugh. And eventually, his words would slur—not that your attention should wane—and he'd lead us to one of the few remaining crystal and linen restaurants in the city where he'd authorize us to spend our budget.

The next morning, customarily, he celebrated Mass in his room. I spared Pen, presumably for the same reason Jack had spared Sophia. I didn't want my wife, who was still mostly proud of me, to see me down on my knees before a caracter like this. I had my own reasons for burying my dignity at times, but, as I had noticed during my stint in the Army, it was almost as if despite a troop's mental or physical attributes, they, the Catholic faithful, could not help but shrink before this duly appointed emissary of God.

Take Mike. Mike who would look to stand toe to toe on any issue which even had a hint of ethics about it but would, now, I noticed, even as a non-believer, accommodate the priest's "fall from

grace" all day long, and still be there in Charlebois'
hotel room when he gathered us for Mass and where
"no sand" Mike habitually became meek Mike. Still
sidling in, but now with hands cupped to take the
host. While I sat very pious for the duration, I could
not go that far.

After Mass, we were to visit the Maronite Bishop
and the Patriarch, but everything got cancelled due
to "events." During the night, all hell had broken
out. Traffic across the green line ceased and even
those who had affected a nonchalance during earlier
militia duels were now preparing their shelters.

Charlebois insisted on leaving for the airport
early since he was concerned about getting blocked
by events. He was damned if he was going "to spend
the summer hunkered down in Mike's cellar." He
said goodbye to Jack and wished him good luck in
Jerusalem, which we learned the night before at
dinner was the offer he couldn't refuse. "Nothing for
him to do there," Charlebois said, "except collect his
pay and keep his staff quiet. That's one place, I assure
you, CRS is not rocking any boats."

This particular airport café was not Charlebois'
territory. We were at a fly-specked table looking at
three warm cokes with sandbags between us and the
windows, waiting somewhat anxiously to learn if the

incoming MEA flight was actually coming. I dreaded the thought of keeping him entertained if he weren't able to leave. He told us about Jack's replacement: a guy who had worked under him on the Cambodian border. "A friend of the Queen of Thailand," he added. We waited for more information about our new boss, but didn't get much. "Yes, our man Joseph should be here in a couple of weeks." Followed by another one of those drags that filled half of his head. I told him that I would probably be evacuating my family soon, which didn't seem to interest him much except to elicit the comment that he expected to meet them on his next trip. Toufic came striding into the café with a duffel bag on his shoulder, looking quite self-satisfied.

"Excuse me, Father: this is what you wanted?"

Charlebois reached down and prodded it. "Thanks." Toufic just stood there at his customary parade rest, as if waiting for more instruction: either that or for Charlebois to look inside at the contents.

Mike and I, however, were looking at Toufic in disbelief.

"The Chouf?" Mike asked. Toufic nodded.

"And how long did that take?"

"Not too long," Toufic said.

Mike was shaking his head and taking out some cash. "You stay in the West tonight, Toufic. Understand?"

"I'm okay," Toufic answered, as if to say, God spare me these gringos' good hearts.

"I mean it," Mike insisted.

"We'll see," said Toufic.

Now Charlebois, who had been acting singularly disinterested, picked up the cash and stuck it in Toufic's pocket. "Salama," he told Toufic, who understood he was being dismissed.

"Salama, Father," he responded. Charlebois rolled the duffel bag over with his foot.

"Just have Farida send them," he told me.

———⊂◉⟩———

Because of various internal imperatives—within Lebanon, within Syria, within Israel and within the PLO—a settling of scores on the battlefield now seemed in all parties' interest. From what we were seeing and hearing on the ground—and by this time we were virtually the only Americans on the road—and what the BBC was telling us from the concerned capitals, the noose was tightening. The community of ex-pats in Beirut was thinning. Those left talked about the airport, looking up at the sky for confirmation of the daily flights from Europe. Without it, we all would be holed up in Ras Beirut. The Maronites would close ranks with Israel, leaving no exit for us to the East or North, and Israel would come up from the South. The PLO would dig in, in Beirut, with us, it seemed. And Syria would occupy the Beka'a. Of course, this assumed the absence of Jordan and Egypt, and then, of course there were a hundred other permutations that kept everyone guessing and in general adding to the pervasive fear.

For us at CRS, the pressure was to stay or get out. Jack and Sophia left for their new post in Jerusalem and, given Mike's reputation as unstable, I was appointed as "interim director," an assignment I dreaded given Mike's penchant for dropkicking waste baskets and the Maronite grip on the rest of the office. There was nothing to do except sit them down in Jack's office, plead with them not to make my life more difficult than it already was, and pray for Joseph's early arrival.

In reality, there was not much to manage other than my own fear. More days than not the Maronites were not able to come in and Mike was either out (it proved too humiliating for him to tell the new dick "where," much less ask permission) or hammering away on the typewriter. Farida moved in with her cousin in the West, allegedly to teach me the ropes, since Jack had passed on nothing to me other than the keys for the BMW. Of course, I commended her for her loyalty.

What else? Not much. Except I did bring Vache back from his paid leave—the compromise Jack negotiated with Mike—which now assured me of my half-dozen Turkish before noon. And on days too dangerous to travel, I would put my feet up on the desk, leaning back in the swivel, and, as was my surcease those days, redesign the house Pen and I would build when our savings account was finally full enough to leave CRS. And breaking with Jack's routine, I sent Khalil, for the first time available to the office, to the Commodore each day with a short sit-rep for New York and an invitation for guidance.

My time at the top, however, turned out to be short-lived. Two weeks after my ascension, Khalil conveyed news that Joseph was arriving the following evening.

We went together, Pen and I and baby Hank, figuring that anyone coming into this should have at least one initial embrace before he was assailed by what lay in wait. Pen asked how to recognize him as we walked around with Hank in my arms. I told her he would doubtlessly get off the plane with sandy hair, khakis and a white cotton shirt rolled to the elbow.

"Like Mike," I said, "but with more flesh." But as it happened, we missed him, waiting for the last bag to be claimed, until we were alone with the soldiers. We were on our way out when a short man with a Van Dyke beard approached us.

"Are you who I think you are?" he asked.

"Why, yes," I said. Pen mocked me with her smile. He was a diminutive gentleman with an embossed leather briefcase, wearing a linen suit.

"I was told to look for 'tall with khakis,'" said Pen, pointing at me.

"Well," he laughed, "you got short . . . for my age, that is." Pen found that very funny.

The next afternoon Damour got hit. We had already put our argument behind us a couple of weeks back, and now without discussion, we packed: baby Hank in her lavender frock and Pen in an embroidered, black and red Palestine skirt. Pen, even in that fly-specked lounge, looked like she had been picking flowers for the last few weeks rather than holed up in our apartment.

That was another photo that somehow survived. Mike took it just before she and Hank boarded. Me in my blue seersucker and black wool tie with my arm around them. But no second thoughts. I watched the KLM rise into the sun till the last trace was gone. I felt my fear receding.

From the first day, Joe drew on me and Khalil, I guess as the only non-threatening people there. Given that he had been chauffeured for so many years in Asia, he now knew no better. Then other departures from the old ways occurred. The BMW got garaged (I didn't want to drive around in anything that precious), and he bought off a departing ex-pat, easily the largest target in all of Ras Beirut, a Chevrolet Impala. In that first month, he was driven over the length and breadth of Lebanon, usually curled up in the back seat in his wrinkled linens, sleeping or reading until he arrived before his next courtesy call, or for an extended lunch, which he thoroughly enjoyed, and a trunk large enough for anything Khalil could pack in it.

They were a good couple, Khalil (at the time our only Muslim) and Joe. Khalil was carefree, single and without obligations since an artillery round had flattened his lingerie shop in South Beirut. "My bra and girdle man," Joe would say, and they would both laugh. Not a daredevil, Khalil, but rather one of those young men who deep down don't expect to get hurt. Joe turned out to be different. He expected it, but was willing to chance it anyway: not seek it, but chance it. I got the impression that he didn't think it would hurt. Death that is.

And then, not long after, the passenger airport closed. Permanently this time, and the Maronites were ever more reluctant to come across. And so Joe, establishing himself with several strokes of a pen, hired a handful of Muslims to pick up the slack, which of course got him called on the carpet the next day by our friend, the Maronite Bishop. By way of reconciliation, Joe promised to pay rent for a CRS branch office in the Diocese: ostensibly to manage CRS investments in Maroniteland. All of which caused Mike to go ballistic and to so damage the trash can that Vache had to go out and buy him a new one, and which, in turn, caused Joe to call me into his office for consultations—often several times a day over the weeks to come. Like Khalil, I was becoming indispensable to him.

He was hard to put together, my new boss. He had a master's degree, but could not do simple math, turning to me in a restaurant and asking me to do the multiplication for tips. Or he'd say, "Here," while

I sat in front of him enjoying one of Vache's coffees, "check this budget, will you, while I read this letter." It was across the board. He lost track of miles gone and miles to go, of how much cash he stuffed in his pocket in the morning and how much he took out at night. There even were times when this man with a master's would hold out his palm, full of cash, and ask: "Do I have enough?"

Joe didn't drive, didn't count, and seldom wrote anything longer than thank-you notes, but these he did write in great numbers on his personalized stationery—often for exotic Bibles, Korans and other rare texts he had received from notables—which, to be fair, I believe he read. At the very least, he was apt at quoting from them.

This dynamic put an additional strain on me. And with Pen gone, the evenings on the balcony ceased. Despite all the talking Mike and I did, it was soon evident that Pen and the spread she provided had been central to its success. And so, I was left with what I had started with eight months earlier: nuts and beers on Mike's sunken terrace, and his antics on the seawall.

With Joe it was more often a sequence: finishing the last coffee at the office, discussing his latest meeting or the failings of HQ, and then having Khalil take us to a restaurant. Usually to the same one where we had brought Charlebois, which continued its effort to maintain standards even as Beirut was closing down. Joe loved a nice thing: a fountain pen in his hand or a bronze lion by his desk. In this case, a linen napkin and a china plate for which he was prepared to charge the parishioner without a second thought. Which of course also put him at direct odds with Mike, whom it appeared was now becoming the self-proclaimed parishioners' representative in Lebanon.

Whereas for me, while fully aware of the depth of Mike's intellect and quite equally aware that we were mostly at a different address with Joe, I considered Mike's ethics, for the most part, hogwash. While the newly arrived little gentlemen did not come from where I had, I could tell you this: if I were going to spend half my day trying to make my back small for fear I'd never see Pen and Hank again, then that parishioner who was flipping his nickel in the basket on Sunday was getting a bargain and, yes, the tequilas consumed before the dinner were on his tab too.

And so over fine dining we unwound. He filled me up with the lore and legend of the previous decade at CRS (Bangladesh, Timor, Vietnam, Cambodia, Thailand), which, as he said, was the decade when

Care and CRS divided the world and most of the competition was internal: when Father Charlebois cut his teeth and prevailed. From that and more I understood, as he talked, that he too cupped his hands for the host from Charlebois, undoubtedly also submissive to his direction.

"Tonnage," he told me, one night. "Capital T. I know you're spared from it here, but in most regions, let me tell you, tonnage says it all. You meet another CRS-er and right after hello, you ask about his tonnage. You see," he continued, "you don't even sit at the same table with someone who does less than five figures annually."

"You must be exaggerating," I said. This conversation was sounding very surreal to me.

"You think so," he replied. "But think. Food. Surplus food which has to be turned over every year in the U.S. Look at the annual report." And here the little man was getting quite enthusiastic. "It's 90% of our program's value. It's even a higher percentage of our stated beneficiaries. And the 5% handling fee we charge the beneficiaries—not to mention what the host country pays us—well, in some countries it's over 150% of our costs." He put his hand over mine. "Don't tell anyone, but it's the greatest gravy train the church has. And, if you've got tonnage then you've got everything from invites to the presidential palace to all the cars you can shake a stick at. Think about it," he said. "We feed nations." At this point, he delicately dabbed his lips with the linen.

"You mean the U.S. feeds nations," I said.

"Not exactly: remember it's our hand on the spigot," he replied, once again placing his hand on mine. "Even though," he conceded, "if so persuaded, it can, on occasion, be Washington's hand at our throat."

"I would hope so," I said.

"Not so simple," he continued. "The Catholic Church with all its resonance among US faithful, has, in turn, its hand on those duly elected representatives in Congress—arm in arm with the undeniable influence of the agriculture and shipping lobbies." He then took his hand off mine and put it over his mouth, while his other hand began a sort of mining exercise with a toothpick, which I understood later to be the custom in Asia.

Tonnage, I considered. I had seen lithographs in Washington. Or murals. With tractors and combines and silos in clouds of dust and chaff, moving across the heartlands to great hulled ships leaving Milwaukee and Houston—all destined to this little gentleman with the Van Dyke sitting on a throne, with one hand on a lever to a great chute from which flowed a river of grain, spreading over a third world's landscape, and into which brown-skinned natives dipped their pails. For a fee.

That, I suspected, probably explains the embossed leather and gold fountain pen. This was definitely not sharing tea on the dirt floor of a hooch. This was manna from heaven: to wit, from Washington. Not that these disappointing realities— the various corruptions of the humanitarian idea— bothered me prohibitively. Actually, it was often the contrary. Cumulatively, they were providing me with a reason to quit and to be righteous about it, as soon as CRS no longer fit with our plans. But now, with baby Hank banging her rattles on the floor in Northbrook, it was convenient employment. Employment which, after all, kept me well out of reach of various plaintiffs. And that afforded me and Pen the additional benefit of keeping us tax-free which had, in turn, kept our little savings nudging inexorably upward every month.

Of course, for the time being, baby Hank was banging her rattle at my parents' house, which bothered Henry no end, a development that was hard for me to accept since Hank was meant to inspire the resurrection of that selfsame family.

"No," wrote Pen, in the last pouch that had made it in by air-freight—the passenger airport now, mostly shuttered. "Henry is vulgar now. He never changes his clothes and has ash holes from his pipe all over his old tweeds and his beard is a mess with remnants of food and pipe tobacco. At dinner last night he muttered, out of nowhere, 'if they're old enough to bleed, then they're old enough to butcher.' Just like that. Like we were talking about the weather or something. And just earlier, Helen had been sharing with me the old black and whites from when they had first met in Australia and was telling me how wonderful he was."

Other news was not much better. "I called the lawyer," she wrote, "but he hasn't answered my call yet. Anyway, Helen says there haven't been any more angry calls or letters . . . so I guess those sleeping dogs are still sleeping. And I should also tell you that I think your mother has talked with your sister. I'm not sure but she let slip something the other day which would indicate such but she is staying silent since at least once a day poor Henry talks about 'getting even,' and I told her that was also one issue which has plagued us as well. But sometimes your mother just lives in La La land and thinks that this whole tragedy just happened, without rhyme or reason. Like an unexpected hailstorm or something."

Her letter included frustrations about seeing her firstborn, as she said, "being showered with all the kid's junk you can imagine and basically everything she wants, which makes it hard for me to attract her to some less attractive life with me unless I drive back up to the hills."

This latter news was quite disturbing since, if we were going to do what was necessary for resurrection, I needed it to be away from whence we had come. It was challenging enough for me to assume the proper responsibilities of being married in a war zone without fighting multiple battles on other fronts: my several disabilities, the sleeping dogs, the abusive lawyer, Henry's deviance from the normal and now, the intimations that the original talks at the Athenaeum were less conclusive than I had imagined. In the return pouch, I told Pen, "Spend as much time as possible with your first daughter, but don't put yourself and Hank back into what we forfeited so much to leave."

Meanwhile, even as Joe affected a certain nonchalance, in my life and in Mike's, the booze and the coffees were multiplying exponentially. There were now long stretches when we could not leave

Ras Beirut and often, when we did, we couldn't push the investments forward anyway. Basically, he and I were stewing, writing some sitreps for New York and engaging in endless debate about the virtues of hunkering down versus flight. We knew our passports would offer us some protection against the Israelis, but the opportunity to present them seemed remote. "Look," Mike argued, "if they take one burst from an apartment building, they take the whole building down: sniper, men, women, children and us." I agreed.

As for the PLO, convincing them we weren't complicit—even as American jets and American ordnance decimated their ranks—well, this wasn't Africa where whites got special attention, where there was that residue of awe for the color white which protected the expats. Shit, here, everyone was white or white enough and few, if any, suffered from any inferiority complex toward their former colonial masters. "Crusader Jews," they called us.

As far as we were concerned, once the commercial airlines had stopped coming, New York was not in charge anymore. It was our three lives, and we'd just cut the communication if New York telexed what we didn't want to hear. What we did want was company; none of us wanted to be off on his own. The choice was drastic. Start moving supplies into Mike's cellar apartment or prepare for a dash across the port. Exceptionally, Joe was not so engaged. As long as we observed adequate deference, he needed us too much to argue options.

When we did get a telex from New York, it was hardly what we expected. It read, in part: "Due to impracticability of project implementation, advise that Joe proceed to Mexico on TDY." We had our own sitreps to thank for that, we figured. We had told them about our "back door."

"Damned sure, this wouldn't have happened on Jack's watch," I said.

Joe was ambivalent about the news, just as he had been ambivalent about the choices concerning Beirut, though he probably distrusted, as I did, Mike's stated reasons for witness. It struck us that in a day or two, he might be leaving us, curled up as usual in the back seat of the Impala while Khalil raced across the wasteland to our back door, Jounieh Port, where presumably George could get him on a speedboat to Cyprus. That Khalil would be a Muslim in Jounieh seemed of little consequence to Joe nor surprisingly, to Khalil. Predictably, however, Mike would have none of it.

"Fuck it," he said. "If Joe needs taking across, I'll do it."

And while Joe could be walked toward almost any point of view, he guarded carefully the trappings of office: the signing of the cover letters or the representation with notables. And so, to have his authority challenged before the staff immediately caused him to close the doors of his office and receive a consultation. His lips were pursed like a sphincter. He repeated several times that Mike needed to grow up, having been here too long, and went on about how he was "not professional."

That night, sadly without Mike, I took Joe out to our restaurant for his farewell, or rather the parishioners took him out and I accompanied. We dined by candlelight, which had the owner visiting us throughout the meal with apologies both for the light and the shrinking menu: he was afraid, I sensed, that his only paying customers would stop coming. One of war's ironies, I supposed, that there was this almost charming desperation within him to stay open, not to succumb. That the taste be exquisite.

There was no one on the street when we left and got into my Chevette. Just trash shifting about and the occasional rat peering into my headlights. It was almost as if we were presuming to impersonate one of those black assassin cars with our maroon Chevette, speeding through the city to the edge of the great carcasses on the green line. In one of them, the former Holiday Inn, the Syrians were stationed, and just down the hill were dives where Filipina whores hung out.

"In Vietnam," I told Joe, as we bumped downward, "around the perimeters of our base camps, GIs would pay to actually stick their dicks into the concertina wire so some native on the other side could pull them off." Well, for these poor girls, half the world away from their home, sucking dick on Beirut's green line was, I imagined, an equivalent desecration. But Joe said he wanted "Asia" for his farewell, and so we parked nearby and ducked down into a dive, about as reckless of an act as could be done. Yet oddly, after spending most of our time praying to get past this or that desolate stretch or armed barricade, we needed, on occasion, an opportunity to break through: to just walk right up to a table full of dog-faced soldiers, salute, and order a beer and a shot in distinctly American English.

They were so far into their drinks, they didn't even blink. And the Filipinas just hustled around, poured more drinks, and took money and coins for the jukebox. And danced if you pleased, or if you preferred, sat on your lap and squeezed your dick. When fear gets distilled then transformed by tequila, it often sends one toward unsustainable ends, which always appear, through blurred eyes, as other wordly.

I took several tequilas, helped her select rock 'n' roll, danced, and allowed her briefly on my lap, thus removing myself inside this dive from the unholy circumstances outside, in the middle of this night.

All the while, Joe was drinking equally, but mostly with the Syrian soldiers who were getting a delight listening to him talk Tagalog to the bar girls. And so, as the pathos of my girl's situation and the imperative to allay fear brought the two of us in closer communion, Joe's party was moving now toward the raucous: shouting at each other and getting rough. I was watching it, pausing any tentative communion, expecting it could soon get ugly and trying to convince him to come down to my end of the table to sit with us.

I stood up a couple times, beckoning him to come down, and the soldiers reacted by getting more possessive and giving me menacing stares. I was starting to think that this is exactly how people die and had a flash of myself lying face down in the beer on the floor. I took the girl's hand off me, told her to wait, and then stood up and told Joe it was time to leave. "We have to go!" I said, expecting he would take it as a further consultation from his deputy, which, to date, he had always followed. But instead he laughed at me, and then, with the Syrians on each side of him, raised his voice.

"You asshole . . . get out of here." Given the gravity of the situation, I did not take his words literally and repeated my advice that we get the hell out. He laughed again, and the two soldiers looked at me, watching him telling me to get lost and then, mouth agape, turning their heads to watch my response, not really understanding the language but presumably understanding the dynamic. I became confused and fearful. Here we were at a table crowded with bottles and ashtrays: I was at one end with a girl, closest to the dance floor, and a couple of her blasé friends, surrounded by a half-dozen Syrian soldiers leading up to Joe at the head of the table.

The soldiers next to him looked like baboons to me, following the back and forth and giggling, and Joe in the middle of them was transformed before my eyes into a man of confident swagger, quite the opposite of the time in his office when his mouth had shriveled up. He was beaming and staring at me. In command. And I was losing interest in any other proximate escape, now seeking to move toward Joe and appeal to our normal relationship, but the girl still had her hands on me, trying not to lose me. I pushed away and managed to move along the side of the table, but a soldier stood up and blocked my advance with his arm. I looked at Joe, beseeching him. "Come on Joe, we gotta go."

But he beamed again, with the baboons watching him, saying, "Go on, get out, asshole!"

By now my sense of self-preservation was kicking in, so I stared at his face and said, "Screw it," and went toward the door. The Filipina scooted after me, provoking me to repel her which, of course, elicited screams, and knowing I could ill-afford any conflict now, I let her follow. But for some reason she wasn't interested in the wad of cash proffered, instead insisting on getting in the Chevette with me. Once inside, she tried to warm me up and get me excited about her, but the earlier notion of some small surcease was long gone, and now I was only thinking about getting free. But I also didn't want to hurt her and so I was trying to talk her down and remove her when right before me, in the morning fog now coming off the Port, Joe appeared with the soldier who had blocked me, now with his arm draped over Joe. The two of them got into a VW bug and drove off.

Less than a week after Joe had left by speedboat for his Temporary Duty, the long-expected invasion began, a blitzkrieg. In the first twenty-four hours, the Israel Defense Forces (IDF) destroyed the Syrian air force, apparently with no losses. Then they started taking out Syrian armor, which took somewhat longer, but with total control of the air, they soon littered the Chouf—that place of wildflower fields and Pen's stone cottage—with Syrian tanks, gutted and smoking.

In the South, I learned later, Bishop Haddad had driven south of Tyre in the early hours of June 6th to confront the Israeli armor advancing on his town. He stood in the road—a solitary priest staring up at the tank turret—and asked that the columns slow down long enough to get the non-combatants into places of refuge. He got an hour. And then the Israelis crushed the place, or rather, crushed any part of it which had had a Palestinian presence or aspect. The PLO camp was surrounded, evacuated and then reduced to rubble. The old men, women and children were soon wandering on the beaches or holed up in warehouses. The PLO fighters, in Tyre and all the way up the coast, beat their way to South Beirut, where they were digging in amidst the general population.

Mike and I soon witnessed the pandemonium. South Beirut was ablaze and smoldering from Israeli airstrikes. The anti-aircraft was putting a thousand puffs of no consequence into the sky. Hundreds of cars went screaming and shooting through the streets, converging on A.U.B.H and other hospitals. Neighborhood fire brigades did what they could to throw water on the flames, while the more invested, those who had hung on to the end, raced frantically across the green line (those who had the right confession, that is). The Christian Phalange, true to expectations, were coordinating their actions with Israel up and down the front. Except for the disastrous and complete collapse of the Syrian air force and armor, it was unfolding as Mike had predicted. It would be war for South Beirut, and if the Israelis hoped to root out the PLO, they would have to reduce a capital to ruin: and that, Arafat was hoping, would be a choice they would not make. He also assumed, or at least had most of his bets placed, that AMAL, as much as they despised the PLO, could not actively be in league with Israel for long.

Within forty-eight hours, most cards had been played. Syria's military, a paper tiger; Israel sucked into a fool's mission; the Phalange tied to a relationship which could not be sustained; and Arafat standing in the midst, watching his Beirut forces blown apart and his civilians wandering the fields and beaches of South Lebanon, destitute and often despised by the Lebanese for their original intrusion as refugees, decades earlier.

As for Mike and me, we were now living on some very high octane: not eating or sleeping anymore, just sucking on cigarettes and downing Turkish. With the first news of the Israel invasion, we had closed down the office, secured the files, cars, and other assets. We agreed to let Vache and his mother hold out in the kitchen. We paid whomever else came in that morning a couple months of salary and wished them God's protection. They expected no more from us, and quickly receded into their confessions and militias for support.

Mike warned me it would be a joke, but after months of participating in the Embassy warden system, I insisted on at least knocking at that door. Presumably there was to be this web of person-to-person communication which would culminate in a convoy out, stars and stripes fluttering among us. Again, Mike was right. The US officials had left secretly in the night, obviously unable to share their intelligence with us. The U.S. mission that day had been delegated to an old Lebanese doorman.

We went to a space which, it seems, each war produces, as I would learn over the next few decades in Addis, Asmara, Luanda, Baghdad, or Belgrade: a hotel which was near the action, still had commo, or failing that, whisky and a decent steak. It was a delicate time. I felt I had to hold Mike in, to keep him in step, but I knew that if he complied, it would only be because of the ethics of friendship, and certainly not because he believed in "flight" or hanging around the Commodore lobby in the company of the huddled media, trying to squeeze in a telex transmission to HQ. This is where you get noticed; on the other side of the stage, from the little reports I had written on the new nets in Tyre.

Here in the lobby, the media jumped on us, me more than Mike, but then again, I made it easier for them. Our names soon went out over their transmissions. And once we had been discovered there ensued little feeding frenzies around one or the other of us which initially had made me feel significant, until later on I also got subjected to the rudeness when after they had taken all they needed for a headline they had scrambled for the telex room (even as one tries, unsuccessfully, to explain that this is only part of the story).

Regardless, during that first hour, after we had walked into the phrenetics of the lobby, we were hot; our names went around the world and also into HQ. I knew from Mike that Joe, Charlebois, and HQ in general would be sweating big time, as Mike put it, about how we described Israel to the press, which, frankly, was bound to be less hysterical and more balanced than most accounts coming from anyone else in Beirut, but still we could not ignore the zeal with which Israel was applying US technology and ordnance, less than a kilometer away from that exact lobby, onto a largely civilian population.

This was probably the principal reason New York telexed us ("with all due precautions for your safety"), to "please implement evacuation to Cyprus."

This suited me okay, since I had no desire to hole up with Mike, living on sardines and Heineken, for as long as it took to get the siege of Beirut resolved. And it helped to relieve the fear of either ending up under an Israeli-induced pile of rubble, or shot in the head and then thrown off the sea wall by some local warrior.

The language was equivocal; it would be easy enough to just hide behind "due precautions." I fell back on our friendship, on our many nights on the balcony with Pen, and asked Mike to please follow me out, which basically meant an hour more of trepidation as we moved from the hotel lobby to our apartments to the Port.

The Sea Queen

Looking back, I find it strange how we were capable of so many hours of deliberation over two days in the lobby but that once we had agreed on "flight," in my case particularly, panic took over. I could hear the seconds ticking in my head, half-expecting to be disappeared mid-flight. I took no care with the departure. Just pulled the sheet off my bed and onto the floor and threw whatever occurred to me into the middle of it—clothes, watercolors, knick-knacks— all in a heap. Then I grabbed the four corners of the sheet, twisted them, and heaved it over my shoulder like Santa with his big sack of toys.

I took one last look from the door, not expecting to see it again, and then took off down the hall, descending the stairwell wildly, knocking my bag about, until the pale blue cotton sheet ripped up the middle in the lobby and the clothes dumped out, knick-knacks skittering across the tile. I looked up at that moment into Mike's face outside, framed in the window of the Chevette. He was despondent to the extent where he did not even smile. I crawled around, trying to rearrange my effects in the ripped sheet, before leaving most behind.

Such ignominy. An armful of stuff thrown in the backseat, Mike sitting silently next to me with all he cared to bring, a Dopp kit, in his lap and me jerking the gears and pedals with such vehemence that smoke started to rise off the hood.

Hardly the Infantry Lieutenant I had been billed as.

In Jounieh Port, Mike began testing me. "Why go farther?" he argued. His logic was hard to dispute. We had communication now, and the Church, if we wanted it: not to mention being wrapped within the Israeli–Maronite alliance. Just across the Port, a besieged city was dying an awful death, and here folks were sipping coffee in crowded cafes, coiffed and bejeweled. An observation which, upon further reflection by both of us, had ended the discussion. We would not stay.

Down by the docks there were the people we meant to join, those others who had not been turned back at the Port gathered in circles according to their kind: a few non-official Westerners like us; some non-Western diplomats; and families with money, not what you usually see at the edge of war, these men and women milling about in tailored suits in the late afternoon, alternately looking out to sea and checking their watches. And then a larger Arab crowd of the more desperate sort milling about, who had by cunning, I imagined, wheedled their way to the port.

The yachts were there—several beautiful craft anchored within the breakwater—and of course the crew was there for the price these folks would pay. But the Israeli military is a different kettle of fish or at least not an Arab one, and so the privileged waited with the rest.

I made some inquiries by myself, since Mike was still moping about, feeling, I assumed, like a deserter, apparently not interested in when we would move out and probably, I feared, half-considering racing back across the Port and into the war.

I was told that the crowd on the dock had already purchased tickets: three of the yachts were already booked out, just waiting for permissions, which sounded to me as if we were a dollar short and a day late, aggravated by a companion with one eye on bolting.

I got directed to the agency which sold tickets for the yachts. But, as it turned out, they had nothing for me. "Maybe tomorrow, who knows?" I returned to Mike down by the water, looking dejected, and told him we might start thinking about finding some rooms.

By coincidence, one of those gentlemen in waiting, a monied man by his appearance, overheard me and asked if I were American. I confirmed it. He pointed to his family: two teenaged pretty ones, and a woman who was obviously haute couture and not particularly enjoying this adventure on the dock. "Do you mind if I see your passport?" I showed it to him. "Ok," he said, "Please come with me." Why not, I felt. Family man, impeccable suit: what could go wrong? Mike stayed back while he led me to the offices of the harbor master.

It wasn't much, allowing that Jounieh was more like a marina than a port, staffed by three men, with the master in the central position behind a desk crowded with communication gear. The two, the master and my wealthy companion, went back and forth in Arabic for a few minutes, glancing at me every so often. Finally, the master shrugged, flicked a couple of switches on the transmitter and invited me to speak. "You are Bravo Charlie for Oscar Romeo. Tell them you're an American and need to leave." I nodded. I got the drift.

The communication was very sharp, very clean. I told the Israeli that I was part of an American delegation which worked with the Embassy and I was coming out. He asked to confirm the Embassy connection. I did. "With them," I said, not "for" them. There followed some transmittal of passport details.

I wasn't prepared for this. I was going along because there was nothing better to do. I mean, an entry-level relief worker does not expect to be negotiating safe passage for other national diplomats and associated men of means. Thus, I was caught in a daze when I was suddenly asked to identify the boat I'd be on. I don't know what I was thinking: we weren't all now just going to wade in and start swimming for Cyprus. I was confused, not to mention somewhat brain-dead from fatigue. I was staring past the harbor master toward the sea when the question was put to me. The question was still bouncing around in my head just as a breeze had unfurled the Southern Cross: the Sea Queen. "The Sea Queen," I said, "of Australian registry." There was a pause at the other end, then he gave me some boarding times and coordinates and told me that was an initial limit.

The harbor master flipped his switches and looked up as if to say, "Well, whaddaya know?" The monied man, however, was now considering me with dismay, tapping what I now understood to be the ticket he had purchased on another yacht. Then suddenly, barging through the door, came a stocky, fair-haired Aussie, who looked like he was going to blast right through me. "You bastard," he said. "You just sold my boat."

True enough, he had been beside himself when, sitting before his radio, he heard me designate his boat for a run across Israeli lines. "The balls," he kept repeating, shaking his head repeatedly. "I swear, if one fucking thing goes wrong with this I am personally throwing your ass overboard." He stared at me. "Got it?" I said I did. "That's if," he added, "we don't all get blown out of the water first." My sense, however, from our subsequent hours together, was that he was not disinclined to ferry well-paying customers to Cyprus. Rather, he had not intended to be a pathfinder and he certainly was not as sure as he would have liked to be about his credentials: me and Mike.

In any case, nothing was twisting his arm to lift anchor or not, other than the risk involved and the profit to be made, and so finally he slapped his knees, stared at me for one long last sizing up and said, "Let's get on with it." At which juncture, my dramatic role receded, at least until we had arrived later at our coordinates. For now, it was he who made choices—in some cases, I am sure, over life and death—about who would walk across his gangplank and who would not. And he did so without any consultation with his credentials. I had no idea about his criteria (money, nationality or humanitarian interest), but sometime before midnight he had accumulated a hodgepodge of about fifty passengers on a yacht that was built for twenty.

At the end of the day, it's an awful lot of what makes life worth living. The incandescence, if you will. Maybe it's lying upstairs on your mattress in Paris looking at the crusted plaster, tingling with revelation, just before the dust balls get you. Or lying on grass after the race, face toward blue sky, feeling your body slowly fill back up after what it gave over 20 kilometers. Or the fingertips to the milk white and coal black, or buried in the orange swatch. But before the time when I was called to the bridge, it was the two of us, Mike and I, standing in the bow, sucking on our smokes: just now passing out of the harbor, past the breakwater with the lights of Jounieh Port receding and the flares drifting down over the fires of South Beirut. This was, we knew, also what can make life extraordinary.

On the deck around us, the socioeconomic distinctions were disappearing fast. Just body after body lying down or sitting in the dark. Families were bound up close, the red coals of cigarettes lighting up faces.

About an hour out, the Aussie signaled me to join him in his pilot house with his wife, the actual Sea Queen (a Scandinavian blonde), and another mate, as he put it. The three welcomed me and offered me coffee. The Israeli captain was transmitting and had questions for me. Were there any Palestinians with me, he asked? I noticed a box of passports on the console. The Aussie was shaking his head. "No," I said.

"Are there any weapons?" he asked.

Again, I looked at the captain. "No."

The Israeli gave us a next set of coordinates. The Aussie captain was confused; it was due South. The Israeli confirmed the new coordinates and ended the transmission. The mood in the cabin had dramatically shifted. The captain looked worried as he made the adjustments to the steering. "They're taking us to Israel," he said.

"What does that mean?" I asked.

"Damned if I know," he replied, "but if they confiscate this boat, I can guarantee you one thing."

That same threatening aspect I had been subjected to with the harbor master had returned. "You're going to buy me a new one, mate."

Soon after, the Sea Queen herself left for the galley to boil some milk for the children onboard and search for spare blankets. I sat on my stool and generally kept my mouth shut. The captain and his mate were discussing practical matters. Then, suddenly, his mate launched off his seat, yelling, "Oh my God, they're firing on us!" Before this, the only Israeli presence was a voice, but now off our starboard was a flash of cannon, lighting up the side of the gray missile boat nearby. The captain crouched down behind the wheel, and I dropped to my knees looking up at him searchingly. I had had this experience before, and was kneeling in prayer that the black would not again come down over me.

I looked at the Aussie face to know whether I was about to die. And for a long time, even when we heard the cannon again, he did not reassure me. Slowly I rose off the floor. To our port was Saida, and the sky over it was lit up by a half-dozen incandescent flares parachuting down over clouds of smoke.

"They're mopping up," I said, and the captain nodded. His mate now also stood up. The wife came in. I had seen aspects of this in Vietnam at the village level, but here it was a city under attack. And I knew what mopping up now meant: Lebanese were telling the Israelis where Palestinians could be found. It was an illuminated hunt for stragglers and sympathizers.

We proceeded slowly down the coast, now under siege by the flares and fires on land. I went out to find Mike; he was surrounded by men clearly scared for their lives, beseeching me, pulling on my jacket and using the deferential "Sir" or "Saidna." I couldn't explain to them why we were not heading toward Cyprus or whether we would be held in Israel, but I could see in their eyes that this was a life-or-death issue for them.

"God knows," Mike said, "who's on this boat. You can buy whatever passport you want in Lebanon, but the Israelis won't be fooled." Even while I talked to Mike, some of the men on board returned, asking me the same questions and just wanting to stay close to me, I sensed.

At 4 a.m., I was called back to the bridge. They told me that we were now at the coordinates and had been asked to wait. The mood was anxious. Some children on the deck were crying. From time to time, a man of means would presume to tap on the door, whereupon the wife or the mate would dismiss them.

Certainly, they were not used to this, I thought. They had stubble and sweat on their shirts and, moreover, wives who looked ghastly.

Then came first light. Rosy-fingered dawn, I recalled, and as the dark lifted, I remember thinking it was like a curtain in a theatre being raised and there, before our wide eyes, was millions worth of gray, deadly technology. A gray ship loaded with a porcupine of antennae, bores, and launchers.

For those of us raised on the war of AKs and RPGs or conventional mortars and artillery, this looked so death-dealing as to take your breath away: especially as you sat, I imagined, with your wife and children on the deck of a wood and fiberglass yacht. The Israeli captain got on the radio again, directing me. He wanted me and Mike in the stern, he said, and everyone else up front.

"No one else in the stern. Understand?" I told him I did.

"With your hands up! Understand?" I told him I did.

"Are you sure there are no guns aboard?"

"To the best of my knowledge," I replied. He paused.

"Listen," he said. "If we see guns, we'll fire on you."

"I understand," I said looking, along with my mates, across a 300-meter stretch at what now had assumed Starship proportions.

A dozen hands reached out to us from the deck. Touching us and wishing God to be with us. And then it was just the two of us, as the captain watched from the bridge—two thin men from CRS facing the Israeli missile boat. Sleep-deprived, caffeinated. Zodiac, a rubber vessel, was coming down the side of the missile boat and, from what I could see, four troops with Flak jackets and M16s were in it, putting toward us. When they drew closer, I could see they were kids, very young considering the power in their hands. If I pulled out a 45, I could have killed them, albeit seconds before our boat was vaporized. I prayed there was no such gun up front.

We climbed into the Zodiac, and you could feel it instantly, especially looking back at the yacht: we crossed those 300 meters from helpless to unchallenged power, but also (the Aussie excepted), from their world to mine. I couldn't help but wonder why those who had touched me on the way to the stern would trust me. In many ways, I was going to my people. I had just been lifted from among the helpless—those who could easily die—to the invulnerable.

We were taken down through the interior of the missile ship and into a small metal room with a metal table and metal chairs. They took the passports, then left us there unattended for more than an hour. Our faces twitched and we squirmed, but said nothing, assuming we were being monitored.

I had been prepared for someone whom I associate with thirty, forty, or one hundred million worth of firepower, but the captain was younger than us. No wrinkles, no gray hair, and a bad haircut. He began by hunching over the table and rubbing sleep out of his eyes. My sense was it could've just as well been his nose, for all he cared. He mumbled, then slid our passports back to us. He asked us about Palestinians on the boat. I told him the captain had no such identities, choosing the word "identities" carefully. He had a good command of American English, but spoke it like a bored kid from Westchester. Or maybe he was just dead on his feet.

And that was it. None of the third degree we were waiting for or of the anticipated discussion of the difference between "with" and "for": the preposition that had put us in this room to begin with. He just stood up and looked at us, the Americans, suddenly rather deferential.

"You still going to Cyprus?" he asked.

This took me by surprise since there weren't many alternatives, although I suppose he might have been inviting us for a lift into Haifa. "Yes," I said. And as he was turning away, wanting to be sure, I asked, "We can go to Cyprus?"

"Yeah," he said. "I'll tell your captain."

It was quite emotional and embarrassing as our Zodiac bumped up against the Sea Queen and we climbed back among the vulnerable. The passengers made way for the captain who helped us up and onto the deck. He smiled and gave me a pat on the neck. "I guess I won't have to throw you overboard, mate."

"They radioed you."

"Yep. Cyprus it is—if the fuel holds."

Then the passengers came in on Mike and me, imitating the captain, all patting us with a multitude of Arab salutations and heartfelt gratitude. For most it had been an excitement of the first order. Others—those who had beseeched me earlier in the night—were now crying and pushing their wives and children on me who, in turn, were embracing me. They searched for things to give me, saying very slow for my comprehension about how Allah would love me.

It was all too much and starting to drive me crazy, so I went off with Mike to the bowsprit and turned my back on them, as if Mike and I had important matters to discuss without them. But even as the voyage was exceedingly long due to the need to optimize the fuel, and even as I had my back turned to them for nearly all of it, a few among them always had a gaze ready to meet mine, clearly eager to approach again and offer a cigarette or a light.

Meanwhile, as the sun rose now to its full strength, the deck began to resemble a shanty town. The Sea Queen was being transformed. Everyone smelled, the can downstairs was a mess, people were doing their stuff off the stern. Blankets were strung up to get some shade. Now, "milk white" was red and blotched. The Sea Queen was running back and forth with water, biscuits, and ointments for the babies and children.

In part bravado, in part, given the sun, good sense, I undid that vestige of civility which I knew had served me well from harbor master to Israeli captain and tied my tie around my forehead. That indeed was the scene as finally we went through the breakwater into Larnaca. Mostly red and blistered, coming in on the fumes, as my Aussie mate said.

The makeshift tents flapped on the deck, passengers rummaged about in the mess to put themselves together, men of means tidied up. Babies were swayed in their mother's arms and, one by one, they approached us, wishing Allah to be with us or for God to bless us. I imagine I looked like swashbuckler with the red and blue regimental stripes around my head. Mike and I were the last off, and the captain came down from the bridge.

"What can I say?" I asked.

He agreed. There wasn't anything to say: just two mates, shaking hands. We started the walk down the quay, where we could see, on the other side of the gate, a crowd now gathered for us. "Memories that are often replayed, like this memory, keep you young," I said to Mike with a grin, quoting something I'd read.

"As long as, if in the making of them, you don't get killed," Mike replied. I put my arm around my stooped sunburned friend with his haystack of hair.

"We made it, Mike."

"I know, I know," he said, laughing and shaking his head. "I'll give you that. You sure do have a way with prepositions."

We crossed through the gate into Europe: the ragged edge, but Christendom nevertheless. Mike with only his Dopp kit and me with an armful of clothes and our cash, wadded in a plastic bag in my shoe.

The reporters closed in, jostling for attention. Other than the earlier Israeli-sanctioned departures for the diplomats, we were the first of what they later described as "those who had escaped," and our flight from Jounieh, our subsequent capture and escort to Haifa, and the sunburned voyage to Larnaca made the next day's front page in cities as distant as London. Dailies carried colored, quarter-page photos of the Sea Queen herself, standing amidst the remnants of the shanties on the deck. Within a few months, a glossy paperback had been published, again featuring her on the cover. But these particular reporters had only pounced on us for their two hundred words and were soon lifting off, when suddenly, I saw Howdy and his ungainly assistant advancing toward us, first on the periphery of the reporter's circle, catching our attention, and then beckoning us with a finger.

The instincts to obey were strong. Despite the Canuck's mauling of the USAID director, the U.S. government did indeed still have its hand on the throat of CRS and could squeeze when it wanted. I did obey, but obeying, at that moment, felt unseemly. These two had holed up in the Embassy while we roamed the wilderness, and then took flight one night courtesy of the Israelis while we were left to our devices and somehow managed to straggle in and now, hardly past the gate, we see Howdy wagging his finger at us. We made a date for a debriefing, then crossed the street to the Sun Hall where we would clean ourselves and get some coffee.

I don't doubt we still looked like beachcombers when they arrived. Both of us in my wrinkled clothes which had Mike looking even more like a scarecrow—a red one—and in my case, with most of the other predictable effects of just coming off our earlier situation: the glassy eyes and chronic hard-on that fame and no sleep produce.

But there was a far more potent influence involved. I had been in a war again, for almost a year at that point. Not shooting folks, as in Vietnam, but still in a place where most of what drove the dynamic was killing. As in Don Juan, death was always there, the crow perched with its claw in your shoulder. And now, from the instant I had left the circle of the reporters in the quay, that crow had flown away. I had been delivered from killing as a milieu. And quite honestly, the tiny little aspects of peace, even in a troubled place like Cyprus, were almost too much for me. A smile sent me over the top. A smile together with a small kindness, and I was as in love as I'd ever been.

As Howdy went on and Mike's friend with the unusual hips chimed in, I was mostly lost to this rush of separation from Lebanon at war. In their eyes, my state was probably translating as sunstroke. They told me that the arrest in Haifa had gone to the Pentagon and back before the boat had been released: I sat there with a moronic smile. Then they were laboring over the preposition, and Mike countered, "Well you tell us, which is it. We know we don't work 'for you' since 'for' doesn't mean you leaving in the middle of the night and not even saying goodbye. So it is 'with' Mush Hayk?"

Before they could answer, Mike, for the first time without his customary deference, continued. "Because if it's not even 'with' then I'll just send my reports to Congress." He leaned in, dead serious. "Now you tell me." At this point, Howdy looked over at his assistant with a very patronizing smile as if to indicate that neither of us—one too spaced and the other too serious—was really competent at this point in time. He suggested that we get some sleep, and called for the bill.

"We'll be in touch," he said.

As it went, Mike did go to sleep. But I was still in the thralls of life without the crow on my shoulder, so I left to walk the terrace alongside the evening sea, moving slowly beside the outdoor cafes toward a dilapidated mosque. A lovely evening. And now, years later, in the throes of sporadic meanness, I wonder how it is that this lovely evening could not have been captured. And yes, the crow did return and again flew off, but the loveliness afterward never got sustained. Something internal, more dangerous than death's crow, eats away, inside out, at the loveliness.

And I thought, now sitting in a chair at seaside and ordering a retsina, that it can't be just the testosterone which follows danger: it must be the rare loveliness that we are not otherwise afforded. It is, in the instance of this evening, the waitress by herself with her smile. The crow has just departed and there is just that brief moment when you still feel, if you will, the wind from its wing, when this loveliness is available and has now been unwittingly brought to me by the Greek waitress who has, I am quite sure, decided to give this sunburned guest a gift beyond the smile, and so bent forward to refill the wine.

And of course, she is disarmed. He is disarmed. Everyone, except the stone-faced killers, is disarmed since everyone can feel, if never articulated, that they have been drawn in as part of the loveliness— and to that, they yield.

The next morning Mike and I decided that our time as "lost" to HQ had run its course and we had better, reluctantly, make contact. We drafted the necessary message for New York and telexed it from the hotel, describing Beirut as we knew it one day earlier and venting on American complicity in South Beirut, describing what we knew to be absent from their daily news and finally recommending our return to the States until a time when we could get relief to the victims.

Then we took the afternoon off and went swimming. When we returned there was a response from HQ, lying there in our key boxes. "Please stay in Cyprus. HQ delegation to meet you there in forty-eight hours. Press coverage widespread. Please no partisan comments. Thank God you're safe." It was signed by one of Charlebois's desk officers. Welcome back, I thought, the loveliness quickly receding.

"They would have found us anyway," Mike said. "Christ, if the Pentagon knows where we are . . ."

It was the dreaded end to being lost. I went upstairs to call Pen. She was very emotional, not wanting me to go back: "Promise me." She told me I had a daughter and must think of that now, and put Hank on to say "Dada" to me, then said "We love you," which got me passionate, imagining her on the other end, missing me so much.

Then she started to talk to me about business and local dramas, and I told her that I couldn't deal with that now and would call her tomorrow. She said she understood, and that Helen was so proud of me. It was in all the papers. I told her to cut them out to save them for baby Hank, and she said she was already making a scrapbook. This caused me to tell her I loved her. She said she loved me too, and that everyone around was very proud of me and thought I was very brave. Through my mind's eye flashed the scene of me crawling about the lobby of our apartment building trying frantically to pick up my clothes and knick-knacks.

It could be like that with Pen. I would not miss her completely until I saw her or spoke to her. Actually, I never had, as far as I can recall, missed anyone from a distance, except Roo who had always been with me as my sister. And whom I was only now just starting to learn how to block from recall: except, of course, when it was presented to me as part of the litigation which was sucking money out of our family. I chuckled. No doubt Pen's family thinks I'm terrific now. Good old press. Putting bright colors on a pretty poor character. And as for the loveliness, when the headquarters contingent disembarked the afternoon plane into Cyprus the next day, its last vestiges were gone.

Charlebois was one of those people who never made sense. He tells you something: you don't understand because it can't be understood. He refuses your misunderstanding and takes you on an extended explanation of the nonsense, which eventually you concede to understand since you don't want to be resented for provoking an even longer explanation. But you and he both know you still don't understand, so he then fixes future events to support his explanation so that now it can, maybe, be understood. The point being, he never had anything to understand, but he sure as hell had an indomitable will to make you understand.

So, there was Charlebois at the airport, cigarette in mouth, pointing out a black leather bag for Joe to handle while a half-dozen Holy Cross Sisters dragged their gear off to a central location: an emergency swat team I learned later, who had worked for Father Charlebois and Joe in Asia.

The initial meeting at the hotel was as I expected: Charlebois running on for an hour and going nowhere, but since we were going somewhere, we did. Then military terms were introduced which, I must admit, sounded funny given the array of Sisters around the table. We were going to launch a pincer movement on two critical fronts. That is, the eight of us were going to split up and follow in the wake of the Israelis and provide sustenance to those hurt or displaced by the blitzkrieg. Charlebois had a verbal commitment from the U.S. on a first installment of one million: it would be cash and local purchase.

"And now, I want to talk to you two pirates, one at a time," he said. "And Joe, I want you here for this. Sister Mary, you find us a place for some grub." The good-hearted Mary asked about a preference.

"Just as long as they can make a good dry martini," he said.

Mike went first, and even before it had begun, I watched him begin to sidle, now with his head down and an apparent unwillingness to look the priest in the eye. Meanwhile Joe was acting very professional: a small joke here and there, a pad for notes for the Father who never in his life took notes, a call downstairs for fresh coffee. I left with the Sisters, then sat outside to wait my turn. Quite a reversal, I thought, from my earlier place on the bridge. I was not particularly worried. I knew that Joe and Father Charlebois were kindred, and that Joe accepted a certain dependency on me and was not aware of my witness to his sinfulness (as defined by the Catholic church) with the Syrians.

As for Charlebois, I observed the obsequites but didn't allow my family to be a witness to them. He knew that. He was very smart about human dynamics. His first question at the airport to me concerned Hank and Pen. Family whom I had not allowed him to meet but whose names he knew. We both knew where the line was and accepted where it was, for the moment.

What Charlebois did to Mike that day was right. And I imagine he did it well: unequivocally and compassionately. In any case, my fellow pirate came out of the room penitent with a weak smile and eyes averted. I approached him, but then Joe was waiting at the door. I took a big breath. "My turn?"

Once again, Mike had called it correctly. The Israelis had indeed pulled up just south of Beirut. Along with the Maronites and the sea they had encircled the city. But now it seemed they were unwilling to try to go further: to root out and kill the PLO forces inside it. Not willing because of those precious boys they'd lose, and for the international condemnation associated with ravaging the city. So I was to take the lion's share of the Sisters—a humorous offering by Charlebois—and fly to

Jerusalem, where I was to arrange for permissions to move north across the Israeli border and to help the victims of the war in South Lebanon, now fully under the control of the Israeli Defense Forces. Jack was to give me his full support.

"And if there's any problem with the 'support' then let me know," he said. I knew there would be problems, and moreover that I would not communicate them to Father Charlebois. The plan, I thought, if there is no more to it than getting food and shelter to those suffering from the recent invasion, was in principle feasible, given that we were as in bed as one can get with Israel on the West Bank already. A novice could grasp it. You conquer a people, little matter whether it's in Vietnam, Iraq, West Bank or South Lebanon; you eliminate its local governance; and then, under the humanitarian flag, you establish a hand-to-mouth dependency, in most cases on U.S. largesse. From the Catholic view, you save God's children from starvation and exposure. They live and their children live to see another day, and presumably, one day bite the hand that fed them.

That part of the meeting was therefore short. My role was familiar, and the cash was in hand. Taxpayers', not parishioners', cash.

Meanwhile Joe and a couple of the Sisters would test the proposition that with the line drawn in Lebanon, our recent breakthrough on the Sea Queen soon would be followed by a more regular—again courtesy of Father Charlebois---boat service between Jounieh and Larnaca.

Unsaid was that our dramatic flight had been unnecessary. The Israelis had pulled up south of Beirut, but no house-to-house search in Beirut had ensued. I admitted to this embarrassment. I was covered by HQ's insistence we leave, but I knew in my heart that HQ could always be manipulated by the information the field chose to give. In the end, we got on the Sea Queen because I had had enough. That crow had been with me too long.

Then Charlebois related what Joe would be doing. "Mercy convoys," he called them, into the Beka'a and Beirut. Actually, I didn't doubt most of the plan had been handed to Charlebois by the same civil servant from State who authorized us the cash. From Maronite land, we would purchase and transport assistance to the Beka'a and Chouf, where, I agreed with them, there would be extensive collateral damage due to the air and armor battle between Israel and Syria. "Moving stuff into Beirut would be dicier," I warned.

If the Syrians and Maronites could collaborate so completely and successfully in the production and transport of hash, I am sure ways could be found to get assistance into Beirut: but not without a tax, seen or unseen, I told them. If they had it in their minds that CRS was going to activate mercy convoys into South Beirut from Jounieh without paying through the nose, then they better think again. And if we were just looking at cost per beneficiary, we could do more for precious lives elsewhere. Such an argument was somewhat disingenuous on my part as I could already imagine the applause back home: the "It's in all the papers" impact of the trucks with CRS flags fluttering off the cabs, en route, right past the cameras at the Commodore, for a quick dump into some warehouse on the edge of the bombing in South Beirut which we all agreed was sure to continue without interruption. "Such assistance will be," I told them, "Unmonitored and, at a minimum, shared with the fighters—most probably handed over in its entirety and this, of course, could be explosive. Imagine the headlines," I said to an unusually focused Father Bob (as the Sisters called hm), "Catholics supply PLO in Lebanon."

It wouldn't take Howdy long, I was thinking, to pull the plug on that. Either way, I predicted, the vulnerable in South Beirut would undoubtedly get what they were now getting in South Lebanon: an empty cellar, septic water, whatever they could buy with their rings and earrings. "In the end," I said, "it would be a trade-off for the taxpayer." The world, courtesy of the press, would know there was a great humanitarian problem and CRS would be invited to explain that in more detail on national television. That would be good for CRS, we agreed. But then again, I argued, our particular public exposure would have to tread so carefully, such that mercy convoys were not in any way to be interpreted as a criticism of Israeli bombings nor as support for PLO terrorists. Media presentations would have to be so shaded with obfuscation as to become virtual lies.

Anyway, I told them, returning to my role in the pincers, working with the Israelis in South Lebanon would give me none of those headaches. I would be in bed from the get-go, as in bed as one could be, and would content myself by getting some food to those Palestinian women and children who at that moment were living under anything that cast a shadow and reduced to picking through Shia garbage for a chance to see next month.

As for the Beka'a, I paused, reflecting. As an American agency, especially given the Iranian presence there, this would definitely have to be finessed, but we could still serve by working our assistance quite anonymously through an acceptable intermediary. Kluiters could help point the way, I suggested.

But the footage of the mercy convoys into the smoke and fires of South Beirut was really what had them going, and I had given all I had to that analysis. Then it occurred to me. I interrupted their excitements, raising my finger in the air, "Mike's the one," I said. "He's the one who can tell you how it can be done." And I paused, looking at the two men whom I had interrupted, but quickly realized I was being inappropriate and then reiterated something about whether it should be done ("I mean, whether the stuff will get to those in need"). Then I trailed off, seeing that a course had already been set.

Charlebois tapped his cigarette on the ashtray and said what I had earlier expected. "Mike's going back with me. We need him back there. Hell, we don't have a clue in headquarters what you jokers are doing out here." This joker, despite the humorous intent, certainly couldn't dispute this statement, but I needed to get to Mike. He wouldn't make it to lunch on his first day at HQ. Despite knowing little about that hallowed place on 1st Ave., I was certain that kicking wastebaskets off the walls was not how any HQ staff vented. And of all people, he was certainly not going for the alternative, slinking around corridors undoing reputations. Christ, I could just imagine him before the press. They'd excommunicate him if he even got that far. Mike still believed that defining the truth was possible.

———⊂▦⊃———

Jack, on the other hand, had a deep-seated sense of the relative and mysterious nature of truth, a sense which, by the time I arrived on his doorstep in Jerusalem, had completely alienated his staff. You see, Jack, by constitution, was incapable of diving into the general righteousness of the Palestinian cause. I suspected it was part weariness born of too many assignments amid mankind at its worst and part of a conscious decision to begin his retirement early. In any event, if the intent of the American Catholic Church was not to rock the boat in the occupied territory, then he was the man for the job. That Jack was considered an outcast by the other agencies was of absolutely no concern to him. He trod on their "sensitivities" regularly. Saw no reason, and wasn't shy to tell them, not to vacation in Israel, nor even for that matter not to dine in Israel: anathema to an expat community for whom solidarity meant living, eating and sleeping exclusively in Palestine.

Just hours after my arrival, in fact, still in the mutual embrace of our Lebanon days, he had walked me into a daily meeting of expat relief workers who were ardently 'sharing' about the situation in Lebanon, passing around petitions to various persons in power, and in general, indulging themselves in outrage and indignation. Stories from the front commanded a hushed respect.

There I was, a credible story in myself, but by mutual agreement with Jack an untold story on that day as we listened to the Oxfam director describe the war to the north. The room was rapt. I, too, while not rapt, found his accounts balanced. The room was perfectly silent as he slowly, deliberately, confirmed their dark suspicions. And, ever loyal to the company which pays me, I sat next to Jack amidst their general reverence for justice, focusing as I was on the speaker, when from my boss came a very full-bodied snore, right at a strategic pause. And when this roomful of ardor stared in disbelief at the desecration, they stared at us. I was certainly in no position nor had any inclination to shake Jack to attention, so I was left affecting this ridiculous position of chin in hand, maintaining my focus on the speaker, as if I were deaf to the snore on the seat next to me, while below the seat I shifted my legs casually, making sure to knock Jack's knee in the process. This caused the old relief veteran to snap awake and instinctively put his finger to his one good ear, and amidst all this rapt attention, bellow out, "What's that?"

We signed no petitions ("Would need Board approval," Jack instructed), and for once, quite like Mike, I certainly did sidle out.

With the exception of an occasional ride from one of the drivers, I would not receive more support: not from any possessiveness on Jack's part, but because he didn't want any complications.

Over the next couple of days, I met with Israeli officials. They were inconclusive, because unlike the West Bank, no one laid claim to Lebanon as a divine right. It was a security issue, no more or less, and what their current occupation meant concerning humanitarian assistance was still confused, at best. I could not even get a hearing.

After forty-eight hours, the only ones who had any opinions were the Israeli military who, upon receiving my suggestions for humanitarian assistance, simply sought to hijack the effort. "You give us the U.S. government monies and we will buy assistance for any Lebanese who may have gotten in the way. Sure, of course, you are welcome to see the distribution. Whenever you want," they said.

"Wonderful," I thought. CRS sets up an office inside an Israeli command post in Tyre and is available to witness Israeli troops pass out food to Lebanese. I feared this concept seemed so logical to the military types I spoke to that I now felt compelled to break off the interviews fast before this concept became unconditional.

Hanging over all this was the code word "Lebanese," by which the Israeli's meant "not a gram for Palestinians." Which could only be considered an absurdity since to a large extent the Lebanese population in the South had been spared. More than that, they had welcomed the invasion. It was, rather, the non-Lebanese who were in need: the Palestinian women, children, and elderly who had their camps demolished and who, for the most part, would die before they would accept help from someone sitting under the Star of David.

I did what would often serve me well over the years to come in this business: I ignored permissions, took a cab to the border, and, amidst all the dust and hollering of Israeli vehicles and long lines of civilians waiting for various permissions, I paid off the driver, threw my backpack over my shoulder and walked past it all, head up, whistling and nodding "Good morning" to all and sundry alike.

The Battle of Karbala

The defining moment in 680 AD when the legacy of Mohamad was riven by the internecine divisions regarding political affiliations as well as the faith and culture that would guide them.

Here, the **slain Imam Hussein** with his coterie of 72 faithful, in a shrinking perimeter on the plains of Karbala, died at the hands of 5000 opposing Muslims .

Henceforth, to this day, the virtues of extreme piety, martyrdom and passion remain prevalent among Imam Hussein's Shia descendants in southern Lebanon and southern Iraq.

Tyre

On the other side, there was business to be done. And for greenbacks or pounds there were cabs for hire, so I was soon on my way into Tyre. And while I should not have been, as Mike had warned me, I was nevertheless shocked by the welcome the invasion had received. From most homes and stores all along the route in and throughout the city, small replicas of the Star of David waved. I imagined how heartbroken those ardent relief workers in Jerusalem would have been: how they would not have believed their eyes.

I was not naïve, attributing most of it to self-preservation, to avoid their homes being reduced to rubble or even for a shopkeeper as a means to make a buck off a visiting army. But even so, a larger part of it, I suspected, was attributable to life in that lull when the PLO hand was off their throat and the Israeli one had yet to be fully felt.

AMAL (the Shia Militia) was everywhere and armed, even on the drive in, sharing checkpoints with Israeli soldiers and the Lebanese Forces (now, the Maronite Forces) who were also parading around. What a strange mix I drove into—Maronite, Shiite, and IDF all dancing on the Palestinian grave. As for Tyre, I had been expecting worse from what had reached me. The town was largely spared. The PLO had indeed left in advance of the Israeli columns. I made a deal with the cab driver, who agreed to be my driver for a week. We drove out to the Palestinian camps and saw where the violence had unfolded, where the uprooting had been done. It was now just a wasteland: a landscape of rubble, those few homes still left being dynamited as I watched. It was effectively an erasure, a harbinger of the massacres at Sabra and Shatila to come. Some cats and an old mad woman were the only living remnants.

"Where are they?" I asked an Israeli.

"Gone," he replied.

"I can see they are gone, but where to?"

He dismissed me. "Gone," he repeated. Though only a teenager, no older than those kids on the Zodiac, already he had the arrogance of a conquering army. Scholars and politicians can

go on ad nauseum about the theological basis for
Zionism or the duplicity of the Arab argument,
but what was undeniable for me that day was that
these Israeli troops were so much like me and my
friends: freckle-faced like Mike's girl, haystacked
like him, or with curls like me. They were us, in
feature and expression. They were not the strange
Yid on the East side, with a glass in his eye peering
into a watch. They were swimmers or soccer players
or disco dancers. And they certainly weren't from
the same tribe as the beautiful creatures Pen and I
had watched from our balcony outside Tripoli. No.
These were not attractive creatures. More like the
American mongrel, but with even less attention to
style. These were, simply put, foreigners in an Arab
world: as much of an intrusion as the Yanks in the
Philippines.

And if you are prone to stacking up the good
against the bad— as I am no longer able—then
Christendom unequivocally is the devil in all this.
The ruthless white Christian who either sanctioned
or turned away from the extermination of the Jew
and then in a post-war pang of shame gave them a
cherished place in an Arab world.

So, this joining of Maronite, Shia and Israeli
for the dance on the Palestinian grave would, I

figured, surely not last beyond the summer. It would start with a landmine over which an unsuspecting Israeli jeep would roll and end with full-scale guerrilla war. I would not be available to see this. But I had seen similar in Vietnam, and you really need only see that teenager at the check point with his practiced arrogance (feet up, reading a Playboy, and listening to a ballgame), to know how much he is an affront to Islam.

Meanwhile, I had work to do. The Sisters were waiting for me to call them forward, and the USG cash was already on deposit at CRS/HQ. So far, my passport had done the job: that together with some little laminated CRS ID and a presumptive self-importance I affected at each potential barrier, as if I had just been sent by no less than the Secretary of State himself. There were now, in the first instance, visits to be made. I needed staff; I needed an independent office; I needed suppliers; and I needed distribution and transport. I also needed, as fast as possible, to set up protection against being used in untoward ways by any party to the process, the latter need being the principal challenge. I knew enough greenbacks probably could take care of the rest, but only smarts could assure our independence.

I missed Mike. He had always been my mentor at times like this. I knew that they were out there: thousands of them in groves, on beaches, in warehouses. Fatah had not taken them with them as they had sped to South Beirut, and once the tanks had arrived at the gates entrance to the camp—well, my guess is they had fled in terror before the first shell ripped through their shelter. But I was also sure that there were enough good hearts in town to staff our effort to help these refugees, who were refugees twice over. For the rest—office, supplies, transport—I needed Bishop Haddad and Rabab, the sister of the Moussa Sadr, the Shia martyr, and now the nominal head of AMAL. But what, I wondered, would be the trade-off. Both would need something for their people, and then how much is left for the Palestinian refugees? Tread carefully, I warned myself.

As had been reported earlier by the BBC, Haddad had risen to the occasion. Many said he had saved the city with his stand on that first day. Now, I was hearing the details of that first night when the faithful had come and gathered in the church and prayed to be spared the onslaught. From inside, huddled in their church, they heard the crank, the whir of the mechanized units, the sporadic gunfire within the city, the detonations here and there. The incessant leveling of the camps.

There was no reason for this small Melkite community of Haddad to be attacked. They posed no threat. On the contrary, they were an intermediary with whom the Israelis could talk. But things go wrong all the time in war. All that was needed here was for some Palestinians to force themselves upon this Greek community and for one of them behave irrationally. The Israelis by inclination and training do not hesitate in such instances. The PLO has always, as a strategy and a tactic, hidden behind civilian populations, and the Israelis have usually pulled the trigger, regardless.

Haddad was overjoyed when I showed up on his doorstep. He couldn't believe his eyes, he told me, and then he gathered me in. "Now tell me: are you here to help? I have rooms for you. You need good people to help you." He stopped here. "You can't be too careful. I will get you good people."

I was thus besieged with hospitality. But I knew no good end could come if you allowed yourself to be captured by such gifts. However, I also knew that in these circumstances, I had to concede something. In the first instance, I needed a bed for the night, and while I could have had any bed in town for a price, choosing hosts at this unsettled moment had some dangerous aspects. And yes, I allowed that the Sisters would be pleased to share his hospitality, but, at every opportunity, I made clear that I could not burden him for more than a few days. Sophisticated and smart as he was, I'm not sure he understood. Debt creation and debt repayment was essential to the culture; the idea of maintaining an independence must have seemed absurd, and frankly wasn't worth the breath to try to explain. It was a fine line that first evening between respectful distance and estrangement. In the end, as we stood around his table preparing to bless the meal, we concluded we would discuss the subject later.

The dinner guests, except for me, were family, nearly all Haddad's relations. We discussed staff and supplies. I explained that where I bought and whom I hired had to reflect both Muslim and Christian constituencies. It was a double-edged sword for them also, I was told: not directly, but as implied by their questions. Who would get the assistance? Meaning, how deeply did the Greeks want to get involved with serving the homeless Palestinians? Other questions were aimed at how discreet I intended to be in doing this charitable act. I explained that though I would approve who was supposed to get it and then see who got it, I also wanted discretion.

That said, we would need to be a credible U.S. convoy to get past Israeli checkpoints where, undoubtedly, I would equivocate on the definition of "Lebanese" and hopefully would have enough Greek and Shia in the cabs to get away with it. So, I told them that could not be discreet, but assured them that once there amidst the refugees, we would do the drop as fast and as quietly as possible, and hope that the local Lebanese would not spoil it. Not this time, I thought. This time the taxpayer got no beneficiary registration nor calculated rations; it would be, in relief parlance, a "truck and dump" with a receipt from whomever was presumably in charge.

The situation I confronted, as I was to learn repeatedly in future such events, was not unusual. There is always that week or two after a conflict when the dust has yet to settle: when the old institutions are shattered and the new ones yet to open. This is the lull when the combatants are still trying to figure out what to do with their victory or their loss, as the case may be, and where there are no reference points for Relief Organizations, but also when the need, the humanitarian fallout from the war, is most tragic. This, I was to learn, is where agencies like

CRS either earn their pay or don't. Agencies with a certain self-confidence use the confusion to their advantage and move quickly through the dust to establish precedent. Those others who wait for the U.N. to establish terms are doomed to irrelevance at the most critical moment.

Thanks to Haddad, it was a good discussion, giving us all much to contemplate. God knows, that was what I was doing—contemplating—as I lay on fresh sheets, sucking away on my smoke and staring at the ceiling. All very confusing. And, then again, why do it? For Charlebois? For Howdy? What a joke. For the taxpayer? Most of them wouldn't even give a shit, should they ever lift a finger to find out. For Haddad? Long, long ago the Greeks here learned how to take care of themselves. For those Palestinian on the beaches? Yes. To that I could say yes, but a truckload now and then was little more than a palliative for what really ails them. For Pen, and Baby Hank? Probably, but then that's only because the papers define "hero" for them and once that stops getting reported, then I'm just absent. Off someplace in the Middle East.

As for me, to tell the truth I could walk tomorrow and not look back. Wandering around South Lebanon, map in hand, clearing up the

humanitarian mess left behind by the various
hegemons did not coincide, I felt, with the only
imperative I ever had after coming out of eighteen
months of neuropsychiatry in military hospitals:
to search for and cultivate as many transcendent
moments as possible. Depressing, these thoughts:
I knew I was just working myself up. I was going
to do it, just as I had raised my hand for Infantry
or in Paris had moved from the table in the living
room to the mattress. As in the past, I'd be driven
by personal momentum.

The next morning, I got to the other confessions.
The Maronite Bishop, who long before had fled
the troubles and his flock, had now reappeared. We
walked around Church property left unattended
since his earlier departure. It was what you would
expect in the lushness of the Litani Valley. Weeds
and seedlings of every variety had taken over the
gardens and walks. He decried the forces that had
caused such degradation.

We didn't know each other. I told him I
represented the Catholic Bishops of America
with a few bosses in-between. "Good, good," he
responded. "As you see, we need your help so
badly." He was pointing to a section of roof where
the tiles had slipped away. I explained that it was

USG money and could only be spent on victims of the war.

"Oh we have victims, many victims."

"From the war?" I asked, perplexed.

"They are poor," he said. I told him that maybe we could fit some of them in, but what I'd really prefer would be for him and his parishioners to reach out to the Palestinian refugees. He was old, and I'm not sure he heard me well, given my French, tainted by an American accent. He was bending over and pulling up a weed.

"You could do distributions from here," I said. He stared at me.

"You really don't understand anything, do you?" I started to answer, to tell him I thought I did but never got that far. He was going on about how pleasant life in Lebanon had been under Maronite leadership, "so tragically interrupted when we, from the goodness of our hearts, opened our land to the Palestinians." He paused. "We invited them into our house and they, in gratitude—they took the house and then tried to kick us out."

We had turned the corner of the old stone residence and were looking at a small plum orchard. Under one of the trees were refugees, obscured by the weeds, save for their heads. My first. The Bishop was concerned, so we walked over. It was one of the camp families, off by its own, missing its able-bodied men. Weathered old men, children entranced, crying babies snatched up by proud women. The Bishop began talking to their old men. To my surprise, he was not really talking but scolding: a high-pitched scolding which apparently was no surprise to the women who had already started to pack their blankets and a few utensils. I just stood there helpless, not understanding much of the Arabic but certainly understanding when the Bishop gestured at them with his hand to be gone, after which the Palestinian women spit on the ground and started moving off.

With the Bible as my guide—graduate of Sunday school and confirmed in the faith at sixteen—and died in the wool agnostic that I am, I was aghast. "Scum," the Bishop said to me as we walked back to the residence. It's all aside, I concluded later. All of it aside or only contributory. In the end, Christ is aside: as is Allah, I suppose. At the end of the day, all that matters is tribe—tribe and their land.

Inside, even in the disrepair there an impeccable Sister to serve us. He had brought several with him, in fact. Fresh orange juice and a bitter Turkish. He directed my attention to the room. Pointed to the outlines of stolen paintings and icons, and then raised both his hands toward Heaven. "God help us," he said. He frowned when I told him I had met with Haddad, but did not offer an alternative and reopened his earlier inquiry into "help." "You see how we are forced to live," he said. "Tell your Bishops." I nodded that I would. He raised his cup. "I will write them, too." I felt like telling him it had little to do with Catholic Bishops: that it was all taxpayer money and that he would get enough to shut him up, but obviously the notion I came with—of Christ's representative reaching out to the victims—was DOA, not a notion to be realized here.

Next stop, Shia, I thought as I gave the driver directions. We would go to Mike's local contractor for 1651. Presumably he would get me to where I needed to go, where we would enjoy the advantages of AMAL's influence. This, indeed, would be terra incognita. With the Christians and the Israelis, there were, at a minimum, some common experiences (however variously interpreted): the Holocaust and America. But here I was entering a more mysterious Shia realm and one which was by no means a monolith. Where I would fit into the various dynamics—stretching from Latif Zayne to the Iranian guards in Baalbek to the ladies from South

Beirut, who had brought the trousseau to Hank, now to Rabab, the sister of the martyred Moussa Sadr—was anyone's guess. However, I was sure of one thing: with the recent erasure of the PLO, the Shia held more consequence than ever before. And so, if inclined, they could easily arrange to see the last of me by sunset. In the end, I was counting on that magnificent contract, 1651, to still rule as Mike had told me at every drunken opportunity. I would be ushered into her presence on the heels of millions of dollars of assistance, once provided from my now-departed friend.

They all bristle to a degree at all the various houses for militia. But here I sensed it was more equivocal. A different disposition to those guards at the Palmyra. It was not some desperate recruit tilted back against the wall with an AK at the ready.

I was taken into the sanctum in the company of Allah's warriors, not a smile among them as I was being directed down the halls. Concrete, black beards, black clothes, and black frames for Moussa Sadr. A somber interior with here and there some striking red calligraphy, advising the faithful. She was at the middle of a semicircle flanked by her commanders: men dressed uniformly, ritualistically going through their beads.

Talk about coal black and milk white. Well, of course, not to compare with those Sunnite creatures dancing in their Paris creations south of Tripoli. But it was against all black that her white hands fluttered like a bird, most often fluttering upward to reveal or to draw closed the scarf over part of her face. For me, a worried soul from northern Connecticut, flanked by commanders and against the backdrop of black Sharia, standing before all this readiness for sacrifice as signaled in the red Arabic script. For me, those white fluttering hands, lifting and closing her veil. For me she allowed a glimpse here and there of a smile and a twinkle: so deftly done that it became an unexpected flirtation greater than I had seen in the West. Imagine, in the midst of all that black death dealing to her right and left, she was now telling a joke which amused the commanders, now pushing peanuts toward me and asking about Jimmy Carter, then drawing the veil on a smile and asking what she could do for me.

So now, completely infatuated, I told her everything I knew: she found such enthusiasm to be amusing and so did her commanders. How I knew of the struggles between Fatah and AMAL but was trusting that she held nothing against families such as I had met in the Maronite orchard and would assist me to help them. "How so," she asked with a smile, which I swear in another world, alone, would have invited an embrace. I told her I wanted three things. She made a sign to one of her men. "Go ahead," she said.

"First, I need to be able to say that you support what I am doing and that if I have problems, I can come to you." She held up two fingers. "Second, I need a few men to help me deliver the assistance." She nodded. "And third, I need a house which can enjoy the protection of AMAL." I stopped and thought for a while. There was no response, for long enough that I was prepared to open up again with some more explanation, but she raised her hand.

"And what can you do for us?" It was a question to which I admitted an ignorance. But by the time I was back in bed at Haddad's residence, sucking my smoke and staring at the ceiling, I was figuring that things were better. My gut was somewhat relieved. I had put nothing in it all day except for a couple of shots of Turkish and the swelling had subsided. It was really a quite predictable remedy I thought: just stop eating and the gut will heal. I shot a few more nice circles of smoke skyward. As for the mission, I murmured, well, the rest of the pieces were starting to come together. Haddad's men would supply me, which made sense, since they were the merchants in town, and it would have amazed me if they couldn't have acquired food under any circumstance. The Greeks and the Shia would both give me university students who would not be at school for some time now. And AMAL had already done what was necessary (I didn't want to inquire about the details) to rent me two furnished houses: one for the office and my bedroom, the other catty-corner across a square for the Sisters, to whom that afternoon I had sent an invitation, courtesy of an Israeli returning home on leave.

The price from AMAL and Haddad was shelter. They didn't want food. But homes, they argued, had been damaged in the fighting. I had some doubts about the extent of the so-called collateral damage from the recent invasion, but if the damage was not held to be specific to it, well then, what the hell. In the end, I figured, as long as we are dealing with some destitute, who cares if we are repairing Israeli damage or PLO damage.

The trouble was that shelter swallowed up a lot of greenbacks for a relatively small number of beneficiaries. But what it did do, the Greek Bishop had countered, was worth more than the repairs. It got people back to work. It gave signs of renewal after years of despair. And so, I was sold. I didn't have much choice, if I wanted the program to happen.

However, I did dig in on one issue. The Sisters and the rest of my staff would qualify and pick the recipients. I was obstinate and they found me such. But I'd be damned if, in diverting 35% of the aid away from those most in need, I would just slide the envelope across the desk the way that Bishop in East Beirut had insisted. "No way," I said. "They come: we register them. We examine their damage and then we approve or not for the repairs." They finally gave up on me, shaking their heads and saying they hoped I'd come to my senses, sooner rather than later.

Later that night, on my mattress, I considered how I had been with CRS for a year now and, other than Vache's mother and Kluiters, had yet to meet any genuine follower of Christ. From my first interview for the job, no employee, it seemed, pursued those higher ambitions. Some like Jack, other than the cross hanging in the foyer of his office, were really no different than any other bloke hurrying on until retirement. And the others were remarkable sinners by any standard.

But Sister Mary and her brood of Holy Cross religious were different. I wondered what the people of Tyre must have thought. I mean, this was eye-catching plain. Denim skirt, white blouse with cross and Dr. Scholl's shoes—spreading their change out on the counter and pointing at a chicken or a carton of milk. They brought no knowledge of the historical forces which had produced the situation they were in. They brought, and I know it sounds preposterous, an uncomplicated faith in hard work, a pleasant demeanor and a humility before their Maker. No righteousness, no mad hunt for a glimpse of His hem, no perch for Castaneda's crow. Instead, there was a tendency to massacre every foreign name in South Lebanon, permed white curls, owl spectacles, and two glasses of sherry after dinner. It was as if Sister Mary had been lifted up from a community in Indiana then dropped into Tyre to do just exactly as she had done in Indiana.

When Sister Mary handed me a half million in greenbacks, she said, "Gosh, now what are you going to do with it?"

It was, in fact, a quandary I had not been able to get around. I would pay the Greeks as much as I could upfront for the trucks and food, and do the same with rent and salaries, but that still would leave me with more than four hundred grand I had no prospect of safekeeping. To complicate matters, this was USG money, and I was, relatively speaking, still a new dick: once we started dispensing cash for shelter repairs, most of the town would know about this unprotected stash. I had little doubt that if it disappeared, I would be suspected.

Curfew was just before sunset, and by the second evening of their arrival, Sister Mary and her team spent their nights catty-corner from my house. She guessed that, contrary to initial expectations, Bishop Haddad had been less than reluctant to see them safely transferred. My sense was that their denim and perms represented a very hot potato within that medieval way of life.

That first night I felt quite vulnerable, alone in this three-story house, fading light outside, in a city with untold scores yet to be settled, sitting for a while by my candle with Tio Pepe, considering tomorrow and then laying down my defenses as I retired up the stairs to my bedroom. "Early warning devices," we called them in the Army. For me it was a series of strings and broom handles, strung and placed across all the ways to my room. Finally, I stood back with my flashlight and reviewed the maze of obstacles I had created. I could see no possibility for an advance on me without an ungodly racket preceding it. Then I tied a rope I got from our fisherman to the leg of my bed, put some knots in, and coiled it by the window.

The cash was in a green pillowcase, next to me in bed. What I would do in an alley in my underpants with a pillowcase of cash I had not considered in detail: there were too many variables. "Now get some sleep," I said, climbing into bed.

Against all the preceding nonsense with Charlebois and then Howdy, and what with failed projects and tribal Bishops, the next morning, I told myself, needed to be the beginning of our relief. Typically, as I've come to know, it is at first light and may be in a courtyard or under a tree. Here it was the circle of young university students and Holy Cross Sisters with our mugs of coffee in the morning chill. We are holding the mugs for warmth. We have no commo and so assignments must be clear. Contingencies must be established as well as rendezvous times and coordinates: and, of course, what we must minimally achieve, and what we absolutely cannot do. Sister Mary and her team would manage shelter and office administration: the students and I, the convoys.

By then the dark was receding, and the first of Tyre's citizens were appearing in the square and noticing this very strange collection shifting their feet, cradling cups, and how, increasingly, the "Ajnabi" in the center was checking his watch.

318

Then we heard the diesels and during the time it took them—deuce-and-a-half's with CRS marked on the canvas flaps—to roll into the square, well, for that ten minutes our circle was electric.

Now we had to move. For the last time I got my wide-eyed students together, watching the presumption and confidence of an American with more faith than it deserved. "I talk to the Israelis. Everyone understand?" They nodded. "Only I," I repeated. "And we stay together no matter what. No truck peeling off to visit his cousin's village. Okay?" They smiled. "And when we get there, no one touches the food until I signal." More nods. Then there was the big respiration, a familiar habit from school-boy races. "Okay," I said. "Let's go."

We were off, down as many back roads as our students knew, seldom hitting a checkpoint and when we did, working it as planned, waving my U.S. passport around, saying, "Gift from the American government for those hurt in the war." They didn't give a shit: the Israelis, that is. Once or twice the Lebanese militia behind them started poking about, but when our relations to Haddad and AMAL were presented, they also backed off.

They had been scattered by the violence. A displaced family in an orchard, several together in

an empty warehouse, others in the rocks by the sea.
There was no throng, no biblical movement, such as
we would see in Ethiopia. No, here they were, from a
bird's eye view mostly invisible. But once you knew
where to look, where they would be secluded, they
quickly added up. To find them I would, through my
students, ask a Lebanese bystander, who most often
would grudgingly point at a building or a place and
walk off, and then my sidekicks and I would enter
the shelter and ask for a leader. Usually, it was an
old man to whom we would describe our purpose but
often not before word had got out and a group of
women had found us.

We tried to isolate the discussion, but that was
sometimes not possible, and then the back and forth
got played out in the crowd. The old men tended to
be thankful, showed us a place to store it, and got
some young boys to help unload. The women were
much more volatile. At best, not stirring, in a corner
looking at us, quite sullen and disrespectful. At
worst, one began a loud harangue, shouting at us to
get out and take our little presents with us. Even as
the boys were bringing in the food, she was breaking
through the others, grabbing at the packages and
trying to throw them back at us. She and some
others were screaming at the students, words I could

not understand but which in one instance caused my sidekick who was translating for me to step away. Whatever they said hit home.

But in the end, the children needed to eat and, in time, a majority were able to quiet the dissent enough to allow the food in. Outside it was not going so well. They were unloading like it was a Sunday picnic, and some Lebanese were starting to gather around: a few of my drivers and students were talking with them. I knew this was playing with dynamite. Too much blood spilled. Not even a modest food drop would be seen as innocent.

"Damn it!" I was yelling at my students. "This is not one bag at a time. Go on, get up there," I said. They balked. They were reluctant to join the Palestinian boys in the unloading. "Damn it," I repeated. I got up on the bed myself and started gesturing at the boys to line up at the tailgate five abreast. Then I grabbed the sack and put it on the first kid's shoulder, then another sack on the next boy. The Palestinian kids were already smiling and joking about the foreigner up on the bed. Then my sidekick got up beside me and others followed. He told me I must get down now: "It's not good for you to be up here."

"Fine," I said. I knew what he was talking about. "But are you guys going to move this stuff?" And so they got into it, finally. When I got off, a bystander came up and asked what this was about. "Gifts of food from America," I told him. "Just for them?" he asked. I looked at his face and could see his intent. New as I was, I knew this could blow up any second into a fight over the remaining contents of the truck and then a fight over Palestinians in their neighborhood. It wasn't hard, at that moment, to envision a mob of Lebanese driving the Palestinians out of their shelter. And once that incident catches the attention of the Israelis, they figure they don't need it and I get detained. "There are shelter programs for Lebanese," I said quickly. "Food for refugees, and repairs for Lebanese whose homes were damaged in the war." He and several others looked at me very circumspect. "Here," I said, giving him our office address. "We register tomorrow." He turned the piece of paper over slowly and then, thank God, walked away.

We've got to get better. That was the gist of my ruminations with Tio Pepe that night. Get our scouts out in the afternoons to do the discussions without the trucks parked outside. It wasn't improbable, I thought, that our little presents could ignite more war. God, what a day. The images multiplied in my mind. The morning huddle in the square; my sidekick pained from the abuse by the Palestinian mother; the dark suspicions of the Lebanese bystanders. Here's to you, Tio, I thought, clinking my glass against the little red sombrero. And not one thank you. The only visible joy we brought was to those twelve-year-olds who helped unload and were probably still laughing at the funny foreigner with the sacks of flour in his arms. It's true, giving implies an inequality. An unjustifiable inequality, I suppose. "Giving," I said, as I slugged down another tequila, "is a very dangerous proposition." Then I screwed on Tio's cap and proceeded up the stairs, laying my protective devices behind me.

The next morning, we did a "lessons learned" in the square and then repeated the exercise. Again, no fuss at the checkpoints, and we didn't bring the trucks up into view until my discussions at the shelters were concluded. And this time the students got their hands dirty: for the sake, I suspected, of that crazy American. They were quickly becoming vets: those that stayed, that is. Two never returned after the first day. Their parents, I suspected, thought the association with Americans or Palestinians or Christians was just too dangerous. But others, more than we could use, showed up at the morning briefing.

When I got back to the office at noon, I was surprised to see that the Sisters had only processed three requests for repairs to war-damaged homes, despite impeccable preparation, registration forms, translators, interview cubicles, questionnaires, and ledgers. Christ. This could have been the loan department at the First National Bank. "Yep," Sister Mary smiled, "All dressed up and nowhere to go."

"What about the three who came?" I asked.

"Zip. You know, I get the feeling this is too complicated."

"What do you mean?" I asked.

"Well, we don't reimburse the person who has already started a repair, we don't give enough for the person who has major damage, and we can't help those with other assets. And that's why it was zip."

"What do you suggest?" I asked. "If we do whole houses, then we're talking thirty homes before the pot is empty. Thirty homes for all of Tyre. And if we take past receipts, my guess is that would qualify half the population, and we sure as heck don't want to hand over our dollars to someone who has two other houses in good shape."

Sister Mary sighed, deferring to my in-country experience, but still looking unconvinced. "I suppose so," she said.

I approached our 1651 engineer and asked why no one showed. And then more directly, I asked, "Did you tell folks?" He demurred. I started to get upset. "I mean, shit, your leaders asked for the help."

To this, he repeated something about the common anxiety over at AMAL: that it was better for them to do it. "We know the people."

That's just the problem, I thought: we don't want to "know" the people. We just want to know the facts. But I kept my mouth shut. There were implicit limits to frankness here, lest I forget that coiled rope by my window. "Look, my friend, if we don't get any clients, the money doesn't get spent and then we all lose," I said. After parting courtesies, he acknowledged my argument and said he'd confer.

There we were in the morning mist, shifting our feet and cradling our mugs of hot coffee, when the first souls emerged from various alleys and streets leading into the square. We initially thought them to be early customers to the port for fish, or the devout heading to an early gathering at the mosque, and so we shifted and sipped and waited for the excitement of the first sound of the diesels.

But soon enough it dawned on us that they were coming at us. A scattered few at first, and then, by the time the trucks had turned onto the square, a distinct trickle. They confirmed they were there for shelter monies. We thanked them for coming, and told them to form a line at the gate to our office. But Arabs don't do lines. The Brits do lines. Arabs do semicircles: whether it be wells or windows at the post office or the gates of the CRS suboffice in Tyre. And so, as we had started to get ourselves up into cabs, we had seen the semicircle form, with all its inherent jostling and reaching. I did have second thoughts about leaving this with the Sisters but after some consideration, figured this is what they do. Plainly, dispassionately, pleasantly, they put order to things. I signaled for the trucks to move.

By noon we had finished with the day's drops and were returning to our neighborhood. I suppose I was not too occupied at the time with the early morning's developments, even as our trucks were slowed down at the periphery of our square. Soon enough, however, the congestion had become enough of a hindrance for me to suggest that we let the trucks go their way and proceed on foot.

We are all familiar with the feeling. We walk toward our place, increasingly amidst many others going our way. We begin to suspect. We start, usually, to think of fire or some such calamity, and we get anxious and quicken our pace. And then we turn the corner.

The morning semicircle of perhaps thirty souls now had spread into a great press of population, a cacophony of shouts and cries, with hundreds pushing toward our one flimsy gate, many waving small pieces of paper in their hands.

It was a sort of "What hath God wrought?" feeling, a moment's hesitation on the edge of it when it occurs to you to just walk away. But then you turn your back on this fantasy and begin wading through the crowd. The students began acting like bodyguards for a celebrity, around whom the town's citizenry was now pushing in, seeking eye contact from me with that long-cultivated Arab expression of weakness and need: seeking eye contact with Saidna.

Said Saidna plowed onward with increasing difficulty toward the gate—his entourage of students yelling for passage—which was slowly being achieved, I sensed, because the crowd wanted to believe that this foreigner held the key to their satisfaction.

The actual gate was the crux of the challenge. It was, at that moment, being held shut by one rather rusty bolt, the weight of all our administrative staff, and one dedicated Holy Cross Sister. To squeeze in without opening the flood gates took all the passion and energy our students could muster. This was a half-dozen young men in the dust and chaos, under the noonday sun, trying to push and harangue what were mostly mothers back a few feet so Saidna could slip by.

Inside, I walked into another fight. Sister Mary, by way of an obviously exhausted translator, was, arms akimbo, repeating "Tell her I said no. It's over." But looking at the woman and the two infants in her arms, it was obvious she was not about to leave, save someone taking a stick to her. She was close to hysteria, waving the paper and menacing the other woman in the room who was giving it back to her.

"Are we glad to see you," said Mary.

"What's this all about?" I asked, now fully appreciating the rising din outside, prompted by my arrival.

"We qualified her," she replied, pointing to the other woman, "but not this one, and now this one is saying—as I understand—that the first recipient is a fraud, something about her husband being in

Texas and having plenty while she can't even feed her kids."

I looked at the women. They had gotten the gist of what Mary had said. The deprived was busy looking pitiful, wiping the kid's nose, wiping her eyes: the other, indignant at the affront.

"She won't go," said Mary, "and I've told our staff no more through the gate until this one leaves."

"What's all this paper in their hands?"

"Receipts," Mary answered. She was smiling kindly at me. "I think AMAL got out the wrong message."

Just then we heard a surge in the clamor outside. I was desperately trying to be calm, in part for these Sisters, who against growing odds were still sticking to their middle-American principles: arms crossed, smiling and hanging onto the rules, albeit a bit white-knuckled. But I was sweating. I had that familiar trickle coming down my ribs, and I was seeing clearly the dam bursting and the building and all its contents being swept away, Holy Cross heads bobbing on the crest and greenbacks fluttering over the spray. My sidekick was looking even more distraught—about ready to quit at the futility of it all—obviously a young man whose life was being changed.

He urged me toward the balcony, and I looked out over the proverbial sea of faces: a small taste of what a dictator must feel. People were nudging each other to be silent. I was lost for words as I gazed over all those uplifted and expectant faces. And so there I was, an odd sight: presenting myself on the balcony, hands on the balustrade. I looked at the student. "Make sure you say it loud and slow." I started by expressing my sorrow at what had befallen the city, not just last week but over the past many years. And I continued by advising them of the long commitment and friendship CRS had had with them—with the fisherman, for example—and now relief was here along with my good staff so as to continue the help.

Many were making affirming motions with their heads. "But now, today, I must tell you that we cannot help you, this way." I swept my hands across the crowd as the translation went forward. "This is not a good way to help you." I could see the mood shifting. People know, particularly poor people, when they are being stiffed. And God knows it is unlikely that my sidekick was doing all this translation honey-tongued. He was a teenager, probably scared to death he would piss his pants for all to see. "So please," I was concluding, "please go home. We will not abandon you. We will visit you."

And now I could see two developments of opposite force. Some, particularly on the edges of the crowd, and more often men, were leaving, but, nearer to the gate, others were refusing and pressing harder. Die-hards. Perhaps half of all those in the square. "Please, louder," I told the student. "Please go away. We will contact you when there is a better way."

But they didn't move. In fact, they put their hands toward the balcony and turned them up and down, gesturing "What about me? Be merciful."

"You better go back in," the student told me. But I was thinking to resume my pleading. He tugged at my elbow, begging me. "Please—they will stay if they see you." In any case, if I did not heed, I would be doing it in English since he, obviously, was not going on.

Inside the aggrieved woman was still dug in, confronting Mary with the injustice of her disapproval, alternately calling the children to attention or shifting arms with the baby and firing outbursts at Mary. It was the abuse of Mary that got me. I had had enough. The blackmail of this woman: that this plaintiff would create such disturbance until we paid her to leave and then, by God, she'd be dripping with Saidna's. I knew poverty was not holes in pants or even flies on the kid's face. This was poverty in its truest state.

But I was too fragile myself at that moment and so I exploded, striding to the door and commanding her to get out. "Now," I shouted in Arabic. She saw that I was about to physically push her out in the next instant if she didn't obey and so she moved from stubborn to ugly. God knows what she said, but the translators would not translate it. I followed her down to the gate, nudging her and her kids with my fist, cold-eyed as I could be. She would not help us. She stuck herself in the small opening in the gate and when I pushed her through into the crowd, she left her children in the gap. And finally, when I had pried their hands off the grate and pushed them out, she dug in into the first row and started exhorting the crowd to demand justice, as was the rough translation.

The gate was beginning to buckle. That one rusty bolt was what was left between us and a riot. Small kids were scaling the pikes, away from the gate with my students admonishing them and prodding their bellies with sticks. Smaller children and one very wizened woman, whom I could see, were being trampled: the children bawling and the skinny, hunchbacked old woman trying to pull herself up on someone's legs. "Let me out," I said.

"No sir," Mary's translator told me. "You can't go out there."

"Why," I asked.

"Because they will step on you."

I pushed myself through the grate and eventually a small pocket—about arms-length—materialized. Roughly a yard, I figured, of some sort of residual awe for the foreigner. But every sense I had warned me that it would be gone in a second. I held up my arms and in my pitiful Arabic I beseeched them to go home. "Closed," I kept saying. "It is closed." But they weren't listening. Some kids crawled into the pocket and grabbed my legs, and then the crush of women and old men followed. My back pressed against the grate, my arms still in the air, I continued my exclamations in execrable Arabic, with some of my students now openly weeping and the Sisters increasingly occupied with those boys scaling the pikes.

And then, as if from Heaven, there were shots. A burst of five. Followed by a few more bursts. I ducked down on my knees, as did some of the Sisters. I looked at the balcony where Sister Mary had cupped her hands and was shouting "AMAL, AMAL" at me and pointing beyond the crowd. I looked up from my crouch and saw the women around me: big in their black-robed abayas, looking down on me quizzically, some even smiling, as if Saidna was now the clown. And then, very fast, they parted, and AMAL militia advanced through, the women advising from the sidelines, presumably about justice, and me, now up from my crouch, dusting off my pants and seeing some serious bearded men coming at me.

There was an immediate hush. I pulled the translator out from the other side of the gate. I began to explain when some of the women started up again. The militia snapped their heads and lowered the AK's: fearful silence resumed. When I had finished, they just nodded. No smile. No questions. They just turned and told the crowd to go home which with, only a murmur or two and some baby's cry, they obeyed, moving off. "They want you to come with them," the translator said. I told her to come with me.

I met again with the cadre: not with the Rabab herself but with a couple of the commanders who had been present that day. It was one of the shortest and most pleasant meetings I was to have in Lebanon. No doubt, the relief of not being at the brink of collapse smoothed the way. I felt delivered, from my back to the gate with a hundred angry mothers and children trying to crush me, and then in one charge, I imagined, occupying my office and house. Yes, indeed, from that to where I was now bringing the demitasse of Turkish to my lips and agreeing that, yes, it was better for AMAL to manage this. In a bid to save something minimal: we would still insist on approving selection criteria and monitoring expenditures, I said. "Well of course, my friend," the commander said, probably fully aware that anything that transpired with selection and disbursement would be surely inscrutable to me.

That evening, after the curfew had prompted the Sisters to leave for their house, I was left again by myself on that same balcony where so much passion had occurred, very relaxed now, looking at the emptiness with my habitual bottle of Tio Pepe and tea glass. Along with my supper, that tonight would be a few packages of high protein biscuits I had requisitioned from the rations.

If I tilted back, the woman's words would ring in my ears, as if absorbed and now emitted from the walls of the office behind me.

The injustice, she had screamed. Many times. The shrill resonance in my ears led me back, through faded memories, to my formative years.

Those years when I would bounce from dilettante to débauche, trolling at sour hour in Saratoga for some cheap loveliness or whetting my appetite for the exotic. Sleeping off inordinate whiskies in an East Side flophouse or holding hands with black Louis from Senegal at the Colonie des Vacances. Or, as wayward student, unwashed and foul breathed, listening to Prof. Kurtz about man's relation to nature and man's relation to man, the whole balance of Earth and Sun reflected in the allied and opposing forces of centrifugal/gravity. The human dynamics of longing for it—the fiery center—and escaping from it. That wonderful dynamic of light and shade. The donkey moving within the daily changes of the shade: the Israelis in South Lebanon for the water, not the PLO.

"So," Kurtz had said—I could see him clearly— his pale face talking to, in my mother's words, what the cat had dragged in. "Sun Shade Water. If you're to understand the Middle East, you must understand those forces. The water above and the water below. Below," he had droned on to a mostly inattentive class, "is the Nile, the Tigris and the Euphrates. It's the allowances which the water below gives to divinity on Earth. The pyramid of control. Which, in these climes, is over sustenance: water and shade.

The dependence on the king for relief from the deadly life-giving forces of the sun."

I would watch him from the back row with his black strands of hair falling over his colorless face, addressing some place midway between the back row and the ceiling. I always wondered how he stood it. These profound emissions filling the air above a class that was half asleep. I, snug in the ratty Army jacket, sensing the uselessness of talking to my neighbors, the Philistines. The bruisers who sometimes had marked me for my high voice or whose instincts had them suspecting my struggles with the "pubic impasse."

"And the water above," he had continued in his monotone. "Falling from a mysterious heaven on every man equally." No earthly hand on the spigot, I thought. "Shepherds with small ruminants. No irrigation systems. Only pastures and grazing." And then he had made his point, as we approached the end of the period. Jesus was the direct descendant of the culture of the water above. He was that part of the human genome which aspires toward the mysterious origins of sustenance and revolts against the presumption of man knowing. Christ as the power emerging for water falling on every man equally. "Christ," he had scribbled on the blackboard, is the "antithesis of human authority." "Funny," he said, mostly to himself as a private joke, I guessed. He was picking up his reference: Genesis, in fact. "Christ as the reputed soul of the Catholic Church which is quite 'water below.'" Again, he chuckled. Then the bell rang and the grunts filed out, and I remained quite confused how he could waste all that wisdom and intelligence on such slope heads.

Of course, it was unjust to deny her. But what was I going to tell her? That we—she and I—were trapped in the water below where even Jesus had been hijacked, where the Justice of Everyman had been violated continuously since the ascent of King David? That I must make decisions within the jurisdiction of the water below, that employs me? At this point in my reminiscing, I rubbed my eyes then tapped my tumbler against Tio's sombrero. "Mush Hayk, my friend."

Within a week, we had our routines, which, with few exceptions, would stay with us until the taxpayers' money had run out. By now, the Israelis knew what we were doing. However, the amounts were so minimal against the need and the fighters so absent among the recipients, that they were largely unconcerned about our morning adventures on the back roads. In fact, it spared them the worry and the expense of having to arrange for those displaced themselves. Particularly now, since the dust was indeed starting to settle.

There was foreboding for them, on two grounds. First, the little Star of David flags which had been waved so enthusiastically the day after their tanks had rolled in were now, just a few weeks later, becoming hard to find. Whatever the practical benefits of having the PLO erased, any further or continued alliance with Israel would be too much of an embarrassment in the Arab and Persian capitals. Word had certainly gotten out. And second, the international Red Cross and some other relief agencies had also arrived, along with some press from Israel. That is to say: there were witnesses now. So that's where we were, Star of David slowly but surely disappearing, but no definitive rupture yet with AMAL, and no grenade yet to roll under an Israeli jeep. Along with more good hearts now snooping around and holding Israel's feet closer to the fire, on humanitarian issues.

Meanwhile, in the North, the situation remained unchanged. The Israeli air force had the PLO in South Beirut like fish in a barrel but yet were stymied by both domestic and international opinion to go in and root them out. And, as yet, I had had no news from Joe on the proposed Mercy Convoys into Beirut. For all I knew he and his pincer were back in Cyprus or drinking coffee with the well-coiffed in Jounieh Port.

Thanks to the Holy Cross Sisters, systems got settled, reports were made, and we had created our own internal interlude of calm. Even the militia was charmed by Mary and her cohorts, who were deferential enough to suit them and so hard-working that the popular joke among the commanders was that Mary must be part Shia. "A good Muslim," the commander smiled. In any case, we managed, far more than we ever had with the Maronite Bishop, to be partners in the process, both selection and monitoring.

In consideration of such progress, I had declared the following Sunday a holiday: "for repairs," I told my students. They looked at me, puzzled. I tapped my head. "To get away."

Which for me meant, to see "neither hide nor hair" of CRS. I had a date with my supplier, one of the patriarchs of the Haddad clan. He had invited me to lunch at his villa in the old town.

From the alley, its inside was evidently meant to be kept secret. You needed to walk some distance down the cobblestones against a broad stone wall to reach one small iron door at the end. Then you had to tread up a dozen stone steps in what seemed like a tunnel, finally, to reach a door which, when opened, took you quite spectacularly into their world, a spacious central room with marble floors, high ceiling fans and a wide array of French doors and windows, all of which opened onto the terrace and beyond that onto the Mediterranean, the curtains waving in the breeze.

On one side of the room was a huge table made from olive wood, as I was told, with some twenty chairs around it, the table bedecked with flowers and fruit. Beyond it were sofas and easy chairs, carpets and brass tables, and though they were numerous, there, in that space, they looked almost incidental, movable in small ensembles or into larger circles. Off on the other side, I assumed, were the bedrooms.

Living was easy here for the rich, whether it was Abdul-Latif on his Nabatiyeh plantation or the Haddad clan in their Tyre villa. It was, as it was at that soiree near Tripoli, the throwing on of a Paris creation over a slender female's naked body, which moved here amidst marble and stone, and damask curtains and the dozen pieces of handmade furniture almost scattered about. Not a sign, not here, of that northern hemisphere disposition for tight boxes full of clutter or bundling in all sorts of layers.

It was amazing how peaceful that afternoon was, only few weeks since the invasion. Leaning back in my seersucker, talking to the merchant on the terrace. And beyond the terrace, a rocky apron, upon which that afternoon were two of those half-clad creations, though hardly milk-white today: brown breasts rising to the sun. And beyond that, the ruins of ancient Phoenicia, and beyond still, an island to which their brother and I would swim later on.

We shifted to the table. Others were already there, dining on the riches of the Litani. The conversations circulated in several languages, guests came and went, plates were removed and replenished, a friendly challenge across the length of the great table. The head of the table patted a chair for someone to come up to him for some conversation. A conviviality amidst plenty. A sunbather asked me what I was doing in Tyre, then picked up an olive and rolled it slowly about her mouth while I answered.

Afterward, the two sunbathers accompanied me and the younger Haddad out to the edge of the rocks from where we were to launch our swim. When I saw they were distracted, shouting something back to the terrace, I quickly took my shirt off, revealing

the pink scars from Chu Lai, and dropped down first
into the swirl around the rocks and then pulled away
a few strokes, seeking to avoid getting dashed upon
them. The younger Haddad joined me. I frolicked in
the waves, porpoise-like, shaking out the sweat and
grime and Tio of the last several weeks. The women
were pulling off their dresses and then, seeing my gaze,
raised their hands high, waving, brown breasts waving.
I rolled back on my abdomen and began swimming in
earnest. It felt like a purification, looking down onto
the seaweed and the colored fish, the silver bubbles
of air surfacing aside my face, the stretch of my long
arm, the cold along my ribs. I remembered myself as
a swimmer since my mother had brought me down to
Rose Bay in the early morning hours, since weekends
diving into the breakers at Bondi.

But it was hard to imagine an imagination so
untouched by reality. The war in Vietnam, hospitals,
dysentery and cholera in Africa. The entrepreneur's
life and the years of Friday night shots for success.
That original madness in Paris. And now a year with
Tio and Marlboros.

And yet, I did not think twice about striking out
from the coast. I am a swimmer. I am an Australian
and American swimmer. It was a mythology which
didn't need proving. And then the bottom started

to get murky, and larger waves slapped across my face when I turned for a breath. My arms began to feel heavy. And, of course, the island seemed as far away as ever. The younger Haddad, practicing his breaststroke with an inner tube around his belly, was now checking on my stamina. An American's stamina. I felt that same old crazy obligation, despite all its sins, to be the American. To be man's best bet, as they say. And so I persisted in pulling my heavy arms through the water. 1, 2, 3, 4, I started the cadence, just like with Sergeant Mitchell in boot camp. Hey Bo Diddly Bo. But then I got an inadvertent gulp of Homer's wine dark sea, and Haddad the younger, feeling a special obligation not to let me drown, tried to push the inner tube on me. I would rather die, and so I told him no, but he persisted, and, feeling he was trying to humiliate the American, I pushed him and the tube away.

By now—between my gulp of Homer's Sea and my struggle with this butterball in the tube—we had drifted down the coast and were farther away than ever. I started to despair about making it to the island, and then shuddered to think I might not make it at all. Period. But without any way out, or too little blood to my brain, I blindly stuck to my stroking, which I guess caused even more alarm up on the distant terrace, for soon there was a launch coming out from around the rocks from where we departed, headed toward me.

Lying on the sheet that night—one hand on my penis and the other on my smoke—I felt shrunken in my own esteem, and in some others', I assumed. My nerves were shot. I was starting to believe that I had had it. At first, it'd been fear, and then it was the constant doses of Turkish and Tio, followed by the increased frequency of swollen gut from that. And now, most recently, after curfew, the loneliness of sitting on the balcony and studying the empty square.

Indeed, we were draining that pot of taxpayer monies. This pincer was working. And we would be all spent or committed in a few more weeks. But I knew the game and knew Charlebois would get us another pillowcase full with a fat HQ overhead attached and that, uncorrected, I could soon enough find myself again looking out the window at the highway from another hospital bed. That debacle in Homer's Sea stirred me to thinking about finding something else for me and Pen and baby Hank.

By midmorning the next day, I was sitting in the office with Sister Mary, signing the financial reports, when I heard a loud, accented rendition of my name. And there he stood—arms outstretched, palms up, and a broad, shit-eating grin—as if he had just been dropped on stage and was now turning before us, to his advantage. He was, at that moment, the frog from rhyme and fable, particularly since he was in green from head to toe. Eli Tsur, Egyptian Jew: sallow frog with an M16 slung over his shoulder.

We didn't know each other very well. He was our Israeli counterpart in the West Bank, and I had met with him a couple of times in preparation for my work in Tyre. But that was then, when he was an administrator, and now Major Eli Tsur was slowly walking toward me, past my staff, his arms still out for an anticipated embrace. And, of course, for me there could not be much more of an embarrassment: a public embrace from the conquering army, and I now in the arms of someone who had been, until his transfer to Lebanon, the man in charge of assuring Palestinian docility.

I rose tentatively and was quickly subjected to his bear hug: right side, left side. And then, still in his grasp, he leaned back with a broad smile and repeated how good it was to see me. I was guessing he must have seen my embarrassment, but was treating it like a character flaw which he was pleased to overlook. All I could think of at that moment, looking past his shoulders at my students, was that based on what they were seeing, it looked as if all my hard-won credentials as an Arab sympathizer were now revealed as a disguise, something that was all too easy for an Arab to believe about an American.

Then, as if there was no other business in that room, he took my elbow and started walking me toward the door. "Come on, let's go," he said, his frog grin lit up from ear to ear. I wish I had had some resolve, just checked my watch and fixed a time at our mutual convenience. But I succumbed, with barely a whimper, to this bully Israeli from Egypt. He put me in his Peugeot, nestled his M16 along his leg, and jammed his combat boot down on the pedal.

What happened over the next twenty-four hours was beyond comprehension. My sense, looking back, was that most of what ensued was for Eli more than for Israel and in the end, as far as CRS ground operations were concerned, it had no effect whatsoever. As Eli explained, this was his new assignment: "To coordinate the relief agencies." Which, given the precedence of our relations on the Israeli-occupied West Bank, meant final approval of every cent "spent strictly and exclusively on Lebanese." He was now clearly looking at me to confirm all this, as we spun out of the city.

I knew prevarication with someone as street smart as Eli wouldn't work. "The money comes from the US Government," I told him, "and is for victims of the war." The challenge was implicit. Did Eli, bully or not, really want a report going back to Washington stating that he was forbidding U.S. taxpayer assistance to refugees? The moment I had said my piece on this, I could see that he was not going to make a stand on that one. A tacit agreement was arrived at before we had even passed the city limits. He would use "Lebanese" to describe my work and, if need be, illustrate it with the shelter program, and I would use "victims." But, as I said, he seemed less interested in the details.

"Eli, where are you taking me?"

"Beirut," he answered.

"Christ, you're kidding me. I've got a program to run." He looked unperturbed. "Eli, you can't do this. This is called kidnapping."

"My friend, my friend," he said in exasperated tone of voice. "We're partners. We have to work together."

"Shit," I was thinking, "Partners nothing." I knew how it worked on the West Bank. You say jump, Jack says how high. I slumped back in my seat, getting myself used to the idea of going North. This frog had teeth behind that smile, and I knew damn well he could make life unbearable for me, if he chose, and for Jack as well, for that matter. And yes, I might win a few skirmishes at the outset, but at the end of the day the U.S. Catholic Church would be mute and the USG unwilling to make a complaint.

Eli manhandled the car, slamming the brake and clutch down with the boot and turning the car with such force, I thought he was going to rip out the steering. This was no strongman. He was, as I said, more the frog. But his treatment of the Peugeot, all the while smiling, was brutal. He hit the brake and asked some Israeli soldiers for directions. We were now leaving the coast and heading inland, into the lushest gardens and orchards in all of the Arab world, where you could reach up to taste the most delicious fruit you've ever had or drop a seed and watch it grow before your eyes.

Eli was googly-eyed and twice almost drove the car off the road. The way I would stare at my voluptuous Pen, he was gorging likewise on the plenty of South Lebanon. For arid, irrigated Israel or for the rocks and gravel of Palestine, this was a cornucopia spilling out, and Eli was the famished boy in its midst. You should have seen this middle-aged paunchy major in his wrinkled fatigues, biting into peaches and plums with the juice rolling down his chin: startled, as I was a year earlier, with such ambrosia, not to be bought anywhere in our own national markets.

That evening was to bring new meaning to "being in bed with." Israeli arrogance never disappoints. Just when you think you've seen the limits of chutzpah, new ground is broken.

I stood at the front desk of the Hotel Alexandria in East Beirut. The lobby was full of second-echelon journalists and relief workers. The receptionist asked, above the general din, whether we wanted one or two rooms, and Eli, the only damn uniform and gun in the lobby, shouted over my shoulder that we will have just one room. He reached over and took the key while I filled out the form. No flies on the frog. I knew what was up. I was his protection: his American protection.

We would occupy our room later and, at Eli's insistence, went up to the roof, which had already drawn a crowd for the nightly round of demolition in the southern part of the city, identical to what we had witnessed from the bridge of the Sea Queen earlier. There were brilliant lanterns drifting down through a pall of smoke, accompanied by the occasional roar of an Israeli bomb: South Beirut was smoldering in its grave, and these journalists were all set up behind tripods, taking their snaps. All was quite safe here in Maroniteland: these guys were obviously more risk-averse than their colleagues closer to the edge in the Commodore, who by now must be running low on Scotch, not to mention a bit shaky from the nightly shocks to their building and the falling lead from all that useless ack ack the PLO put up.

And then some wise-ass relief worker told Eli that no guns were allowed in the hotel. Eli just smiled widely at the guy, then told me that we'd seen all we needed to see and walked away, as if the wise-ass had just asked him if he wanted another drink.

We saddled back up in the Peugeot, and I guided him down off the hill and north to the casino on the Maronite coast: a black glass monster which for some reason Eli said he needed to see. Thinking back, it must have been something to do with class that made Eli want so much to see the slender creatures in the Paris creations, the silver-maned traders with their beads and white linen pants.

Israel had no such finery or elegance. Israel had wrinkled uniforms, messes of hair, and blotches and blemishes from a tribe not used to this sun. Tenacious, they were. Smart, heroic and certainly exacting with their terrible swift sword. But unable to have what was in that casino. And my guess is that Eli, the boy raised in Alexandria, missed the glamour—maybe even ached for it at times.

But we didn't get far, and this time Eli was out of his depth. A hotel staff in impeccable attire cut across our path on the carpet in the foyer and simply said. "Yes?" with arched eyes. Eli pointed past him at the gaming room where we could see glimpses of the beautiful people exercising their options. Eli, unheeding, walked on. At this point, two other staff, similarly dressed, walked over from their stations and blocked his way.

"Yes?" asked Eli, trying to make light of it and provoke a grin, but no grin was forthcoming from these gentlemen's gentlemen.

"Some other time, sir," one said, and put his arm on Eli as if to escort him out. Eli looked at them, and put his finger to his eyes.

"Maybe just to see?" I felt sorry for him.

"Some other time, sir," they repeated.

After his dispatch by the casino Mafia, Eli didn't loom so large. He had had his feathers plucked by the Arab underworld and now it was the forlorn Egyptian who was manhandling the car, and me, back to the hotel. Regardless, I had had enough of Eli's personal reconnaissance into the wonders of Lebanon. This was not business and he had extended his authority over me as far as it would stretch. There was a free press in Israel, and if I so chose, I had enough on Eli now to get him crucified for negligence, which I had no intention of doing as long as it was understood that about one second after I had drained my last coffee at breakfast, my time as tour guide was finished and I was going back to my "truck and dump" for the victims. But that would be tomorrow. For the moment, I was advancing to our room without even a toothbrush to my name in the company of Eli and his M16.

My heart sank when I saw there was only one bed in the room—something between a single and a double—a nice tight accommodation for Eli, me and the M16, which I knew would not leave his side under any circumstances. So there was a precious moment when I lit the candles—the shadows of Eli and his gun looming on the wall—while we considered the bed.

Not for long, however, as we both seized upon the alternative simultaneously, pulling the top mattress off and laying it (following Eli's directions) in front of the door. Eli then draped a blanket over it, and looked at me the same way he had when he had walked into my office in the morning, with his arms stretched out, palms up, wearing his "frog went a courting" smile.

"You don't mind, do you?" he asked.

Hell no, I didn't mind. On the contrary, having my own blanket and mattress was my heart's content. Of course, given my own preoccupation with early-warning devices, I now fully appreciated my own position: lying prone across the doorsill.

"Good night," Eli said, and blew out the candle.

"Good night, my friend," I replied, as I heard him shifting the M16 around, presumably to blow a hole in the door at the first sign of interference.

Christ, I laughed to myself, I sure hope the cleaning people don't start work early. Not at all the way Eli would want to conclude his tourism, I'd imagine.

The next morning at breakfast, I laid it on the line with Eli. I was going back, with or without him. I was quite surprised by his reaction: he was hurt. Quite genuinely, it appeared, hurt that I was being so "hard" as he characterized it. It was mind-boggling, the personality divide. He did not sense, it seemed, any inconsistency between kidnapping a guide and friendship. Like a courtship by way of rape, I thought. I wasn't sure whether his aggression was organic or rather a work-related aggravation: by work, meaning

Eli's job managing dependency programs in the occupied territories.

He was a weird guy, proud as hell when we had driven through the graveyards of Syrian tanks in the Chouf or watched the firestorm in South Beirut, but also undeveloped: his childish fascinations with the luscious fruits of the Litani and the casino were like a little boy on tiptoes looking into the window of a candy store. Sort of pathetic, if he weren't so dangerous. I didn't doubt he could pull the trigger on his lethal companion piece, if he so chose.

On the way back, Eli decided to become very professional. Somehow, as if slighted for friendship, he now was concentrating on his overseer role, annoying me with numerous questions on the mechanics of my program and probing my relationship with the Palestinian refugees. On this issue, I told him to take it up with State, since I was directed by the USG to help victims. He dropped me off in the square, alerting me that he would be back from time to time, and then manhandled the Peugeot out of the square: not at all consistent with the embrace he had offered me the day before.

The next couple of weeks proved almost routine, considering the environment. We were drawing down our stocks without interruption—it was down to almost a milk run—and my green pillowcase was finally empty, with the last of the monies now on deposit with the Greeks and AMAL.

Then we finally received some mail by the good hand of Jack and then the Red Cross: brief notes. The big news from Jack was that CRS Mercy Convoys into Beirut were underway, and Joe and a HQ spokesman had been on all the networks. And there were now increased rumblings about a U.S. buffer zone: the two not necessarily connected. That was one Mike had never predicted.

Interesting, I thought. Israel backs off, the bombing stops, the U.S. fills the breach south of Beirut, Fatah fighters get safe passage out, and the Shia regain control of South Beirut. If it materialized, that would mean federal monies by the basketful for repairing what Israeli had wrought. And which also meant—I could see it already—Charlebois' swagger reaching unbearable proportions. Yes, the spigot was on full stream for CRS and more so than ever thanks to the publicity associated with Joe's Mercy Convoys.

The other note was from Pen, and equally brief: "I have no idea whether this will ever reach you—just to let you know that we are all okay and that we pray you will stay safe. And Hank is walking now, which everyone says is very advanced. Not too much, I mean, just a few yards—but walking. And oh yes, the big news is that CRS was on TV last night, and we all looked for you but only somebody from HQ was on, with some film of CRS trucks going into the fighting. We all really miss you and need you to come back to us soon. No matter what, it's not worth your being there anymore. I mean, crippies, can't CRS send you to a family post? Don't they know you have a baby?"

"Yeah probably," I thought, "if I remind them."

But I wasn't reminding them, mainly because I didn't have things figured out in my own mind. Our last convoy was fast approaching and unless I made a noise, God knows how long it would be before they transferred new monies. It was all there in Sister Mary's reports, but I was under no illusion that they were getting much attention: especially not when everyone, including my wife, was getting all worked up over the convoys into Beirut.

Other than nearly drowning at Haddad's and my twenty-four-hour tour with Eli, one day followed another now, and frankly, except for my presence in the front cab, Sister Mary was running the show. And, yes, CRS would probably transfer me if I made a stink, but where the hell to? I was still a new dick, with a very thin commitment. Was I ready for Djoubti, if that's what popped up?

Either way, my year was more than up, and my R&R was due. And as soon as the paper on the last convoys was done, I would take off for two weeks, at least. But I dreaded the thought of returning to Connecticut, of being surrounded by that original mess the minute I stepped off the plane: lawyer's avarice, family vengeance, the ever-unfolding heartache around Pen's first child. I feared, soon enough, I'd just end up in the backyard beside the willow, getting stoned.

The evenings were most difficult. Curfew was earlier as we approached fall, and the political environment was tense as the presence of the Israelis and their Maronite partners wore thin. At 7 p.m., it was as it had been from the beginning: just me and Tio with my feet up on the balcony railing.

I often talked to myself those days. "I mean," I said, clinking my glass against Tio's red sombrero, "the sensible thing is obvious. Turn this over to Sister Mary and bring me back to Beirut to work with Joe. But I don't want that, Tio," I said. "He has cold water in his veins. I'll bet at this very moment he and Khalil are driving those deuce-and-a-half's right into the worst of it. And, my friend, I can't handle that. My nerves are frayed. Abused them in Chu Lai." And then, "Shame on me, Tio—hold on, let me just fill my glass to overflowing again—yes, shame on me. But if I am to say the truth, what I really need for R&R is to go back to Larnaca and sit at that café by the sea and be served by the waitress again. Just the smile, mind you, Tio. Just the smile and the colored lights strung up over the tables and the seafood and retsina."

In short, I was becoming quite distraught, spending half my life alone in my house with increasing amounts of Tio Pepe as comfort for what ailed me, one significant part of which was getting up each morning and chasing around after these God-forsaken refugees with my tidbits of solace.

"But not tomorrow," I shouted out onto the square. "Tomorrow, we're doing it up 'brown,' as they say, Tio. You may be unfamiliar with the expression, though, not at all I imagine, unfamiliar with sticking your dick up loveliness. Not unfamiliar with that, are you, Tio?" I staggered up the stairs, unwilling to set up the devices. "Fuck it, all they'd get is an empty pillowcase."

The next morning, we gathered as usual in the square, cradling our cups and waiting for the sounds of the diesel entering the square, me with a worse than normal hangover (though not much worse).

"This will be our last until my government sends more," was all I cared to say to my students, as I called them. "For a while, now, you will all work on shelter." And then there was a cheer for the cargo now turning into the square. This would be my last hurrah, at least with these grant monies, and was the best I could do to bite the hand that fed me. We pulled back the flaps to verify our purchase. It was there in all its glory, and my students just stared for a while, trying to size it up. Marlboros—three trucks' worth of red and white cartons, and one filled with Arabic coffee. I turned to my sidekick. "This is really what those old men and women want, isn't it?"

He smiled at me and patted my back. "You got it, man."

We made our runs. The checkpoints all knew us by now and as long as the Israelis were with them, would not have sought any personal profit anyway. The fact that it was tobacco and not food would not have raised any eyebrows. On the contrary, it would have seemed perfectly appropriate. And so, we plied the back roads to the beaches, warehouses, abandoned buildings, and orchards, stopping just long enough at each place to unload coffee and smokes and be on our way. I certainly didn't want any noise about this, and we had all our drops to do in just one day. The U.N. would hear about it— since they were starting to consolidate and serve the refugees, and God knows Mary sent each and every receipt—so what I did would be known. But as long as there was no splash which attracted higher attentions, this little infraction would hardly be a footnote.

"We finally connected," I said to my sidekick. "Just think, weeks of deliveries and hardly a thank you. But you saw her today, didn't you?" He nodded.

"Even that woman who hated us came over. She was holding up a carton of Marlboros and said 'CRS, okay.' Coming from her, that's a standing O. Got that, my friend? Standing O. When you get back to AUB, tell your professor we got a standing O."

He smiled, "All right, man."

A few days later, I said my goodbyes to the staff and counterparts and told them I was going home for a couple of weeks. I would be back, I promised. And then I had my student drive me up to the border. In my heart, I wasn't certain at all I'd be coming back. But they'd get over it, except maybe my sidekick, with whom I was very close by now: many hours in the cab together, and some dicey moments, too, though none to compare with our shelter riots. He could tell I was equivocating: he knew me well enough, this Shia youngster. God knows, I thought, how he is going to reconcile sitting at my knee all these weeks—at the American knee—with what will surely be expected of him as he grows older. In the end, I couldn't lie to him. I shook his hand with a meaning that, I hoped, might serve if I didn't get back. And then, at the last minute, before walking into Israel, I sailed my Giants baseball cap over to him.

We waved at each other intermittently as I walked toward the Star of David, now mostly disappeared among the Lebanese—and then I got in a taxi and said, "Jerusalem."

Jerusalem

Man's flying contrivance. In the beginning, I was still young enough for the stewardesses to tousle my curls and at every opportunity, to give me flying medals and insignia, when I was making the long Trans-Pacific journey to Australia. I had made the newspapers for my travels. "Boy, nine years of age, traverses Pacific for the fourth time." These were images even now I could pull up. Nose pressed to the pane in the pitch of night, flames leaping out of the far engine, descending down through war clouds and thunderclaps. Breaking through at first light. The beautiful necklace of surf as we coasted into Fiji. For me it was being with Biggles, the rat-a-tat-tat of his machine guns over the South China Seas. I had told a reporter in Sydney that I liked Fiji best because the women didn't wear clothes. The headline: "Boy, seven years old, enjoys state of undress in Fiji."

And now I may as well have been in a cattle car, crammed in, with the food trays dealt to you like cards. I slowly digested my bun, hoping to ease the pain in my gut. Once again with my nose to the pane, sweat beading in my palms, once again a scant inch from air too thin to sustain me, from cold that would turn me purple in an instant.

I had managed a couple of days with CRS / Jerusalem before the flight. A large part, on my back at the American Colony, trying to get the swelling down in my gut. I did get a short trip to our projects in the occupied West Bank and a dinner with the Israeli counterparts. I was daunted by these Israelis. So many had heroic stories: truly heroic. Sort of hard to imagine these days in American Suburbia where heroism is a home run in the bottom of the ninth. Despite their courtesies, how could they not have considered me a slouch? These were the ones with hollow eyes while I had been sitting on the piano at sour hour in Saratoga Springs. The hunchback Ibrahim was jumping from the Talmud to European history to contemporary American politics, while others on his terrace were veering off into other disciplines and—quite apart from those two techies from Oxfam at Mike's one and only dinner—as a bystander, I could only gawk at their scholarship.

But what I couldn't get, I pondered, as the stewardess zipped by for the third straight time, looking away, presumably so that she could get this chore done and get some serious time in the back with her Winston's and Vogue—what I couldn't get was how they all missed the essential. Or, perhaps I had missed the essential. It had been like *Tender Is the Night* at Ibrahim's house on that confiscated land. The lights sparkling in the valley, ice clinking in our cocktails: but all on captured Palestinian territory, or reclaimed territory, as some say. And yet the scholar next to me could not broach it.

Everything had been so familiar from the minute I left my sidekick. At first, the vast irrigated farms and then, the familiar hate: from out of the blue, the taxi driver, feeling so sure of his ground, without any invitation began complaining about Palestinian scum and how their women were all whores. With zero compunction. Just some fat-assed Sephardic spouting venom without even the first tentative feeler about how disposed I was to hear it.

I looked at the Orthodox kids with their ringlets in the row of seats across the aisle from me. I knew already baby Hank wouldn't stand a chance:

especially not with us as parents. These were the next generation of hollow eyes, shuttling between Jerusalem and New York.

And then only the day before—an imprint for me, one more freeze frame—that these scholars must see a hundred times a month. It was this Israeli settlement on the West Bank, on the crest of a hill as always. And directly below, well within its fields of fire, was the Palestinian village where CRS was working to cap a pathetic well which, by Israeli mandate, could not go deep enough to fill a fraction of their need. I then remembered, sitting in the plane, looking up at the concertina perimeter and over the surrounding fence beyond it: every half-minute or so I could see a body fly through the air, followed by the thud of the diving board.

Milk and honey. Bullshit. Teenage Israelis at checkpoints undressing Palestinian elders in front of their grandchildren and laughing about it. All that was what we skirted on the terrace. We talked on the greatest themes, the hunchback Ibrahim and I. My friend Ibrahim, I should say. Such a gentle, hollow-eyed Jew from London. We talked about everything but what the brutalization was doing to them. Don't any of these men write essays or novels about drinking cocktails on confiscated land? And then, if it is not confiscated, then, Christ, where does the world go with that?

Here I was, knees up to my chin, the stewardess ignoring my desire to pass her the tray, which I hadn't eaten anyway. I wanted to get it off my gut. I hated the agony of knowing that the swelling was trapped there for this whole miserable flight to New York. That it would be at least another day of rice and water before I had overcome the rot imposed by Tio and the morning Turkish.

And how long would events in Northbrook allow me to rest and recuperate? Lying up there on the second floor of the Cape with Henry causing a disturbance every half hour, Helen nagging her wayward son about what needs fixing, and Pen starting to creep back into the carnival she had sought to escape: which, I was discerning, despite the pain she had suffered there, was still attractive, that world of mixed-up accusatives and nominatives. Dread. That was it. I dreaded going home. Even my beautiful, white-haired baby Hank was too young to console me. Sitting there hunched up, in pain, I wished to hell I had just flown back to Larnaca and bathed in the loveliness there for a while.

When I first arrived back in America from Australia, my life was the life of Huck Finn: swimming holes in a muddy brook, lolling about on the banks with my friend, Dickie, making dams and diving boards, and swimming bare-assed. We put buttercups in our pee-holes. We spent countless summer afternoons waiting for the tug on our lines. We were very close, we two revolutionaries, in that countryside. There's hardly a time I can remember when various parents had not forbidden their children to play with us.

There we'd be, the two of us sitting on the stoop in August, hatching new adventures, usually construction projects: dams, tree houses, and tunnels. Traps and bombs also. I would slip out my window after my parents were asleep, and rove the fields, barns, and forests with Dickie until first light. There in the backyard was also loveliness, as sure as that smile in Larnaca. And, as before, I needed to dwell in it. Just as poor is not really one's ribs showing, so too, cripple—cripple that Pen and I were and are— is not as simple as the limp or stutter. For us, it was the fundamental inability to live very well in the world as we found it. Cripple, so defined, had Pen and me clinging to each other. Cripple had us go to Lebanon. And now cripple had me insisting on recollecting my childhood with Dickie.

In our last year together, we discovered sex. Had our first stirrings together in the tops of trees where we sat on planks, and I read out aloud passages of books Dickie had discovered in his attic: descriptions of voluptuous women along with a variety of disguises for the man's intention. Not graphic as they would be two decades later, but our imaginations took up the slack. We burrowed in tobacco fields, built mazes of underground tunnels where we also read by candlelight, in silence, chewing our nails, and sometimes, without any thought about perversions, showed our fledgling erections to each other: the way we would a wound or an honor, incurred in some misadventure.

Too soon, those idyllic times ended. My great partner in mischief, my fellow "shithead," as we were often described by irate farmers, was severed from me absolutely. He took up mechanics and carpentry with an early exit from school and I advanced to college preparatory school. I didn't understand yet how much difference that would make, but even then I knew our forts and dams and traps would now all decay and collapse: would end up, years later, as just a board hanging by a nail from the cottonwood or a depression in a tobacco field. And only a few smudge marks left of that intricate console we had drawn on the back of the bus seat in front of us, where, during that half hour to school, we had excited ourselves amidst galactic fire storms, ricocheting around, bouncing off infinity.

My homecoming was in late fall. My wife and baby were still resident these past months in this countryside turning suburbia: a circus to be sure. What with Henry now, as Pen had written, unshaven for weeks and stationed at the end of our driveway all day, or, after nightfall, compounding the tragedy with sudden upheavals, as he roared "Bugger it," and went crashing off toward the bathroom, invariably messing himself before he got there. And Helen was now insistent on her boy stepping up and becoming head of household, but not in filial imitation of poor Henry. There would be no homecoming hurrah for a son in a chair on the back lawn, staring mindlessly up at the bare branches of the cottonwood, unshaved and running into the woods with great urgency, and paying less attention than she would have hoped to who might see him squatting there.

This pretty much described my state, as seen by another. My gut needed repair: both bland diet and circumstances peaceful to its digestion. But not here, not with a raving father as a shadow of himself, a righteous mother, and baby Hank, who was certainly not gathering any myths here. Rather she was pulling down and sometimes shattering the relics and souvenirs that Henry had brought back from distant lands. Baby Hank, Habibi, was scared of this new man in the house, and I of course was impatient for a love that was not forthcoming.

And so, even as the last leaves were falling, I felt it necessary to escape to my chair by the cottonwood: sometimes stargazing, but often returning to those times with Dickie and my mortal combat with the little men, and of course to the 'how now, brown cow." Both the lawyer and CRS were waiting in the wings for me, waiting for me to make my next move, and yet I was getting dangerously close to incoherence.

Continuing residence—the notion of presiding over this circus as head of household—made my head spin. But so too did the notion of resuming with CRS: a circus by another name.

Finally, in the face of Pen's and Helen's disenchantment with my homecoming, such as it was—I guess in such stark contrast with the heroics described in all the newspapers—I agreed to see the lawyer. It was a complete humiliation from beginning to end. He kept me waiting, then read the file while

I sat silent like a delinquent before the principal's desk. He asked me a few questions, the answers to which had already been conveyed, and then took the concluding time to lead me in fond remembrances of Henry. Even as I had become somewhat stupefied by my retreat to the back lawn, I did raise my hand, literally, to ask this joker—who was still swallowing my Army disability check each month—questions about resolution and its implications for Henry and Helen.

He replied that I should be okay as long as I was gone, and that no judge would come down hard on someone who is facing so much tragedy, such as my mother now was. That was it: this bespectacled Rotarian confirming that yes, the unsatisfied suppliers were still very much at large, that the Dane and Roo were in absentia and that I was gone. My only stateside assets had been either seized or were now offshore, and my mother was visibly aging in the midst of tragedy. Given all that, he said, we seemed to be "okay" for the moment. And then he started rising from his chair.

As for CRS, they had both immediate and long-term concerns. Yes, of course, they understood the strain of separation on a family. But wouldn't the war be over soon? "No," I said. Mike and I had sent so many memos on that same subject I was now convinced HQ just asked for info to assert control, not because they absorbed it. Then there was silence on the phone, as if they were waiting for proof. Finally, only getting my deep breathing on the other end, she asked if I would take a fine young man back with me and whether, as soon as he was "up to speed," I was willing to go to Tunisia.

"A family post," she added. Still in the midst of my incoherence, I told her I needed to deliberate. As for the present, there was an upcoming talk show on Hartford radio, she said: would I participate next Saturday night?

"I would," I responded immediately. I sensed that this indeed would help elevate my standing within the household. Not to mention with neighbors and Pen's extended family. Of course, my public appearance would be at odds with the bespectacled counsel's advice about being gone. But hiding under a stone had an equal price attached. And I knew my 'yes' was not the result of any reasoned debate in my own mind, but rather an instinctive rush for the limelight, rising up now as an alternative to slinking about.

As for CRS, the instructions were predictable. Repeat the name and telephone number as often as possible and stay away from political statements concerning Israel. I tried; got cleaned up that morning and then poured black coffee down me until I was as far removed from "laid back" as I had been a week earlier in Tyre. The show began as CRS would have liked, with some introductory words from the host about my bravery on behalf of humanity and my ensuing description of the Mercy Convoys and shelter programs. But then the red lights, indicating incoming calls, became less frequent, and in an effort to light up the board the host started prying into the bombings. Was it true that Beirut was in flames?

I couldn't deny that Israel kept its losses low by taking full advantage of its technological might. And that yes, women and children were often "in the way." At the host's urging, I described the military exchange as "a Palestinian pop-gun against Israeli cannon." And so, despite some initial forays into the techniques of relief, some of the truth of the larger situation was now leaking out, and suddenly the switchboard went ablaze. Among the calls, some of the vitriol got broadcast. Frankly, it wasn't much different from the demonization all countries need to sustain war, the difference here being that these were presumably Americans. I would say refugee, and they would say terrorist. I was a terrorist sympathizer.

"How could the Catholic Church employ someone like you?" Thus the conversation ended. The host, of course, was delighted.

Unfortunately, some of the calls followed me home. From early Sunday, the phone was ringing off the hook, as Helen put it: "People saying terrible things about you." Pen then took the calls and soon enough received death threats. With everything else going on in the household, this made it worse, and served to ricochet me back into the backyard chair. On Monday, while Pen was getting an unlisted number for us (Helen found it disgraceful "that we should now have to hide like criminals"), CRS called to say that the local Bishop in Hartford had called to inform them that relations between the Catholic and Jewish communities had suffered irreparable harm.

Come Tuesday morning, Henry was in the front yard doing his Salaam bows to each passing vehicle and being, by turns, otherwise disinterested or vulgar, while his son spaced out under the cottonwood. Amid this, Pen's first daughter came for the afternoon.

She was bicycling up and down the road, when suddenly I heard a car skid, the sound of metal on metal and then screams. I figured Pen would be all over it and, at that moment, not able to deal with crisis, I stayed in my chair and waited for Pen to bring the news of resolution. In any case, I knew from the kind of screaming that neither death nor disability had resulted.

Pen was beside herself. "Yes, it was only a scrape, but how could you have possibly known that?" She looked down at me in disbelief. "You didn't even bother to get up out of the damn chair. Who the hell are you, anyway?"

Assailed on all sides, there was now no question now about flying the coop, and being quite incapable of new starts, I called HQ and agreed to Tunisia, for no fewer than twenty-four months. And with this, as I put the phone back in its cradle, my preoccupation with war in the Levant came to an end. Yes, I would return to Lebanon as a visitor on Temporary Assignment, and even much later as a regional overseer. But now, in late 1982, once again a fugitive and still with no inklings of a career, I made a different step down the same trail: a trail of assignments that would take us eventually across the Maghreb and down into West Africa.

Of course, the war in Lebanon would rage on during my own advancement elsewhere. Bits of news would reach me, sometimes quite dated and often tragic. My Jesuit friend Kluiters was assassinated not long after I left and thrown down a well where he was discovered by villagers. Whether it was our well, I would never know. A truck did indeed, as the whole world would learn, barrel down my hill loaded with explosives and take out the U.S. embassy. Howdy died instantaneously and Mike's liaison was crushed so badly it took years to repair her.

Meanwhile, Joe continued to carelessly ride with fate, and as fate would have it, was spared for the two years he was there. This, despite two direct hits on our office: one at night, one during a staff celebration in a nearby restaurant. "Allah is merciful" was what Joe told me the next time we met in Cairo. The little gentleman was then transferred to JWB by a new CEO at CRS to replace Jack who was unceremoniously retired. Joe's replacement (Father Jenko), also as the whole world would learn, was taken hostage two months after he arrived and remained in captivity for eighteen months, at which point CRS prohibited any more assignments for ex-pats, and management was turned over to national staff with better results than expected.

The war maintained its ferocity, seemingly immune to the strong arm of the U.S sixth fleet, which, despite its power to destroy empires, left the Lebanese coast—a massive gray battlement—with its tail between its legs, throwing up a few farewell

2000-pounders onto the Chouf as spite for the ignominy inflicted.

As for me, I returned with the fine fellow HQ personnel had acquired through the good graces of the Cardinal's office. Our relationship was a fiasco from the moment we met. As Joe said, "he arrived on Lebanese soil unbuttoning his fly," not accepting the constant advice that "everything there in Lebanon was to see; nothing was to touch," save the Filipina whores. This rogue, the Cardinal's man. Unable to walk up three flights of stairs to interview a beneficiary, as "his heart would not allow it." Flipping out his spare change in South Beirut, and managing in the time I had looked away to get us both nearly killed by a mob of street urchins. Two weeks after I had left for Tunisia, he was excused from Lebanon employment for what HQ called "comportment issues."

As for Mike, he never came back. In fact, after his talk with Charlebois in Larnaca, he left CRS for two years to pursue a master's in accounting at The University of Texas. Such courses I imagined to be a workaday outlet for his internal righteousness. The news was a disappointment to me: it seemed a paltry outcome for a man so recently consumed by his need for redemption or, alternatively, for death in its pursuit. And, Farida, ever on fire, left Lebanon not long after I did, in the arms of a Brazilian painter, for a new life in Rio. As for Vache, he started a fire in the kitchen at Rue d'Amerique and nearly burned down the entire building. The landlord forbade him ever to enter the premises again.

Carthage

The Academy had introduced me to Virgil. One of those more ambitious books like Milton or Rimbaud that under your arm gave a secret signal to those few other precocious students that also were intent on moving below the surface. Often, a different surface in my case. In *Islands in the Stream,* my man, shot up in a firefight, was lying on the deck of a small craft in flight, and said he was really learning fast at the end.

"Dead weight" were the last words I remember. My men lugging me to the bed of the slick. And one, my RTO, saying "God, he's heavy." And then the chopper went hell bent for leather, low across the paddies, with my head hanging out the bay and my mangled body laid out, inside. The rim of my helmet liner was pinched between the sill of the slick and the bone in my neck, with the rest of the liner tilting out, off my skull. Everything that preceded and that might follow lay in that balance. Amidst everything else—the mangled body, the deaths in my platoon—I was only fixed on that liner and was sure that if it fell off and down onto the paddies, I would die, be no more. And there was nothing to do about it: my arms were dead, and the pilot was unaware. I, too, was learning fast, learning that despite all my earlier flirtations with the darkness, I clung to life with an abandon that belied it all.

And so, despite the transformation of the dust balls in Paris and the dissolution of the corporeal, Aeneas, Dido, and Daedalus would be converted into a pleasant mythology for the family, rather than the vain boast they presented under my thin arms at the Academy.

I went ahead of the family to Tunisia and rented an apartment close to where Aeneas had landed, courted Queen Dido, and departed. With two bedrooms this time, surrounded everywhere by relics of Rome and Phoenicia, with a large marble floor where baby Hank would race around on her plastic wheeled horse, named Aeneas.

Thus, Pen and Baby Hank and I were united again in the winter of '83' in Carthage, from whence I would commute past the city's great stinking lake to the CRS office in Tunis and also from whence, most always at sunset, we could drive to the coast where Pen would sit on her blanket at La Marsa and watch me walk knee-deep up and back along the coast with baby Hank in my arms, still the Habibi with the white hair in her Shia lavender dress. As we walked, I spoke over her head about the great voyages to Carthage from her birthplace in Phoenicia.

A recovery ensued, alongside the pain of withdrawing from the war. Initially it was leaden. The gray skies and cold drizzle of Tunis in winter. The unsmiling faces under the heavy hand of state-managed socialism. A dreary little office for CRS: a priest's apartment until the current director replaced him a decade ago. Our office was in what had been the priest's bedroom. A desk was set up in the hall for the accounts, and another room held half-dozen desks pushed together for the food and nutrition monitors. Mold spread from the corners and over cold stone walls. Some of the office staff wore gloves with the fingertips cut off. There was a hole in the floor of a freezing little WC with miniature squares of wax paper for the ex-pats and a rusty faucet for those who were used to it.

The office brought to mind Joe's education on the might of the zeros: how you could parade around if there were enough tons of US government food on the CRS waybills. Here, the grandeur of the zeros had not occurred to anyone in decades. My predecessor had been expelled seven months earlier for (as Dali, the head food monitor described) an incautious affair with a married Minister of State. She'd been caught in his company, rock climbing in a bikini, driving an already timid director to risk management in extremis.

And I, burned by the sun, with the regimental stripes around my forehead, the swashbuckler on the bridge coming into Larnaca on the fumes, now sat beside the dank WC trying to reconstruct by hand the numbers into various ledgers—not a very long step from a boy filing the dog-eared pink at Phoenix Insurance as a summer apprentice. And now I worked for a shadow of a man, who, quite incredibly—when you have been bossed by the likes of Charlebois and Joe— insisted on keeping the key to the wax paper and pen refills.

I'd been reduced to the most humiliating of circumstances, suffering from long hours of transferring numbers and the silence of same: playing havoc on the still-active streams of adrenaline cultivated so ardently by Tio Pepe, Turkish. and a year of war.

That was it. There were no more new parishioner-funded projects after the scandal with the minister: only two residuals by the time I got there. One was rather large project involving rabbits, which sought to introduce gigantic, New Zealand rabbits, but which had gone belly-up when the chef de projet went on vacation in August and no one cared to water them. At least that was the official reason, but I suspected (viewing it through the Lebanese looking-glass) some fast profits from pelts and meat while the boss was gone.

The other project was introducing balloons to the deaf in Bizerte: apparently, the hearing-impaired could learn to feel the vibrations of music on a balloon's distended skin.

However, the balloons for the deaf that winter were neither here nor there for me, bent as I was over my ledgers, then seven months in arrears. I spent my days calculating the arithmetic concerning PL 480—17,000 tons of American grains and vegoil, from Port to hundreds of nutrition sites for Tunisian children.

And so, grudgingly at first, the adrenaline receded, reluctantly in the first several weeks, when nails got bitten to the quick and I was often seen stepping just a few feet into the WC, where I could grab a rusty pipe, pull myself up, and hold it until I could bear it no longer. In this way, my recovery ensued.

Every day at 5, I packed away my pencil and
pen and took my Peugeot 104 back across the
stinking city lake to our refuge. This time of the day
was blissful and complete. Once in the door I got
the last of it out. Push-ups and sit-ups were done,
feet anchored under the couch, while baby Hank
involved herself with each lift and recline and Pen's
sauces brewed next to us in the kitchen. We were
three for dinner on our balcony. The sauce now all
over baby Hank's face with a great mound of pasta
before Pen and me, drinking our glass of Tunisian red
with the sea just visible beyond a line of eucalyptus
trees. And then, kisses for my Beiruti and a novel for
Pen while I resumed the aborted work from Paris:
never to get lost in it again, it seemed, since there
was only the time between that kiss for baby Hank
and my reclination on the mattress in our bedroom.

Weekends, even in the drear and drizzle, and
even though I had idiot's work, were beautiful. Each
a holiday really. I went everywhere with Hank. She
became as much a part of my back as if she were
growing from it. Strapped into the rucksack, as we
wandered through the exotica of spice and fruit
stalls, of beheaded chickens, with the crazy donkey
(me) under her repeating the first common words for
her (pole, ball, path) while the overloaded baskets

pulled the donkey's arms inexorably closer to the ground. We were interrupted occasionally by women who touched my arm and asked for permission to kiss the Habibi or touch her hair.

And the strolls through the Old French Cathedral grounds on our hill with Pen describing what grew and pinching off a petal for us to smell. And daddy pointing to the thunder and lightning moving across the sea toward us and ecce miraculum anticipating its thunder with a finger to the sky, for baby Hank. And running finally down the path toward our flat, as the first drops fell and the oleander began swaying in the wind and slapping at our feet.

Through the winter and into spring, Pen and I climbed about the cliffs, Hank strapped in, to unvisited caves where we three were pinned between sea and rock face. Where we, purple and goose-bumped, swam and then brought our blood back wrapped in blankets, while Hank got deep into sand tunnels, soon to become sluices and canals as the tide advanced and pushed us closer to the cliff which just at dark, we confronted by pulling ourselves up, hand over hand, Hank on my back, grabbing branches of scrub to get me and Pen up and over the crest before the sun was gone.

ACKNOWLEDGEMENTS

Helen Majorie Swanton...Nursed me in our basement after Vietnam

Ann Patrice Swanson...My dearest partner during the Lebanese war

Michiko Ota...Professor and biblical scholar on the Holy Lands

Mike Nolan...Mentor and fellow traveler during the Lebanese civil war

Virginia Konchan...copy-editor for **'The Water Above'**

Leslie Kreiner Wilson...Editor of my first book-- **'The Avant Garde of Western Civ'**

Ali Hijazi...Friend and sidekick from south Lebanon

Zevart Nadjarian...God mother for 'Baby Hank' and the bravest colleague we had in Beirut

Marian Lewis...Helped me to make a book out of a manuscript